Encountering the Sovereign Other

Encountering the Sovereign Other

Indigenous Science Fiction

Miriam C. Brown Spiers

MICHIGAN STATE UNIVERSITY PRESS | *East Lansing*

♾ The paper used in this publication meets the minimum requirements of
ANSI/NISO Z39.48-1992 (R 1997) (Permanence of Paper).

Michigan State University Press
East Lansing, Michigan 48823-5245

Printed and bound in the United States of America.

LIBRARY OF CONGRESS CATALOGING-IN-PUBLICATION DATA
Names: Brown Spiers, Miriam C., author.
Title: Encountering the sovereign other : indigenous science fiction /
Miriam C. Brown Spiers.
Description: East Lansing : Michigan State University Press, [2021] |
Series: American Indian studies series | Includes bibliographical
references and index.
Identifiers: LCCN 2021016774 | ISBN 9781611864052 (paperback) | ISBN
9781609176808 | ISBN 9781628954470 | ISBN 9781628964417
Subjects: LCSH: Science fiction, American--Indian authors--History and
criticism. | LCGFT: Literary criticism.
Classification: LCC PS153.I52 B78 2021 | DDC 813/.0876209897--dc23
LC record available at https://lccn.loc.gov/2021016774

Book design by Charlie Sharp, Sharp Designs, East Lansing, Michigan
Cover design by David Drummond, Salamander Design, www.salamanderhill.com.
Cover art is *Sequoyahzilla*, by Roy Boney Jr., 9" x 12", watercolor & pencil on paper.

Michigan State University Press is a member of the Green Press Initiative and is committed to developing
and encouraging ecologically responsible publishing practices. For more information about the Green
Press Initiative and the use of recycled paper in book publishing, please visit www.greenpressinitiative.org.

Visit Michigan State University Press at *www.msupress.org*

Contents

Acknowledgments

I am grateful for the wisdom and support of Jace Weaver, Christopher Pizzino, and especially Channette Romero, who challenged me to become a stronger writer and a more thoughtful scholar while giving me the tools and encouragement I needed to do that work.

I have been fortunate enough to live in several places and have many communities to support me while writing this book. Thank you to my colleagues and students at the University of Georgia, Miami University Middletown, the University of California, Merced, and Kennesaw State University. I could not have completed this project without my writing partners: Rachael Maddux, Mary Lee Cunill, Leigh Bernacchi, Kate Schaab, Liz Miles, and the Spring 2019 Manuscript Completion Project group.

My Athens Team helped me survive grad school, offered much-needed advice and comfort, and cheered me on through this long process. I am extra grateful to Laurie Norris and Beth Kozinsky, who found a way to visit no matter where I moved. I've been welcomed into homes, fed, and supported by too many folks to name. But I have relied especially on the friendship of Dan Rosenberg and Becca Myers, Elizabeth and Ben Steere, Gabriel Lovatt, Sarah Rose Nordgren and Brandon

Dawson, Dave McAvoy and Maureen Hattrup, Mark Warren and Stephanie Saline, Catherine Koehler, Yogita Maharaj, Matt and Christy Snyder, Rex and Angela Kreuger, La Shonda Mims and T Rosser, Leah Benedict, Rudy Aguilar, Michelle Miles, and JoyEllen Williams.

I have also benefited from generous mentors at each of my academic homes, including Laura Adams Weaver and Barbara McCaskill at UGA; Marianne Cotugno at MUM; Tom Hothem and Anne Zanzucchi at UCM; and an entire community at KSU, including Laura Davis, Robbie Lieberman, Letizia Guglielmo, Stacy Keltner, Griselda Thomas, Ashley Shelden, Chris Palmer, Katarina Gephardt, Kim Haimes Korn, Laura McGrath, and Marshal Chaifetz.

I have long been guided and nurtured by my community at the Native American Literature Symposium, which has graciously supported, corrected, challenged, and encouraged me. Thank you all for doing the hard work of creating and maintaining this space—especially Gwen Westerman, LeAnne Howe, Gordon Henry, Margaret Noodin, Jill Doerfler, Niigaan Sinclair, Theodore Van Alst, Jesse Peters, Becca Gercken, Julie Pelletier, Scott Andrews, Stephanie Fitzgerald, Carter Meland, David Carlson, David Stirrup, James Mackay, Nancy Peterson, Martha Viehmann, Karen Poremski, Brian Burkhart, Smokii Sumac, Shannon Toll, Amy Gore, Jessi Bardill, Steve Sexton, Brian Twenter, René Dietrich, Mandy Suhr-Sytsma, John Gamber, Billy Stratton, Kim Wieser, and Jeremy Carnes. I have also relied on the support and guidance of other colleagues in Native American and Indigenous studies, including Melanie Benson Taylor, Eric Gary Anderson, Kirstin Squint, and Deanna Reder.

I am grateful to the three anonymous readers of my manuscript, whose insightful critiques have helped me craft and better articulate my arguments, and to the editorial team at MSU Press—especially Gordon Henry, Julie Loehr, and Catherine Cocks. I am delighted and honored that Roy Boney allowed me to use his art for my book cover. I owe many of the ideas that became the introduction to the University of Georgia's Summer Doctoral Fellowship award. I could not have finished this project without the assistance of a Manuscript Completion Program grant and a Scholarship Support Grant from Kennesaw State University's Radow College of Humanities and Social Sciences.

A portion of chapter 1 appeared in an earlier form as "'The Yellow Monster': Reanimating Nuclear Fears in Cherokee Science Fiction," *Native South* 12 (2019). A portion of chapter 4 appeared in an earlier form as "Reimagining Resistance: Achieving Sovereignty in Indigenous Science Fiction," *Transmotion* 2, nos. 1–2 (Fall

2016). The feedback I received from the journal editors and anonymous reviewers refined and strengthened my ideas.

I am thankful to my family for their love and support. I am lucky to have parents who filled our house with books and insisted on watching *Star Trek: The Next Generation* on Saturday nights. They always prioritized my education—especially my mom, who did everything from checking my homework each night when I was growing up to babysitting my son while I revised my manuscript twenty years later. My brothers, godmother, aunties, cousins, and in-laws all asked questions about my work and indulged me when I gave overly enthusiastic replies. My grandparents, Ruth Claire Keeling and Ralph Darwin Frey, and my uncle, Ralph Darwin Frey Jr., aren't here to talk through these ideas in person anymore, but they gave me a path to follow.

This book would not exist without John and Theo. Theo, thank you for sharing your mama with her writing, for bringing me presents, and for giving me the biggest hugs. John not only took care of Theo and kept our lives running smoothly (during a pandemic, no less!) so that I could write; he also found the time and energy to listen to my ideas, respond to endless drafts, and proofread each chapter multiple times. The book and I are both so much the better thanks to your patience, enthusiasm, and love.

Introduction

ndigenous science fiction—science fiction written by Indigenous authors, as opposed to science fiction that simply includes Indigenous characters—is a relatively new genre, and the question of how we might define it is still under discussion. The development of such a definition is complicated by the conflicting theoretical approaches of Native American studies and science fiction theory, as highlighted by the questions raised in the very act of naming the genre. Even the choice to refer to a collection of texts as "Indigenous science fiction" has implications: first, the word "Indigenous" shifts the emphasis from the tribally specific to broader social and literary categories; second, the generic definition of "science fiction" emphasizes Euro-American rather than Native literary traditions. Given that Native literary critics, particularly those who heed the call of American Indian literary nationalism, have fought to establish a critical approach that recognizes Indigenous literatures as both tribally specific and separate from the Western canon, this problem of naming is a serious one.

Native American studies scholars have proposed various names and definitions for the genre, from Grace L. Dillon's "Indigenous futurism" to Dean Rader's "the Indian invention novel," but each term encounters its own definitional difficulties. While Indigenous science fiction (or "sf") certainly has the capacity to introduce new, Native-specific categories of storytelling, I argue that it also has the ability to challenge and expand the mainstream critical definitions of the genre itself. An analysis of Native science fiction should, of course, be grounded in both the tribally specific readings of American Indian literary nationalism and the broader theoretical perspective of Indigenous knowledge. But Indigenous science fiction is not simply traditional Native storytelling under a new name—it consciously interacts with the tropes of mainstream science fiction. Additionally, then, Native sf can be usefully interpreted through the lens of Euro-American science fiction theory. Because the genre exists at the intersection of two disparate critical approaches grounded in two separate worldviews, an analysis of Indigenous sf from only one perspective will always be incomplete. Moreover, where Indigenous knowledge intervenes in science fiction theory, it questions basic Euro-American cultural assumptions and expands the boundaries of the genre as a whole.

We might think of this expansion in terms of Hans Robert Jauss's concept of the "horizon of expectations." According to Jauss, any new text "evokes for the reader (listener) the horizon of expectations and rules familiar from earlier texts, which are then varied, corrected, changed, or just reproduced. Variation and correction determine the scope, alteration, and reproduction of the borders and structure of the genre."[1] In other words, genre is not simply a normative set of textual features, but also a structured and ongoing interaction between the author, the text, and the reader. The ways in which a genre is defined change over time, depending not only upon the text itself, but also upon "the impact of a work within the definable frame of reference of the reader's expectations: this frame of reference for each work develops in the historical moment of its appearance from a previous understanding of the genre, from the form and themes of already familiar works."[2] Following Jauss's theoretical approach, it becomes clear that the boundaries of any genre are flexible, expanding and contracting as new texts invite readers to rethink their definitions, thus contributing to the ongoing "dialogue between work and public" that is inherent to our relationship with literature.[3] Thus, as a broader audience is introduced to Indigenous science fiction, the boundaries of sf may be revised and expanded to include Indigenous worldviews.

Through this method, Native writers who adapt sf's normative generic tropes can initiate a conversation between Native American studies and science fiction theory that illuminates both fields' treatment of identity and the Other. Influential science fiction author Philip K. Dick has proposed that the defining characteristic of science fiction is the "shock of dysrecognition" it produces in its readers.[4] Because Indigenous peoples in North America share a history of European and, later, American, Canadian, and Mexican colonization and have thus experienced frequent encounters with alterity, Native writers have much to contribute to a genre that is concerned with such encounters. Individual works of science fiction may use this confrontation with alterity as a metaphor for exploring human relationships and discovering similarities between groups, or they may make a genuine attempt to encounter an Other, to imagine something beyond their own comprehension. Many Indigenous authors situate their science fictional novels as a response to these older discourses: their texts reinforce a desire for Native people's humanity to be acknowledged—but not assimilated—and they also embody the nationalist demand that Indigenous peoples be respected as distinct political entities and thus recognized as sovereign nations.

The title of this book, *Encountering the Sovereign Other*, reflects the necessity of maintaining this balance in both the individual and the political spheres. As much of the scholarship in Native American studies makes clear, Native peoples demand to be seen as distinct in several ways: primarily as distinct tribal nations with their own languages, cultures, histories, and worldviews; but also as distinct from other minority groups in the United States and Canada, who share a common history of oppression but not the nation-to-nation relationship with the federal government that has shaped the history and experiences of Native American and First Nations peoples; and, finally, as distinct from the assimilative pressures of mainstream Euro-American and Euro-Canadian cultures, which have worked so persistently to erase the presence of Indigenous peoples on this continent. In these capacities, Native peoples are indeed an "Other," remaining outside of categories that have served to elide and deny the distinct cultures, histories, and political realities of tribal nations.

And yet, the concept of the "Other" generally carries negative connotations. For instance, in her discussion of bodily subversions, Judith Butler cites Iris Young's use of Julia Kristeva's theories to suggest that "the operation of repulsion can consolidate 'identities' founded on the instituting of the 'Other' or a set of Others through exclusion and domination. What constitutes through division the 'inner' and 'outer' worlds of the subject is a border and boundary tenuously maintained for the purposes of social regulation and control."[5] In other words, humans construct our identities by establishing boundaries, a process that necessarily requires us to identify an Other against which we can define ourselves. Through this process, we identify "the 'abject,' [a term that] designates that which has been expelled from the body, discharged as excrement, literally rendered 'Other.' This appears as an expulsion of alien elements, but the alien is effectively established through this expulsion."[6] Although such a theory offers an accurate description of the ways that European and, later, American and Canadian settlers have responded to encounters with Indigenous peoples, I will focus here on the relationship between the Self and the Other that develops after the initial process, as outlined by Kristeva, has already taken place.

Here I turn to science fiction theorist Michael Pinsky, who draws on Emmanuel Levinas's understanding of ethics as the moment when the Self recognizes the demand of the Other (a definition that I will discuss in further detail later). For now, it is enough to say that, in Levinas's and Pinsky's constructions, the Other can become something besides the abject; it is simply understood as that which is separate from the Self, but which makes a demand upon the Self. This definition brings us to the other half of the phrase, the "Sovereign." Although the term "sovereignty" generally refers to political sovereignty, Native American studies scholars have applied it in a variety of other contexts, including literary sovereignty, educational sovereignty, food sovereignty, and digital sovereignty. In each case, "sovereignty" implies not only the right to self-determination, but also an inherent demand for *respect* from outsiders, who must acknowledge that Native peoples are not only entitled to, but are fully capable of self-governance and decision-making in each of the areas listed above. Given the long history of paternalism in the United States and Canada, such respect would mark a distinct change from both historical and contemporary policies and attitudes affecting Indigenous peoples. And it is precisely this demand for respect that Indigenous science fiction invites its readers to embrace. As Rebecca Roanhorse argues, "Indigenous Futurism also advocates for the sovereign. It dares to let Indigenous creators define themselves and their world not just as speaking back to colonialism, but as existing in their own right."[7] Through the generic tropes of sf, the texts I examine here resist the continued portrayals of Native peoples as doomed either to be assimilated into hegemonic, mainstream cultures or, incapable of survival and self-determination in the "modern" world, to vanish. Instead, these novels advocate for a balanced approach. In the new worlds of Indigenous science fiction, Native peoples are depicted as culturally and politically distinct but also fully human—in other words, as *Sovereign Others*.

Defining Terms: From Indigenous Futurism to the Indian Invention Novel

The concept of Indigenous Futurism was first popularized by Dillon in her 2012 anthology, *Walking the Clouds*. In the critical introduction to that work, Dillon makes two important claims: first, that Indigenous science fiction has "the capacity to envision Native futures, Indigenous hopes, and dreams recovered by rethinking the past in a new framework," and second, that "Indigenous sf is not so new—just overlooked, although largely accompanied by an emerging movement."[8] While I share Dillon's optimism for the possibilities of the genre, I am concerned about the potential consequences of reclaiming older texts as examples of science fiction. For instance, Dillon introduces the category of "Native slipstream," which "is intended to describe writing that does not simply seem avant-garde but models a cultural experience of reality."[9] Such a project has obvious value for Native literature and Native communities, but Dillon's definition raises other questions about the nature of Native worldviews. If examples of the Native slipstream "model a cultural experience of reality," then why categorize them as science fiction in the first place? What separates such texts from the multitude of other Indigenous stories that reflect "a cultural experience of reality" through interactions with ancestors, wendigos, or tricksters?

Though he does not address Dillon's work directly,[10] Rader illustrates some of the complications that might arise out of such broad definitions. To distinguish between science fiction and the "cultural experience of reality" that Dillon describes, he introduces the term "Indian invention novel" as a replacement for the concept of "Indigenous science fiction." According to Rader, the Indian invention novel

> draws from all of the motifs of science fiction that make it fun, fanciful, and forward looking, but, unlike the "science" and "fiction" components of sci-fi, Indian invention tropes are neither scientific nor fictional. They arise out of the diversity of Indian narrative—its humor, its disregard for the laws of physics, its trickster traditions, and its sense of circular and unending time. The novels of Indian invention play with creation stories, shape-shifters, coyotes, and all that is atemporal, creating a new genre that takes indigenous aesthetics to new planes.[11]

Rader's distinction between science fiction tropes and the "diversity of Indian narrative" draws attention to the dangers of collapsing categories, especially when we rely on mainstream, Euro-American critical categories to describe Indigenous literatures. By labeling texts that reflect Indigenous worldviews as "science fiction," we run the risk of trivializing Native voices and communities, of reducing lived experiences to primitive superstitions. Just as Toni Morrison has resisted the term "magical realism" because "it was a way of *not* talking about the politics. It was a way of *not* talking about what was in the books. If you could apply the word 'magical' then that *dilutes* the realism," so too could Dillon's reclamation of earlier texts imply that all Indigenous literature is simply fantastical.[12] Although this is clearly not Dillon's intent, readers who are unfamiliar with Native cultures may unintentionally use these new categories as another way of reading Native literature as myth—as a fascinating but naïve interpretation of reality that ultimately allows those readers to dismiss and disregard Indigenous cultures. In effect, although Dillon aims to demonstrate the ways that such texts model resistance to colonization, the fraught nature of these categories might actually serve to reinforce such structures.

A related though distinct critique has been raised against J. K. Rowling, whose story series *History of Magic in North America* incorporates actual Native traditions, including medicine men/women and skinwalkers. As Adrienne Keene has argued, "Native spirituality and religions are not fantasy on the same level as wizards. These beliefs are alive, practiced, and protected. . . . If Indigenous spirituality becomes conflated with fantasy 'magic'—how can we expect lawmakers and the public to be allies in the protection of these [sacred] spaces?"[13] Keene further points out that "Indigenous peoples are constantly situated as fantasy creatures" and, moreover, that "there is also a pervasive and problematic narrative wherein Native peoples are always 'mystical' and 'magical' and 'spiritual.'" The issue, as Keene explains, is that Native peoples "fight so hard every single day . . . to be seen as contemporary, real, full, and complete human beings and to push away from the stereotypes that restrict us in stock categories of mystical-connected-to-nature-shamans or violent-savage-warriors."[14] The conflation of Native peoples and spirituality with the genre of fantasy in general, and with the Harry Potter franchise in particular, is bound to reinforce those stereotypes—just as, in Rader's argument, the conflation of creation stories and tricksters with the genre of science fiction is bound to misrepresent the reality of Native spirituality and worldviews. Dillon's reclamation of earlier texts is clearly not equivalent to Rowling's appropriations, but in both cases there is a similar concern: when real Indigenous beliefs are collapsed with fantasy or science fiction, uninformed readers may "make a logical leap that Native peoples belong in the same fictional world as Harry Potter."[15]

In contrast, Rader's concept of the Indian invention novel resists reductive readings. His term is intended to highlight and celebrate the reality of Indigenous narratives and worldviews. As important as this concept is, however, the existence of Indian invention novels does not necessarily refute the presence of Indigenous science fiction; it just asks audiences to reconsider how we define the category. The Indian invention novel makes perfect sense when applied to certain texts—Rader's examples include Thomas King's *Green Grass, Running Water* and LeAnne Howe's *Miko Kings*—but it overlooks a handful of texts that engage with both Native worldviews *and* mainstream science fictional tropes such as alternate and virtual realities, Monster or Creature stories, postapocalyptic narratives, and time travel.[16] *Walking the Clouds* includes excerpts from some texts that draw on traditional sf tropes, such as Stephen Graham Jones's *The Bird Is Gone: A Manifesto* and Nalo Hopkinson's *Midnight Robber*, but the anthology's categories often combine such excerpts with texts that might be better understood as Indian invention novels.

Notably, both Rader and Dillon claim Sherman Alexie's novel *Flight* to illustrate their arguments:[17] Dillon includes an excerpt from the novel under the category of the Native slipstream, while Rader argues that it is one of the best examples of the Indian invention novel, an overlap that draws attention to the root of the disagreement between the two theories. Dillon refers to *Flight* as an example of "thought experiments by Native authors," while Rader contends that the novel contains "remnants of trickster tropes."[18] Dillon connects *Flight* to a variety of non-Native texts: she refers to the narrator as "an Indian Holden Caulfield" and highlights similarities to both the "popular early 1990s television series *Quantum Leap*" and Afrofuturist author Andrea Hairston's short story "Griots of the Galaxy."[19] Meanwhile, Rader observes that *Flight*'s "relation to American Indian storytelling traditions was, surprisingly, completely ignored by the reviewers."[20] While Dillon notes that moving through time allows the narrator, Zits, "to move beyond the self-loathing of internal colonization that Alexie might argue typifies reservation youth today," Rader argues that *Flight* emphasizes "Zits's role as a storyteller, the novel's community of voices, and its circular notion of time."[21] Ultimately, Dillon's description of the novel focuses on the way that a "thought experiment" carried out through the mainstream science fictional trope of time travel can lead to empowerment for Native readers, and Rader takes issue with the idea that *Flight* is using mainstream science fictional tropes in the first place. He argues that, while Alexie was clearly inspired by Kurt Vonnegut's *Slaughterhouse-Five*, the narrative structure is at least equally influenced by American Indian traditions.[22] Ultimately, these readings point to both the overlap and the disparity between the two arguments: Dillon and Rader position *Flight* as a positive intervention into Indigenous concerns in the twenty-first century, but Dillon sees Alexie using mainstream narrative approaches to achieve that end; to Rader, the narrative is primarily Indigenous. This conflict is only one example of the tensions that can arise when trying to reconcile Native storytelling traditions with the generic tropes of science fiction—particularly without examining the theoretical arguments that underpin science fiction as a genre in its own right.

Due to the limitations of these categories, as well as the way that some works seem to consciously engage with two distinct discourses, I propose that such texts can be more effectively situated at the intersection of two critical approaches: Indigenous knowledge and science fiction theory. In addition to the term "Indian invention novel," Rader proposes the concept of "engaged resistance," which he defines as "a fundamentally indigenous form of aesthetic discourse that engages both Native and American cultural contexts as a mode of resistance against the ubiquitous colonial tendencies of assimilation and erasure."[23] The works of Indigenous science fiction that I examine here are also all works of engaged resistance. They engage with multiple cultural contexts, but their engagement does not point to assimilation or hybridity; rather, such texts reinforce tribally specific values and emphasize the applicability of Indigenous knowledge in the twenty-first century. As Roanhorse suggests in her discussion of Cherokee author Daniel Wilson's *Robopocalypse*, Indigenous science fiction "dares to imagine that Indigenous knowledge offers the larger world something that might just save it."[24] For instance, the protagonist of William Sanders's *The Ballad of Billy Badass and the Rose of Turkestan* uses a Cherokee tobacco ceremony to defeat a radiation Creature from another dimension, while Blake M. Hausman's *Riding the Trail of Tears* follows a group of Nunnehi, or "spirit people,"[25] who interfere with a virtual reality game that monetizes the Trail of Tears and exploits its Native employees. Texts like these depict the "cultural experience of reality" that Dillon describes, but they *also* incorporate mainstream science fictional tropes that have little or no basis in Indigenous worldviews. Fewer texts fit into this category, but those that do have the ability to reinforce Native narrative structures and worldviews while simultaneously challenging and expanding the theoretical definitions of science fiction as an academic field.

Indigenous Science Fiction in Conversation with Postcolonial Studies

While the genre of Indigenous science fiction is still emerging, the related field of postcolonial sf has already established a critical foothold. Although postcolonial studies remains separate from Native American studies in key ways, the critical arguments surrounding this field point to some of the possibilities of science fiction to tell stories that have historically been silenced. Indeed, Indigenous peoples and those living in postcolonial societies share many experiences of colonization, and thus, many of the arguments established in a critical discussion of postcolonial science fiction may shed light on the possibilities of Indigenous sf. For instance, speaking broadly about her experiences as "a person of colour writing science fiction," Jamaican author Nalo Hopkinson suggests that "arguably, one of the most familiar memes of science fiction is that of going to foreign countries and colonizing natives. . . . For many of us, that's not a thrilling adventure story; it's non-fiction, and we are on the wrong side of the strange-looking ship that appears out of nowhere."[26] Similarly, Istvan Csicsery-Ronay Jr. points out that "the dominant sf nations are precisely those that attempted to expand beyond their national borders in imperialist projects: Britain, France, Germany, Soviet Russia, Japan, and the US."[27] He suggests that the presence of empire and imperialism in science fiction is no coincidence; rather, "all the social and creative endeavors of imperial peoples are shot through with the institutional violence that makes them materially possible. Imperial violence is so powerful that it must expand; contained, its society would implode like a black hole."[28] In other words, works of science fiction that are written within this context will necessarily be tainted by the colonial power structures upon which the nations themselves have been built. Thus, it is unsurprising that they often repeat the meme described by Hopkinson.

And yet, Csicsery-Ronay is also careful to distinguish between larger structural patterns and individual writers:

> To say that sf is a genre of empire does not mean that sf artists seek to serve the empire. Most serious writers of sf are skeptical of entrenched power, sometimes because of its tyranny, sometimes because it hobbles technological innovation. This is one reason why some Marxist critics consider the genre to be inherently critical, despite the fact that careful social analysis rarely plays a central role in sf narratives.[29]

Despite his sympathy for individual artists, however, Csicsery-Ronay seems to suggest that writers from imperial nations are necessarily trapped within these notions of empire. And yet, he does not explicitly address the position of artists whose nations have been colonized, including Indigenous writers. Are they, too, doomed to repeat and reinforce imperial values? Or might they more successfully resist, given that their very existence is in opposition to the aims of empire? Dean Rader might argue that such authors are better prepared to incorporate "careful social analysis" and, thus, to create works of engaged resistance. Jessica Langer articulates this argument more fully when she suggests that "in its concerns with alienness, marginality, utopian exclusion, and colonialism generally, [science fiction] is a useful site in which to explore the concept of (post)coloniality in its various guises."[30] Indigenous authors, like other writers from marginalized and oppressed social groups, have much to contribute to a genre that deals in "foreign countries and colonizing natives" because their lives have in many ways been shaped by such encounters. By writing stories that reimagine this "familiar meme," Indigenous authors may literally write back against a dominant culture that romanticizes colonization, supports an imperial agenda, and alienates Native peoples.

For this reason, postcolonial scholars have sometimes included Indigenous texts in their analysis of science fiction. While the critical attention paid to these texts contributes to a larger discussion, readings that are grounded in postcolonial methodologies may also overlook the tribally specific readings that are so important to Native American studies. Two of the most notable sources of postcolonial science fiction, both of which engage with Indigenous texts, are Langer's book-length critical work, *Postcolonialism and Science Fiction*, and *So Long Been Dreaming: Postcolonial Science Fiction and Fantasy*, an anthology edited by Nalo Hopkinson and Uppinder Mehan. Hopkinson and Mehan include Haisla/Heiltsuk author Eden Robinson's short story "Terminal Avenue" in their collection, as well as a fantasy story by Cherokee/Scots-Irish writer Celu Amberstone. In the conclusion to that collection, Mehan describes "postcoloniality" as a term that includes "those of us who identify ourselves as having Aboriginal, African, South Asian, Asian ancestry, wherever we make our homes."[31] Because there is little critical framing within the anthology, this is the extent of the text's theoretical discussion of the relationship between "postcolonial" and "Indigenous."[32]

In *Postcolonialism and Science Fiction*, Langer deals more directly with that relationship. She acknowledges that there is an important distinction between the two fields, but she ultimately follows Hopkinson and Mehan's lead by choosing to include an analysis of Robinson's "Terminal Avenue" in her text. To supplement her postcolonial approach, she "makes significant use of some of the questions raised in the First Nations cultural context provided by Dillon's 2007 article "*Miindiwag* and Indigenous Diaspora."[33] Essentially, Langer acknowledges the larger theoretical argument and then circumvents it by relying heavily on a single critical article about Indigenous science fiction. She notes that her own contribution "build[s] on Dillon's work and link[s] the stories themselves to wider postcolonial and science-fictional critical practices" and then goes on to summarize Dillon's argument while connecting it to broader critical discussions—most notably by approaching the story through a Foucauldian lens.[34] Langer's reading of "Terminal Avenue" illustrates the loss that occurs when postcolonial and Indigenous theoretical frameworks are collapsed: although she acknowledges many differences between the two disciplines, she nonetheless approaches Robinson's text from a Eurocentric critical perspective that is inappropriate to Indigenous literature.

The article that Langer relies upon, Dillon's "*Miindiwag* and Indigenous Diaspora," more productively models the possibilities of reading Indigenous science fiction through the lens of Native American and Indigenous studies. Dillon begins by acknowledging that "Native intellectuals have for decades questioned the 'post' in postcolonial."[35] While she accepts that Robinson and Amberstone have been categorized as "postcolonial," she supplements that categorization by performing her own analysis of the two stories, which she performs "as a means of achieving a serious reflection on the past that contextualizes activism rather than breeding nostalgia."[36] Thus, rather than becoming entangled in an argument over terminology, Dillon provides a culturally and historically specific framework that is more appropriate to an Indigenous literary approach. Her reading of Robinson and Amberstone demonstrates the useful work that can be done when Indigenous texts are read within a Native context rather than being forced into a Eurocentric critical model. By demonstrating the ways that the future world of "Terminal Avenue" echoes the very real history of banning potlatches throughout Canada, Dillon draws attention to the culturally specific oppression faced by First Nations citizens, as opposed to reading the story as a broad, universalist allegory. Although she also steps outside of a tribally specific framework when she discusses the work of a Haisla/Heiltsuk author through Anishinaabe and Okanagon frameworks, Dillon's article nonetheless demonstrates the importance of situating Native science fiction within a specifically Indigenous framework.

Indigenous Knowledge in Conversation with SF Theory

In addition to contextualizing Native sf within Indigenous histories and traditions, it is also important to situate these works within a critical discussion of science fiction itself. Unsurprisingly, there is widespread disagreement among critics and fans about both the basic definition of the genre and its origins. In fact, John Rieder argues that "the collective and accretive social process by which sf has been constructed does not have the kind of coherent form or causality that allows one to talk about origins at all."[37] Similarly, Csicsery-Ronay suggests that "by sf, we should understand not an ideal category with a putative social or aesthetic logic, but what national audiences understand sf to be—which is less a class than a jelly that shifts around but doesn't lose its mass."[38] Defining the genre in more theoretical terms, Rieder draws on Jauss's reception theory to argue that "there cannot be a first example of a genre, because the generic character of a text is precisely what is repeated and conventional in it." Thus, rather than defining science fiction as a set of specific characteristics or tropes, Rieder proposes that we understand genre as a historical process in which "categorization . . . is not a passive registering of qualities intrinsic to what is being categorized, but an active intervention in their disposition, and this insistence on agency is what most decisively distinguishes an historical approach to sf from a formalist one."[39] In other words, as they decide how to classify particular texts and tropes, individual readers, authors, critics, and publishers all participate in the ongoing formation of the category that we refer to as "science fiction."

This is not to say that a discussion of sf tropes or icons is irrelevant, but it does mean that the genre cannot be defined by those tropes alone. Csicsery-Ronay offers a quick rundown of the most recognizable icons, including "the spaceship, the alien, the robot, super-weapons, bio-monsters, and the more recent additions, wormholes, the net, the cyborg, and so on." He further observes that "it is not difficult to link these [icons] to colonialist and imperialist practices."[40] That observation is shared by Roanhorse, who echoes Hopkinson when she argues that "Indigenous Futurisms is a term meant to encourage Native, First Nations, and other Indigenous authors and creators to speak back to the colonial tropes of science fiction—those that celebrate the rugged individual, the conquest of foreign worlds, the taming of the final frontier."[41] No matter how these tropes are deployed in individual works of science fiction, such lists demonstrate the accuracy of Rieder's underlying argument: the genre cannot be defined by the presence of any single icon. Rather, the repetition of those icons in various combinations across texts, and their categorization as sf by writers, readers, and publishers, cements the definition of the genre as one that includes these tropes. Such a process is "historical," as Rieder argues, precisely because the definition of the genre will continue to change over time as new tropes are added or old ones fall away, much as Csicsery-Ronay lists both conventional and more recent icons.

Though Rieder refutes definitions of sf based on particular tropes or formal distinctions, he does not simply give up on the notion of definition. Instead, he proposes that a common understanding of science fiction could be located at the intersection of these competing definitions, arguing that science fiction is

> the product of the interaction among different communities of practice using different definitions of sf. The multiplicity of definitions of sf does not reflect widespread confusion about what sf is, but rather results from the variety of motives the definitions express and the many ways of intervening in the genre's production, distribution, and reception that they pursue.[42]

Rieder's theoretical framework serves as a useful starting place for understanding science fiction not only because it acknowledges the genre's flexibility and willingness to adapt to historical conditions, but also because it is inclusive of diverse voices and traditions. It makes way for both academic and popular interpretations of sf while also granting legitimacy to science fiction writers and artists from historically marginalized groups. By including and giving equal weight to the "multiplicity of definitions," Rieder envisions a welcoming space where new traditions, such as Indigenous science fiction, can contribute to and expand upon the existing canon.

Practically speaking, how might we apply this broad definition of the genre to specific texts and theories? Rieder proposes that critics should not look "for the appearance of a positive entity but rather for a practice of drawing similarities and differences among texts."[43] To locate some of these major similarities and differences, I turn to Carter Meland, who, following Brian Stableford, suggests that "there are two broad types of sf writers."[44] First are those who focus on the strictly scientific, such as H. G. Wells and Arthur C. Clarke. Second are those writers who "are unconcerned with the rigors of scientific discipline and aim instead to 'disturb settled routines of thought,' in Stableford's words." Perhaps the most famous example of this second type of writer is Philip K. Dick, who "claimed that the aim of sf was to create a 'shock of dysrecognition' in the reader's mind."[45] As Dick explains, this shock occurs when the reader encounters an idea that is "truly new," one that "unlocks the reader's mind so that that mind, like the author's, begins to create."[46] Such an idea, which Dick argues is at the heart of *"good* science fiction," must imagine a society that "is predicated on our known society," but that has been "transformed into that which it is not or not yet."[47] In other words, according to Dick, the most important element of science fiction is not the scientific theory that explains *how* a new society came into being so much as it is the author's ability to present readers with a "distinct new idea."[48]

Dick published this definition of science fiction in 1981, near the end of a prolific career as an sf writer and just two years after the publication of sf theorist Darko Suvin's book *Metamorphoses of Science Fiction*, which offers a similar—and extremely influential—definition of the genre.[49] Suvin proposes that the defining characteristic of sf is the presence of a "novum," or "strange newness," a term that echoes Dick's "shock of dysrecognition."[50] Just as Dick emphasizes the importance of a new idea that "sets off a chain reaction of ramification ideas in the mind of the reader," Suvin's novum must become a catalyst for the rest of the story.[51] A new idea that is simply a casual detail will not suffice. According to this logic, we ought to be able to locate at least one novum in any work of science fiction (or, as Dick would have it, *"good* science fiction"). For instance, the novum in H. G. Wells's *The Island of Doctor Moreau* is found not in Moreau's unsettling humanoid animals, but in the medical procedure that he has developed to create them. That concept is built on a late nineteenth-century understanding of vivisection, but it is a new idea in that Moreau extends the work of actual surgeons and anatomists like John Hunter to imagine that beyond the "transplants and grafting operations" that were actually performed, it is possible "to transplant tissue from one part of an animal to another, or from one animal to another . . . and indeed to change it in its most intimate structure."[52] This new concept is at the core of Wells's story. Without it, the events of the novel could not occur.

Suvin argues that in addition to serving as the catalyst for the plot, the novum must also be produced through the "interaction of estrangement and cognition."[53] He suggests that estrangement occurs in works of fantasy as well as science fiction, but cognition "differentiates [science fiction] not only from myth, but also from the folk (fairy) tale and the fantasy."[54] *The Island of Dr. Moreau* continues to serve as a useful example here, as Moreau's invention meets both of Suvin's requirements. First, it is clearly an example of estrangement that is both new and strange to readers. The scientific knowledge itself is unfamiliar, as are its results: hybrid animals that combine the characteristics of an ox and a boar, or a hyaena and a pig, which are then engineered to resemble humans. But that estrangement, which is here combined with something like the horror of the abject, is only half of the equation. As Suvin notes, a work of fantasy could easily include talking animals and animal hybrids—think, for instance, of a centaur, minotaur, or Pegasus. What distinguishes science fiction from fantasy, according to this theory, is the presence of *cognition*. Because Moreau is a scientist whose research is based, at least loosely, on real scientific theories of the nineteenth century, there is some logical explanation to justify Moreau's process. The animals were not conjured by a sorcerer who waved a wand but instead created in a laboratory by a scientist whose work reflects a logical extension of medicine as it was understood in Wells's time. So, according to Suvin, any text that is considered science fiction must have a clearly identifiable novum that puts the narrative into motion, and that novum must be, as in *The Island of Doctor Moreau*, an example of cognitive estrangement.

Though Rieder reasonably points out that Suvin's theory "has to be understood partly in the context of its opposition to the commercial genre practices Suvin deplored,"[55] his definition must also be understood as "the core critical approach specific to the genre, against which almost everything else has been obliged to define itself."[56] It is also a particularly useful way to approach Indigenous science fiction because Suvin, perhaps surprisingly, takes a theoretical approach that demonstrates awareness of his own epistemological position while also acknowledging the validity of other worldviews. He defines "cognition" both as a stand-in for "scientifically methodical cognition" and as "intrinsic, culturally acquired cognitive logic."[57] He further argues that "cognition is wider than science" and suggests that we might take "'science' in a sense closer to the German *Wissenschaft*, French *science*, or Russian *nauka*, which include not only natural but also all the cultural or historical sciences and even scholarship."[58] These broad definitions encompass Euro-American understandings of "science" but *also* make space for alternate kinds of cognition, such as the Indigenous epistemologies that determine the underlying logic in many works of Native science fiction.

Here we might turn to Tewa scholar Gregory Cajete, who explains that "when speaking about Indigenous or Native science, one is really talking about the entire edifice of Indigenous knowledge."[59] This edifice "can be said to be 'inclusive' of modern science," just as Suvin suggests that "cognition is wider than science."[60] So, where Suvin argues for the importance of the "cultural or historical sciences," including "sociological, psychological, historical, anthropological parallels" in understanding mainstream works of science fiction,[61] Cajete observes that

> in Native languages there is no word for "science," nor for "philosophy," "psychology," or any other foundational way of coming to know and understand the nature of life and our relationships therein. Not having, or more accurately, not needing, words for science, art, or psychology did not diminish their importance in Native life. For Native people, *seeking life* was the all-encompassing task.[62]

Both writers make the argument that "science" cannot be so easily broken down into distinct categories, acknowledging that the various epistemological approaches all contribute to the same end. Likewise, in the act of distinguishing between science fiction and fantasy, Suvin establishes a definition of sf that includes non-Western forms of cognition and thus makes room for an Indigenous understanding of science as a holistic framework encapsulating a variety of disciplinary approaches that usually remain distinct within a Euro-American worldview.

Other elements of Suvin's theoretical framework similarly reflect science fiction's openness to alternate worldviews and the inherent possibilities of the genre to tell new stories. He avoids terms loaded with inherent value judgments, such as "magical realism" or "the supernatural," replacing them with the concept of the novum, or "strange newness."[63] Suvin is also careful to distinguish between objective reality—which, he argues, may well exist but that is difficult to define—and "the author's empirical reality," a term that allows for differences in perspective and experience rather than reliance upon the concept of a universal worldview.[64] He further argues that science fiction "sees the norms of any age, including emphatically its own, as unique, changeable, and therefore subject to a *cognitive* view."[65] Such a view is also capable of "confronting a set normative system with a point of view or look implying a new set of norms."[66]

To see Suvin's theory in practice, we can turn to Ursula K. Le Guin's 1969 novel, *The Left Hand of Darkness*. That novel follows the story of the Envoy Genly Ai. Genly represents the Ekumen, an intergalactic governing body somewhat similar to the United Nations. He has been sent to the planet Gethen to persuade the Gethenians to join the Ekumen. He is repeatedly frustrated by the rules governing this encounter, which require him to arrive alone with limited technological resources and no weapons with which to protect himself. And yet, by the end of the novel, Genly comes to appreciate the logic that undergirds the Ekumen's rationale. Speaking to his closest friend on the planet, Estraven, Genly explains:

> I thought it was for your sake that I came alone, so obviously alone, so vulnerable, that I could in myself pose no threat, change no balance: not an invasion, but a mere messenger-boy. But there's more to it than that. Alone, I cannot change your world. But I can be changed by it. Alone, I must listen, as well as speak. Alone, the relationship I finally make, if I make one, is not impersonal and not only political: it is individual, it is personal, it is both more and less than political.[67]

As Genly learns to understand Gethenian cultures and is necessarily changed by his experiences on the planet, Le Guin illustrates the importance of acknowledging and respecting multiple perspectives. At the beginning of the novel, Genly clearly believes his own species and culture to be superior to the ones encountered on Gethen. But, during the course of the book, he also learns to recognize and critique the "set normative system" that has shaped his own worldview. Through Genly's model, Le Guin encourages her readers to confront their own perspectives and learn to appreciate a "new set of norms."

One of the most famous aspects of *The Left Hand of Darkness* is the Gethenians' biology, which differs from that of people on other planets, including Genly Ai's. Whereas most humans are "bisexual," a term that Le Guin uses to refer to the division of the species into two sexes, Gethenians are neuter, neither male nor female, for most of their lives. Once a month, each Gethenian enters kemmer, a sexual cycle in which their anatomy changes to become either male or female. They mate only while in kemmer, and afterwards their bodies return to the same neutral state. Genly is initially disgusted by the idea of the Gethenians' anatomy, which he also collapses with their gender presentation as he struggles to interact with people whose sex and gender remain ambiguous. But it is not just differing gender norms that cause problems for Genly: he is equally frustrated by *shifgrethor*, an unspoken principle and cultural touchstone that governs most interpersonal relationships in Karhide, the nation where he spends the majority of his time on Gethen. As Genly slowly comes to understand and appreciate these major differences, he also comes to accept that the norms that have governed his own life are, as Suvin suggests, both "unique" and "changeable."[68] In fact, as he acknowledges in his speech to Estraven, the process by which Genly changes his perspective is actually built into the Ekumen's protocol. Or, as David M. Higgins points out, "the Ekumen is dedicated to the continuous productive failure of its own identity in favor of a continuous (and nonimperial) dialectical process of becoming."[69] In other words, through the Ekumen, Le Guin demonstrates the importance of flexibility and openness to change that is so important to Suvin's theory of science fiction.

Considering the relationship between ethical theory and Le Guin's novels in greater detail, Higgins argues that she

> accomplishes what contemporary theorists do not; she imagines, through the Ekumen, how cosmopolitan ethics and values might be embodied in normative practice. She can achieve this where [Judith] Butler and others cannot because science fiction offers a space where extrapolative thought experiments—difficult for abstract theory to undertake—can be conducted.[70]

Higgins's explanation of the important work done by science fiction is echoed in Suvin's emphasis on change and the importance of analyzing normative perspectives critically, as well as his willingness to acknowledge that different authors may experience different empirical realities. Both Higgins and Suvin point to science fiction's distinct ability to tell non-normative stories and challenge mainstream Euro-American worldviews that accept Western Enlightenment rationality as the "correct" lens through which to interpret the world.

Despite the space that Suvin's theory creates for previously marginalized voices, it also clashes with many of the underlying principles of Native cultures—and, thus, with concepts common in Native science fiction. The source of the problem lies in Suvin's understanding of religion, which he introduces when he defines science fiction against other genres. He argues that myth also makes use of estrangement as a formal device but claims that it is distinct from sf because it uses a "'timeless' and religious approach" and is "diametrically opposed to the cognitive approach since it conceives of human relations as fixed and supernaturally determined."[71] This pairing of "timeless" and "religious" hints at Suvin's understanding of religion as that which is "fixed." He is bothered by such a perspective because it suggests that humanity cannot change—a belief that goes directly against the goals of a genre that seeks to inspire Dick's "shock of dysrecognition" and thus to present "the norms of any age, including emphatically its own, as unique, changeable, and therefore subject to a cognitive view." As a result, he situates religion as the polar opposite of science fiction, a genre that hinges upon the possibility of change.

However, Suvin's binary definitions of science/religion and science fiction/ myth remain grounded in a Euro-American perspective that simply fails to consider alternate definitions of "religion." In order to understand why Suvin sees religion as fixed and static, as well as how we might redefine the term, we must bring Suvin into conversation with Vine Deloria Jr., who outlines the distinctions between Western European and Indigenous religions that Suvin's critique overlooks. As Deloria explains it, "The very essence of Western European identity involves the assumption that time proceeds in a linear fashion."[72] This attention to time stems from religious beliefs: "From the very beginning of the religion, it has been the Christian contention that the experiences of humankind could be recorded in a linear fashion, and when this was done, the whole purpose of the creation event became clear, explaining not only the history of human societies but also revealing the nature of the end of the world and the existence of heaven."[73] This belief originates, logically enough, in the life story of Jesus Christ. As Deloria argues,

> The whole basis for the Christian belief in life after death was the alleged resurrection of Jesus after he had been dead for three days and his subsequent ascension into heaven. . . . When Jesus failed to return within the lifetime of those who had been his closest associates, the religion should have folded. But . . . the initial prediction was continually modified so that while the basic idea had been an immediate conclusion to history through divine intervention, its immediacy gradually became symbolic, not historic.[74]

When Suvin criticizes the mythical or religious approach, he is criticizing that approach as it appears specifically in Jewish and Christian cultures. What he considers to be "timeless" and "fixed" is the concept that the past two thousand years of human existence, as well as all future events, happen in between two unalterable points in linear time: Jesus's birth and his eventual return. Suvin considers such an approach antithetical to science fiction because there is no real possibility for change so long as all events are contained between those two points; in other words, we already know how the story will end. Moreover, such a philosophy bothers Suvin because, as a Marxist, he is ideologically invested in seeing history as a different kind of linear progression—one that leads from the rise of capitalism to its downfall and, eventually, to the rise of socialism in its place. Thus, when Suvin claims that the religious or mythic approach is "diametrically opposed" to science fiction, he is relying upon a very particular understanding of religion, as well as a specific historical and ideological approach.

On the other hand, many Indigenous religions emphasize the importance of space rather than time.[75] Where Christianity focuses on linear progression, "the vast majority of Indian tribal religions . . . have a sacred center at a particular place."[76] Because Native religions are spatially, not temporally, oriented, within Native communities, "it was not what people believed to be true that was important but what they experienced as true."[77] Or, as Deloria reiterates in a later text, "experience is not limited by mental considerations and assumptions regarding the universe."[78] In other words, because Euro-Americans generally understand the world as a temporal progression based in a religious belief, they make certain assumptions about how the world works and what is possible within it. On the other hand, because Native peoples tend to focus on what happens within a particular place, they do not share this set of assumptions or expectations based in the linear progression of time. Where a Western European worldview defines reality by "what you allow your mind to accept, not what you experience," Native peoples are more easily able to recognize and respond to whatever events occur, no matter how unexpected or unlikely they may be.[79]

Indeed, a Native religious approach, antithetical to its Western European counterpart, might much more successfully engage with science fiction as a literature of change and difference because it emphasizes the transitive, causal relationship between religious beliefs and the "present," "ongoing" world, as opposed to Suvin's understanding of religion as a "static" entity.[80] As Deloria demonstrates, a culture that defines reality in temporal terms does indeed maintain a fixed understanding of the world. This perspective may be counterproductive to science fiction, which depends upon the possibility of change both within the story and in its readers. On the other hand, a worldview based on spatial relations allows for greater flexibility and, thus, a more open attitude to change. We can see the benefits of this worldview reflected in Indigenous science fiction, which often depicts Native characters as better prepared to accept and respond to elements of cognitive estrangement than their non-Native counterparts. In these stories, Euro-Americans often refuse to acknowledge that a problem exists because it does not fit into their fixed notions of the world; meanwhile, Native characters recognize the presence of a novum, assess its effects on the community, and react accordingly. So, in a genre that is defined by encounters with the unknown, an Indigenous approach models a more effective—and even a more ethical—response to alterity.

An Ethical Approach to Science Fiction

To make sense of the ethics of science fiction, we must consider the nature of the genre's relationship to the real world. Suvin suggests that science fiction is ultimately metaphorical: "Whether in space or . . . in time, the new framework is correlative to the new inhabitants. The aliens—utopians, monsters, or simply differing strangers—are a mirror to man just as the differing country is a mirror for his world."[81] We can apply this metaphorical approach to various works of science fiction. In H. G. Wells's *The Time Machine*, for instance, the protagonist of the novel travels into a distant future where human beings have evolved into two distinct species: the Eloi, who live above ground, and the Morlocks, who live below. The Time Traveller theorizes that this split occurred because of "the gradual widening of the present merely temporary and social difference between the Capitalist and the Labourer."[82] He goes on to propose that in the London of his time (1895), there is already "a tendency to utilize underground space for the less ornamental purposes of civilization," such as the subways and "underground workrooms and restaurants." "Even now," he continues, "does not an East-end worker live in such artificial conditions as practically to be cut off from the natural surface of the earth?"[83] The simple, childlike Eloi and the horrifying, abject Morlocks are simply a metaphor for the extreme socioeconomic divisions that existed in Victorian England. No matter how estranged these beings may seem at first, they are a "mirror to man," a reflection of the cruelty and inhumanity wrought by capitalism and extrapolated to its logical conclusion: a world in which the lower classes are banished underground, the upper classes are reduced to helpless idiocy, and one group quite literally cannibalizes the other in order to survive.

In contrast to Suvin's metaphorical view, Pinsky argues that the genre has the capacity to imagine a genuine encounter with alterity or the Other. For Pinsky, "the real issue is the relationship between the two poles of technological disposition (the actuality of an other) and the absolute external 'truth' of the Other, and how this very relationship is articulated through the space of science fiction."[84] He goes on to propose that "the space of science fiction" foregrounds a discussion of ethics, claiming that "we exist already in the world, and any understanding of ourselves must go hand-in-hand with an understanding of ethics and our relationship to others."[85] In Pinsky's conception, then, the "shock of dysrecognition" is important not because it mirrors a world that is familiar to its readers, but because it presents a genuine attempt to imagine something outside of ourselves.

If we reconsider *The Time Machine* according to Pinsky's framework, then we must accept that both the Morlocks and the Eloi are truly distinct from humanity. We may extrapolate how humans evolved into these two distinct species, but there is nonetheless a real difference that makes it impossible to see ourselves reflected in these creatures. An ethical approach to the novel demands that we acknowledge this difference and recognize the demand of the Other, including both the Eloi and the Morlocks. Here we might say that the Time Traveller succeeds in acknowledging the Eloi though he fails to recognize the demand of the Morlocks. Although the Eloi have lost most of the characteristics of humanity, the narrator nonetheless treats them with respect. When he first encounters them, he describes one "as being a very beautiful and graceful creature, but indescribably frail."[86] A few pages later, he realizes that the Eloi "were on the intellectual level of one of our five-year-old children."[87] Despite the Eloi's intellectual and physical limitations, the narrator befriends one of them, Weena. He saves her from drowning, and she thanks him by giving him "a big garland of flowers."[88] When he returns to the present day, the Time Traveller brings Weena's flowers with him. One of his colleagues asks if he can study the unusual flowers, to which the Time Traveller replies "certainly not."[89] His refusal to relinquish the flowers—even in the name of scientific research—demonstrates his emotional attachment to Weena and reinforces the idea that though the Eloi are not recognizably human, the Time Traveller still regards them as *people*.

On the other hand, when faced with the more difficult task of recognizing the ethical demand of the Morlocks, both the Time Traveller and the novel itself fall short. Although the Time Traveller catches several glimpses of the Morlocks, he does not encounter them directly until he seeks them out by descending into the underground tunnels where they live. When he finally comes face-to-face with a Morlock, he says that "You can scarce imagine how nauseatingly inhuman they looked—those pale, chinless faces and great, lidless, pinkish-grey eyes!"[90] The narrator's own emphasis on the Morlocks' "inhumanity" is telling: it is this, rather than any specific threat, that so unnerves him. Although he will later realize that the Morlocks survive by eating the Eloi, this description comes well before that realization. Where the narrator compares the Eloi to children or "the more beautiful kind of consumptive,"[91] the Morlocks are instead compared to "abysmal fishes."[92] When he comes face to face with the Other, then, the Time Traveller is able to respond ethically to the Eloi, building a relationship with them across difference, but he fails to respond similarly to the Morlocks. Instead, he treats them as the abject, in Kristeva's sense of the term: he insists on their inhumanity and thus "discharge[s them] as excrement, literally rendered 'Other.'"[93]

As illustrated by this example, Pinsky can help readers make sense of Indigenous science fiction because he challenges us to acknowledge that alterity does in fact exist, that the entire world cannot be reduced to a metaphorical representation of the Self. Moreover, Pinsky's theory challenges audiences to consider our ethical responsibility in those inevitable encounters with the Other. Suvin's understanding of sf as metaphor can help readers bridge the gap between the human and the alien, but Pinsky's approach cautions us against extending that metaphor too far. It is important to recognize similarities, to see an unfamiliar Other as a person with dignity, but if we reduce the Other to a mirror for the Self, we may unintentionally assimilate, and thus do ethical violence to, that Other. As my earlier discussion of Euro-American and Indigenous worldviews demonstrates, significant differences may exist between people from various cultures, and universalizing one's own perspective leads to the marginalization of other voices. By confronting the presence of the Other and asking us to consider the ethics of that encounter, Pinsky challenges readers to reflect on our own responses to alterity: When faced with real difference, are we able to accept the existence of other perspectives, or do we insist on reproducing dominant narratives and enforcing those narratives upon the Other? Because science fiction emphasizes the importance of change and asks us to question normative assumptions, it also encourages us to consider how we engage with change and difference in our own lives.

To explore these questions, Pinsky draws on a Western European philosophical discussion of ethics. Situating his argument between Martin Heidegger's concept of *dassein*, or Being, and Emmanuel Levinas's ethical theory, he proposes that

> the individual self within the collective expands its parameters through consumption, the assimilation of other objects on the basis of their similarity. Reproduction of the same takes place within this enclosure, as a cloning of perfect copies. Any alterity is subsumed within the collective and assumed to no longer exist. The past of such a being is based on a certain certainty of memory. Its future reflects a certain enfolding order, which we call Progress. This Progress is goal oriented, obsessed with the production of meaning within a closed system.[94]

This explanation addresses several key concepts, but we might begin by observing that, according to Pinsky, each individual self within the collectivity of human culture is engaged in expansion, assimilation, and reproduction of Self, generally at the expense of the Other. Assuming that this description is universally true is problematic at best. Since Pinsky is working within the framework of Western European philosophy, it seems more likely that such a description applies specifically to Western European and Euro-American cultural responses, just as Suvin's definition of "religion" must be placed within its cultural contexts. Indeed, Pinsky's claim seems more plausible when repositioned within Vine Deloria's religious framework and understood as a discussion of Western European cultures that have been heavily influenced by the development of Christianity. Deloria's discussion of the Western European focus on temporality is echoed in Pinsky's suggestion that the individual situates itself in linear time, where it understands itself as moving into a future that reflects Progress with a capital "P." A narrative of continuing progress is, after all, a core component of the Western belief in Enlightenment rationality. Pinsky's definition might help us understand the Western desire toward expansion, colonization, and assimilation, which are explained here as part of the goal-oriented movement toward Progress.

Pinsky is not necessarily endorsing this concept of Progress, nor is he uncritical of it. But he *does* claim that all human beings attempt to assimilate alterity, to transform Difference into Sameness, by establishing a narrative of Progress through time. Even as Pinsky advocates for an ethical response to the Other, then, he assimilates that Other by making universal assumptions about the value of Progress and the human response to alterity. Such an attempt to assimilate the Other is precisely what Deloria critiques when he argues that "Western man must quickly come to grips with the breadth of human experiences and understand these experiences from a world viewpoint, not simply a Western one."[95] Deloria's argument demands that Western peoples acknowledge that other perspectives exist and may offer a more effective way of understanding the world. Indigenous peoples, who already ground their worldviews in space rather than time, are more aware of the limitations and dangers of this Progress narrative, both from a philosophical perspective and because of their historical encounters with those who have espoused such narratives. For several hundred years, Native peoples have been attacked, assimilated, and violently erased by Europeans and Euro-Americans who valued the kinds of Progress and assimilation that Pinsky describes. Such encounters have damaged both Native and non-Native peoples, as well as the earth itself, but Deloria is encouraged by non-Native people's growing interest in "American Indian religious traditions."[96] For Deloria, American Indian understandings of land and life "may provide the larger society with the conceptual tools to rescue itself from its own destruction."[97] Following Deloria, we can see the ways that Indigenous science fiction has the capacity to resist the assimilationist impulses that Pinsky describes and, moreover, to model an alternative approach to his idea of an ethical encounter.

Ironically, even as Pinsky notes this pattern of assimilation, he fails to acknowledge that such a pattern might be culturally specific. By assuming that this is how "human culture" behaves, he also absorbs all perspectives into one, applying a distinctly Western European experience to all humanity.[98] If we take Deloria's advice instead, we can step back and note that for cultures that are grounded in the spatial rather than the temporal, the individual might *not* feel the inherent desire to subsume the Other into a narrative of Progress, with its linear conception of time. Moreover, because many Native cultures also prioritize the community over the individual, members of such communities might be better prepared for an encounter with the Other. Only cultures that place a high value on individualism will be threatened by the existence of anything beyond the individual. So, before proceeding, we might make this distinction: while Pinsky's claim that there is a Self that will encounter an Other seems reasonable enough, his argument that such a Self will attempt to assimilate the Other should be understood as describing a culturally specific set of circumstances and responses, just as Suvin's critique of science fiction relies on a culturally specific understanding of religion.

What we might more usefully take from Pinsky's argument is the acknowledgement that Otherness does in fact exist—that no matter how humans respond, there is an "unassimilable alterity" that through the "Law of Chance,"[99] we might encounter at any time—and that science fiction creates a space where we might explore such encounters. To illustrate this point, we can return to Le Guin's depictions of sex and gender in *The Left Hand of Darkness*. Contemporary readers may be tempted to interpret Genly's response to the Gethenians as a metaphor for transgender and/or gay rights, but such a metaphor falls short. In fact, terms like "transgender" do not apply to Gethenian experience because people on their planet do not rely on a binary understanding of sex or gender in the first place. Instead, almost all Gethenians are effectively neutral, lacking both sex organs and secondary sex characteristics for the majority of their lives. Only when Gethenians enter into kemmer do they develop either male or female anatomy and seek out sexual partners of the opposite sex. Unless they become pregnant during the few days of kemmer, their bodies return to a neutral state. In fact, even when Gethenians do become pregnant, their bodies will return to the same state after giving birth.

Genly Ai, by contrast, comes from Terra, a planet with a binary system of sex and gender that reflects Euro-American cultural norms of the 1960s. Although he understands Gethenian anatomy from a logical, scientific perspective, Genly struggles to apply his understanding in his daily interactions with actual Gethenians. Early in the novel, Genly admits that "though I had been nearly two years on [Gethen] I was still far from being able to see the people of the planet through their own eyes. I tried to, but my efforts took the form of self-consciously seeing a Gethenian first as a man, then as a woman, forcing him into those categories so irrelevant to his nature and so essential to my own."[100] Genly's admission echoes Pinsky's description of "unassimilable alterity," suggesting the unbridgeable differences between Gethenians and Terrans. As Higgins suggests, their encounter with Gethenians catalyzes "members of the Ekumen, like Genly, [to] reconsider the way they understand divisions of masculinity and femininity."[101]

We see Genly struggle with this reconsideration throughout the novel. When we first meet him, for instance, Genly struggles to respond to Estraven, the prime minister who has guided him through his first two years on Gethen. He first describes Estraven's behavior as "womanly, all charm and tact and lack of substance, specious and adroit," before admitting that he "disliked and distrusted" him precisely because "it was impossible to think of him as a woman . . . and yet whenever I thought of him as a man I felt a sense of falseness, of imposture."[102] Although it takes nearly three hundred pages, Genly ultimately comes to understand that he cannot force Estraven into masculine/feminine binaries that hold no meaning on Gethen. Instead, by the end of the novel, Genly has learned to recognize Estraven as both alien and human:

> And I saw then again, and for good, what I had always been afraid to see, and had pretended not to see in him: that he was a woman as well as a man. Any need to explain the sources of that fear vanished with the fear; what I was left with was, at last, acceptance of him as he was. Until then I had rejected him, refused him his own reality.[103]

Genly at last recognizes the demand of the Other, a demand that has existed since Genly and Estraven first came face to face. Pinsky would argue that science fiction offers the tools necessary to explore such an encounter with Otherness—something all humans experience.

Drawing on Levinas, Pinsky suggests that when this encounter between Being and Otherness occurs, the arrival of the Other will result in a "disruption of time and space" that will "destabilize the ordered Self. The Self reproduces itself through fusion with alterity: a self-becoming-other."[104] Because this encounter disrupts both time *and* space, it might also be more applicable to Indigenous experience as Deloria defines it. And because the focus here is spatial as well as temporal, it is reasonable to accept that this claim applies more broadly than those arguments centered in Western culture alone. In a practical sense, we know that encounters between Indigenous peoples and Europeans have often led to a destabilizing spatial disruption for both groups. But, while Euro-American traditions tend to read the European as the Self who is disrupted in such narratives, Indigenous science fiction encourages us to reverse that reading, to see the European as an invasive Other whose presence destabilizes the Indigenous Self.

It is also important to note that although encounters with the Other lead to "a self-becoming-other," this is *not* the same as suggesting that the Self becomes a hybrid. It simply suggests that the Self's former understanding of itself, of its boundaries, is called into question. As Pinsky explains, the process of becoming-other "renders hypostasis in time and space (became, being, becoming, as absolute positions) indeterminate, due to the fact of disruption."[105] But rather than losing one's identity in this moment, such an encounter actually defines the Self in relation to the Other because that moment of self-definition is also the moment of ethical encounter. Pinsky, again relying on Levinas, defines ethics as "the recognition of the prior Other and the accounting for the possibility of change with regard to anticipation. It is an acting for the future and for the other that arrives from the future."[106] Whatever claim the Other makes, and however the Self responds, this moment of encounter, when the Self recognizes the very existence of the Other, is itself an ethical demand.

In Indigenous cultures like the ones that Deloria describes, the response to this ethical demand may differ greatly from the response that Pinsky predicts. While a Western European or Euro-American may immediately attempt to assimilate the Other into the Self, an Indigenous person who has learned to understand the world from a tribally specific perspective might be able to accept the moment of disruption and form an ethical response based on Indigenous epistemologies and the sense of communal responsibility grounded in Native worldviews. In either case, an encounter with the Other serves to remind us that the world is not fixed and unchanging, and that change occurs over time—as the Other could indeed, at any moment, "arrive from the future." While such a realization may understandably destabilize those individuals who interpret the world as a fixed, linear progression, Pinsky's sense of the world as changing and fluid echoes Suvin's argument that science fiction hinges upon the possibility of change.

Pinsky imagines a Self inherently threatened by the presence of the Other and the concept of change but fails to acknowledge Indigenous readers and writers of science fiction, whose ethics are more likely to be grounded in actual, lived experiences and an openness to change and adaptation. As Deloria describes it, Indigenous "ethics flow from the ongoing life of the community and are virtually indistinguishable from the tribal or communal customs."[107] Since Native peoples understand the world through space rather than time, an Indigenous individual might be able to accept the presence of the Other without feeling threatened, without getting swept up in a narrative of Progress and assimilation. Finally, those raised with Indigenous values are more likely to allow lived experiences to inform their decisions, whereas those raised in Euro-American culture are more likely to try to force reality to fit into their preconceived notions of how the world should be.

Just as science fiction occurs at the border between the familiar and the unfamiliar, between the reader's known world and the "shock of dysrecognition" that initiates change, the ethical encounter that Pinsky describes occurs at the border between Self and Other. Thus, Pinsky argues that the ethical encounter, the "becoming-other" is itself "a border-construct . . . [that] is able to exist simultaneously in multiple states."[108] At a meeting of the Self and the Other, the "relationship of dominance and power become unstable fields" where "boundaries . . . are transgressed," and each body "is unique and context-specific."[109] Because of their spatial orientation and emphasis on the community over the individual, many Indigenous peoples already understand themselves within such constructs. Furthermore, most Native cultures are both polycentric and geocentric, which means that it may also be easier for Indigenous peoples to acknowledge and transgress borders while recognizing that the Self and the Other share "a common identity."[110] As Deloria explains, since "Indian tribal religions . . . have a sacred center at a particular place . . . this center enables the people to look out along the four dimensions and locate their lands, to relate all historical events within the confines of this particular land, and to accept responsibility for it."[111] Indigenous peoples, who establish Being within a particular place rather than within a particular time, are already aware of the existence of an Other in the world and can further acknowledge that the Self's own experiences are not necessarily the universal rule. Indigenous cultures are therefore equipped to encounter and respond to difference in ways that Euro-American and other colonizing cultures struggle with, as they must first reorient themselves to understand the world through space rather than time.

Here again, Indigenous science fiction suggests alternate models of the ethical encounter. Because Native peoples are already aware that cultural Others exist, they are better prepared to acknowledge those Others and accept the "shock of dysrecognition" that accompanies the ethical encounter. By incorporating Indigenous knowledge and ethics, such stories can suggest a more productive relationship between the Self and the Other. In addition to Deloria's explanation that Indigenous ethics are rooted in the community, we might also turn to Anishinaabe scholar Niigaanwewidam James Sinclair's definition of ethics as "a responsible curiosity," a responsibility that we all share to build a "mutually beneficial home."[112] Sinclair grounds this concept of ethics in the act of the round dance, during which participants must work together to find a common rhythm, establishing unity among disparate individuals. Such a concrete example, grounded in physical action and an ongoing process, offers an alternate approach to Pinsky's conception of the assimilative ethical encounter. Indigenous science fiction reiterates that approach, reminding readers of our shared responsibility to both the Other and the world around us and modeling the ethical encounter, not as a threat to identity but as a process of building community.

To demonstrate the possibilities of Indigenous science fiction, I examine four novels that employ science fictional themes to resist the traumas of colonization and imagine an empowering future for Native peoples. Each of two central sections discusses a pair of novels as a means of exploring formal experimentation alongside a particular generic convention. In the first section, the trope of radiation monsters opens a space to address the medical and environmental issues raised by nuclear testing, uranium mining, and the disposal of toxic waste on reservations. In the second section, I examine virtual and alternate realities, two related conventions that allow authors from Southeastern nations to reimagine and resist the forced removal of their peoples. I conclude by looking beyond the genre of the novel, considering ways that Indigenous authors are adapting and appropriating science fictional tropes in other forms, such as the short story, digital animation, and comics.

This analysis is far from exhaustive. I analyze just a few sf conventions employed by Indigenous authors; the field has grown exponentially in the past ten years, and it is beyond the scope of this project to catalog—much less analyze—all related texts. Rather, my goal here is to map some of the ways in which Indigenous science fiction might further expand the possibilities of the genre and offer its readers a new method of approaching the ethical encounter. Although Pinsky's argument falls short where he relies too heavily on a Euro-American understanding of ethics, he also seems eager to move beyond that position, and he makes a persuasive argument for science fiction as a genre that might help us rethink our relationship with and responsibility to the world around us. In his conclusion, Pinsky reminds readers that contemporary philosophy, quantum physics, and science fiction all "seem to have evolved parallel to one another as distinctly twentieth-century articulations of our relationship with the world around us, and the world of the future. . . . We anticipate further collisions among physics, metaphysics, and fiction that might help us understand our being in the world."[113] Such a claim echoes Deloria's observation that "the view of the world which formerly dominated Western peoples and which currently dominates Western science is being transformed into an ancient and all-encompassing attitude toward life, best characterized by the American Indian cultures and traditions."[114] Because Indigenous knowledge draws connections between disciplines that are considered distinct in a Euro-American approach, because Native cultures are rooted in space rather than time, and because Native worldviews are already open to the possibility of encounters with alterity, Indigenous science fiction has the ability to expand and complicate the boundaries of this historically Euro-American genre in ways that are beneficial to both Native and non-Native audiences.

PART ONE

Modern Monsters, Modern Borders

The trope of radiation exposure may initially seem outdated and out of place in contemporary novels, since the fear of radiation and its harmful side effects is often associated with mid-twentieth-century American political fears that have largely subsided since the end of the Cold War. In fact, radiation exposure is but one iteration of a trope that both pre- and postdates Cold War anxieties. In a discussion of science fiction films that describes the characteristics of the genre and thus applies to science fiction (sf) novels and short stories as well, J. P. Telotte points out that, by the 1930s, the "various icons, plot devices, and themes" of science fiction were "already well understood by filmmakers and audiences," including a thematic concern with the "combination of apocalyptic destruction and eventual salvation—at the hands of both science and technology."[1] In other words, even before the development and deployment of nuclear technology, "one of the genre's most telling characteristics" was its ability to "speak both positively and negatively about science and technology."[2] Thus, although films produced "in the immediate postwar period" tend to link "science and technology to new sorts of weapons, reflecting widespread cultural anxieties about the Cold War and atomic power," this anxiety is just one version of a common sf trope that spans the twentieth and twenty-first centuries.[3]

Even as we acknowledge that science fiction reflects anxieties about technology well beyond the scope of the Cold War, it is also useful to consider the way that anxieties about atomic technology have appeared throughout mainstream science fiction. Nuclear power as a trope can be subdivided into at least two categories: first, the communal threat of total annihilation represented by the existence of the atomic bomb and the inevitable consequences of nuclear warfare; and second, the individual threat of radiation exposure leading to a wide variety of individual transformations and mutations. Texts in the first category tend to depict events surrounding nuclear apocalypse, including "the post-holocaust novel of survival."[4] Describing the relationship between technological anxiety and the mainstream production of science fiction during the mid-twentieth century, Aris Mousoutzanis notes that

> a rather peculiar relationship between science, fiction, and reality can thus be found at the very start of the Nuclear Age, which became typical of nuclear catastrophe fiction, most of which condemns nuclear war but also gains an awkward legitimacy from it. Many sf narratives suddenly began to appear more plausible and realistic, and the atomic bomb served as a starting point for many sf classics. These either described the irreversible total extinction of the human race or the aftermath of a nuclear war . . . or focused on the possibilities for rebirth and revelation in a much more distant future.[5]

The actual existence of nuclear weapons led to an increase in the production of a specific brand of apocalyptic science fiction, which we see explored in novels such as Judith Merril's *Shadow on the Hearth* (1950), Walter M. Miller Jr.'s *A Canticle for Leibowitz* (1959), and Pat Frank's *Alas, Babylon* (1959).

Each of these works imagines the aftermath of nuclear warfare at different scales. Merril's domestic novel maintains a tight focus on a single suburban family and their experiences in the week after a nuclear attack on New York. Frank broadens the scope both spatially and temporally, telling the story of how a small town in Florida survives the first year after nuclear war. And Miller paints a much larger picture: *A Canticle for Leibowitz* begins several hundred years after nuclear war has effectively destroyed civilization, and it imagines the rebuilding of that civilization over thousands more years. Each novel depicts the horrors of nuclear aftermath in order to argue for the importance of achieving peace in the present. Notably, these large-scale stories of impending apocalypse were most popular in the early days of the Cold War, as Americans struggled to comprehend the concept of nearly total destruction.

The second category of nuclear sf, which focuses on individual or smaller scale experiences, includes a wider range of stories produced over a larger time span. Among these are the monster movies of the 1950s. Godzilla is first described as a Creature from the Jurassic or Cretaceous period who was "driven from its sanctuary" by H-Bomb testing, while the giant ants featured in *Them!* were transformed by lingering radiation from the atomic explosion at White Sands, New Mexico in 1945.[6] This subgenre also includes a wide variety of Marvel Comics superheroes like Spider-Man, The Fantastic Four, and the X-Men, all of whom can trace their superpowers to some type of radiation exposure.[7] The original *Godzilla* film was released in 1954, while the Marvel heroes first began to appear in 1961. Both franchises have continued into the twenty-first century, suggesting the ongoing relevance of their themes. One of the clearest examples of the genre's continued relevance is Hideaki Anno and Shinji Higuchi's 2016 film *Shin Godzilla*, which "pointedly replicate[s] scenes from [two] 2011 disasters": "a massive earthquake and tsunami [that] cause[d] a meltdown at the region's Fukushima nuclear power plant."[8] While apocalyptic fiction depicting the aftermath of nuclear war has become less popular in the twenty-first century, concerns about containment of and exposure to radiation remain relevant.

Indigenous sf engages these concerns from a unique perspective. Radiation has historically been—and continues to be—the source of much legitimate destruction and fear in Native communities. In addition to the nuclear testing that took place near reservations in New Mexico, Utah, and Nevada during and after World War II, many uranium mines are located on or near Indigenous lands in the Southwest, particularly in the Four Corners region.[9] The Native people who worked in these mines were not informed of the risks of exposure and were not provided with proper protection, and many more have since been affected by the legal and illegal disposal of nuclear waste on or near their reservations.[10] The medical and environmental issues caused by such exposure are a source of ongoing concern for Southwestern Indigenous peoples. As Sarah Alisabeth Fox notes, "Long after the dust has settled and the politicians have claimed victory and the historians have penned their summaries, cancers and illnesses will continue to manifest in the bodies of ordinary people, erasing the supposed boundaries between soldiers and civilian and making us all survivors and potential victims of a war we thought had ended."[11]

Beyond the regional issues related to mining and testing, the harnessing and wielding of nuclear power continues to affect Native communities locally while also threatening large-scale disasters that could cause significant harm at national and international levels. As Fox notes, "Ultimately we all live downwind of a nuclear test, but some people live closer to ground zero than others do."[12] These processes have led to the poisoning of natural resources such as air and water, as well as to the contamination of meat, dairy, and produce grown near test sites.[13] Moreover, human exposure to radiation leads to genetic mutations that "can accumulate in both intensity and complexity" as they are passed down.[14] In both mainstream and Indigenous sf, radiation exposure is generally unintentional, but the effects of exposure are at least partially positive for non-Native characters like Spider-Man or the Hulk. In Indigenous sf, however, the effects are decidedly negative: in *The Ballad of Billy Badass and the Rose of Turkestan*, illegally disposed toxic waste attracts and strengthens a radiation Creature that very nearly destroys the world. In *It Came from Del Rio*, prolonged exposure to fragments of a radioactive meteorite transforms the novel's protagonist into a gruesome and toxic zombie who poisons anyone who gets close to him. There are no underlying positives to these situations. The existence of nuclear power causes gruesome death and destruction under any circumstances, and once it has been unleashed, no one can effectively or responsibly control that power.

As both Sanders and Jones make clear, the environmental as well as the human effects have inevitably spread beyond the boundaries of Southwestern reservations. Thus, we must acknowledge that political and even temporal borders will ultimately fail to contain the long-term effects of radiation exposure.[15] Illustrating the wholly negative effects of nuclear power production—a process that begins with the extraction of radioactive minerals and ends with the ineffective disposal of nuclear waste—Fox reports that some Navajos have begun referring to uranium as "the yellow monster."[16] Considered in this context, it becomes clear that by writing about radiation monsters, William Sanders (Cherokee) and Stephen Graham Jones (Blackfeet) have appropriated an unnervingly relevant genre convention not just to tell an entertaining story, but also in order to draw attention to an issue whose relevance for both Native and non-Native communities persists well into the twenty-first century.

CHAPTER ONE

The Yellow Monster

Reanimating Nuclear Fears in *The Ballad of Billy Badass and the Rose of Turkestan*

Cherokee writer William Sanders's 1999 novel *The Ballad of Billy Badass and the Rose of Turkestan* reimagines mainstream science fiction (sf) tropes in order to challenge colonial notions of geographical and political boundaries, insisting that, although regionally and tribally specific distinctions are quite real, we must simultaneously acknowledge the network of relationships that extends far beyond such borders. Sanders tells the story of Billy Badwater, a.k.a. Billy Badass, a Cherokee veteran of the First Gulf War who follows his Kazakh scientist girlfriend from Oklahoma to a Paiute reservation in Nevada. There, he and his friends encounter a radiation Creature from another dimension that threatens to consume the entire world. By pitting humans against literal and metaphorical monsters, Sanders suggests that people must form alliances rather than building walls in order to survive. As he revives and adapts the science fictional trope of the radiation Creature, Sanders resists philosophies of strict regionalism, nationalism, and isolationism, instead encouraging his readers—both Native and non—to embrace an Indigenous ethical approach grounded in recognizing and respecting differences even as we cultivate alliances.

Sanders is hardly the first Native novelist to write about the dangers of nuclear power, although he is perhaps the first to bring that power to life in the form of a radiation Creature.[1] Other works of Native literature—most famously Leslie Marmon Silko's 1977 novel, *Ceremony*—have also drawn attention to the lasting damage done by nuclear power. In fact, one of the central arguments of *Ceremony*, as of *The Ballad of Billy Badass*, is that the creation of the atom bomb has established a deep connection between the local and the global. As Kyoko Matsunaga explains, the protagonist of *Ceremony* "realizes . . . that nuclear colonialism of the Southwest reflects the threat of destruction that the atom bomb poses to the world . . . these instances . . . expose fundamental connections between Laguna and Japan: territories victimized by the production and use of nuclear weapons."[2]

Writing about the same history and landscape—and also drawing on the tropes of genre fiction to do so—Navajo and Laguna Pueblo writer A. A. Carr similarly condemns uranium mining in his 1995 novel, *Eye Killers*. In that book, Carr tells the story of Falke, a European vampire who has fallen in love with and kidnapped a Diné and Keresan teenager, Melissa. As her grandfather, Michael, and her teacher, Diana, search for Melissa, they drive through the desert beyond the Pueblo. Diana recalls that "a huge uranium mine existed there . . . or had existed. It was only just recently shut down."[3] Where the mine had been, they see "a landscape that had been blasted and torn apart. . . . Nowhere could Diana see any signs of life. She had hoped to see a deer or a rabbit at least. A single blackbird flew above the wrecked, voided carcass of land. At what level did radiation remain? Had anyone ever bothered to check?"[4] Later, they visit a Navajo elder who explains that there are no sheep or deer in the canyon because "the mine scared them all away. . . . [The miners] have taken all of what they needed . . . and left us a bunch of money, but they haven't shaped the earth back into what she was."[5] Just as Sanders makes a metaphorical connection between the radiation Creature and the misuse of nuclear power, Carr points to the similarity between the companies responsible for mining uranium and vampires like Falke: both have preyed on Native peoples, extracting resources at the expense of Indigenous bodies and lands.

Although uranium mining has most pervasively damaged the Southwest, where many of the mines were located, it is important to recognize that the harmful effects are not confined to that region alone. The Manhattan Project appropriated land across the United States—not just in the Southwest, but also with headquarters in New York and facilities in Cambridge, Massachusetts; Dayton, Ohio; Hanford, Washington; and "dozens of other sites."[6] One key facility, located in the traditional

Cherokee homelands of the Southeast, was the land that became Oak Ridge, Tennessee, in the 1940s. The area was selected "as the site for the pilot plutonium plant and the uranium enrichment plant," which meant that "Manhattan Project engineers had to quickly build a town to accommodate 30,000 workers."[7]

Cherokee Appalachian author Marilou Awiakta writes about her experience of growing up at Oak Ridge during the late 1940s. Like Sanders, Awiakta recognizes the potential—both positive and negative—for multiplicity and connection represented by atomic power. The poems in her first book, *Abiding Appalachia*, as well as in her later work, explore the tensions and double meanings that inevitably accompany the creation of nuclear power. Poems like "Test Cow"—about a milk cow dying of radiation exposure—focus on the explicit dangers of exposure, while others, such as "The Fence," struggle to reconcile that horror with the freedom that paradoxically accompanies increased governmental protection at Oak Ridge. Perhaps the most compelling poems are those that simultaneously acknowledge the increase in both risk and reward. In "Disaster Drill," for instance, Awiakta begins with a description of children evacuating their school, an image that she connects to the removal of Anne Frank by German troops.[8] Implicit in such a poem is the recognition that the children of Oak Ridge are endangered by the presence of the labs and machinery—and yet, that risk is tempered by the fact that the power contained therein has the potential to save children on the other side of the world. Here, as in *The Ballad of Billy Badass*, there is a recognition that the local is undeniably connected to the fate of the global.

In order to reconcile such disparate structures, *The Ballad of Billy Badass* demonstrates the necessity of alliance building. Such alliances may be formed between members of different tribal nations, as when Billy befriends Mickey Wolf, a Mohawk-Irish preacher who was once a Catholic priest, or between Native people and other U.S. citizens, like Sarah Aronson, a Jewish doctor from New York who runs a clinic on the Paiute reservation. These alliances further extend to Indigenous people from other parts of the world: Billy's girlfriend, Janna, is a Kazakh scientist whose experiences with the Russian government closely mirror the treatment of the Cherokee by the United States.

At first glance, these characters may seem like token representations, chosen merely because stories that threaten the end of the world usually involve an ensemble cast of eclectic characters coming together against all odds. In such stories, individuals often stand in for entire nations or cultures, and ultimately, most of them exist to support the Euro-American protagonist who eventually saves the day. We see this trope at work in texts like Roland Emmerich's 1996 film *Independence Day*, or in several incarnations of the *Star Trek* series, where, as Carter Meland has argued, a multicultural crew rallies behind a Euro-American captain whose decisions ultimately reinforce mainstream liberal American values.[9] David Higgins also points to the way that the original *Star Trek* series reproduces imperialist relationships, arguing that the

> Prime Directive (Starfleet's General Order #1) ... explicitly enshrines a cosmopolitan imperative to foster ethical relationships between people; at the same time, however, Captain Kirk's perpetual violation of this directive reflects an ideological commitment to American exceptionalism that justifies U.S. neoimperialism during the Cold War and beyond.[10]

Higgins suggests that where actual cosmopolitan sf "entails restraint on the part of the advantaged party (either on its own initiative or as part of a multilateral coalition) in the name of a nonexploitative equitability between both entities," *Star Trek*, like many other works of mainstream sf, reflects "an unresolved tension between imperial and cosmopolitan attitudes."[11] These tensions may result in a weak cosmopolitan discourse that "refer[s] to nothing more than capitalist globalization ... serv[ing] as a celebratory enabling logic of global capitalism."[12] Such texts "disregard asymmetries of power between actors who are positioned differently on a global terrain."[13]

Consider *Independence Day*, in which the band of heroes who unites to save Earth includes the American president and first lady; an MIT-educated scientist; an alcoholic Vietnam veteran; and a Marine captain and his fiancée, who works as an exotic dancer.[14] Among these protagonists, there exist obvious power differentials grounded in race, gender, and socioeconomic status. Nonetheless, the film depicts them all as equal players. Despite the vast inequity of their lives before the alien attack, they are now united by a common goal: in the face of total annihilation, those seemingly insurmountable differences in race, class, and gender become inconsequential. This is perhaps most clearly illustrated by the narrative arc of the first lady, whose racial and socioeconomic privilege cannot protect her from injury and eventual death. Ultimately, *Independence Day* encourages viewers to overlook very real systems of oppression in order to band together as Americans—a national identity that is intended to inspire unity despite disparity, both within the film itself and presumably among its viewers.[15]

As opposed to this oversimplified "melting pot" approach to diversity that ultimately "valorize[es] the emergence of a Cold War neoimperial hegemony,"[16] *The Ballad of Billy Badass* focuses on a very specific group of social outcasts working together to solve a geographically specific set of problems—although those problems threaten to expand beyond the local to a national or even global scale. It also depicts a more cosmopolitan relationship between its protagonists, as Sanders devotes a significant portion of the novel to exploring the similarities and differences in the characters' intersectional experiences. The Creature that Billy and his friends face is certainly an invention of science fiction, and Sanders acknowledges that "there is no Blacktail Springs Reservation in Nevada," but the kernel of the story is quite specifically realistic.[17] In the author's note that prefaces the novel, Sanders points out that "the matter of legal dumping of radioactive wastes and other toxic materials is, of course, a nationally notorious reality," and "the information . . . concerning Soviet nuclear-weapons testing in Central Asia and the effects on the population of Kazakhstan is factually correct according to the author's personal sources."[18] It is this reference to historical events, as well as to tribally and culturally specific beliefs and experiences, that sets *The Ballad of Billy Badass* apart from other similar sf stories. By ensuring that individual voices are not silenced, the novel repeatedly acknowledges the "asymmetries of power between actors who are positioned differently."

A major strategy for recognizing individual experiences and forming alliances in this novel is for characters to tell stories and share beliefs. We begin with Grandfather Ninekiller's explanations, then follow Billy as he explains Cherokee culture, and, with him, we listen to Janna describe her experiences in Kazakhstan. Because Billy, like many U.S. citizens, is unfamiliar with this history, readers do not need to feel self-conscious about their lack of knowledge; instead, they can follow his example, especially when Janna relates her people's experiences of trauma. After she describes some of the atrocities that the Russians have committed against her people, "Billy didn't know what to say."[19] His response allows space for readers to feel the same way; with Billy, we can respect Janna's experiences without becoming overwhelmed or trying to take ownership of her story. At this point, readers may also begin to acknowledge "asymmetries of power" among groups, which is the first step in "recogniz[ing] the face of the Other rather than . . . automatically subsum[ing] otherness in the reductive dialectic of self/not-self."[20] Through Billy's example, the novel encourages readers to reflect on our own experiences and consider the best way to exercise restraint as we build personal relationships and political alliances.

Although *The Ballad of Billy Badass* models the process of building relationships across difference, it stops short of building such relationships with the radiation Creature itself. Instead, its presence challenges readers to confront alterity quite directly. When we first meet the Creature, for instance, the narrator explains that

> it possessed an awareness—rough and chaotic, but rapidly developing—of itself and its surroundings, but this awareness had no resemblance whatever to the consciousness of man, beast, plant, or computer. There are no words in any human or electronic language to describe what it used for thought processes.[21]

From this first introduction, the novel emphasizes the Creature's difference and inherent strangeness. Finding language to describe it is a struggle, and the best that the narrator can do is explain what the Creature is *not*: it cannot be compared to any living thing on our planet, and our languages inevitably fail to describe it because no metaphor can establish an accurate relationship. In fact, in the midst of trying to describe the Creature, Sanders says that "none of these statements means anything."[22] Although he tries to describe the Creature through language, all language can ultimately do is, paradoxically, acknowledge its own failings.

Even as we learn more about the Creature, the narrator continues to alienate readers rather than helping them understand or make sense of it. He repeatedly highlights the failure of human language and concepts, explaining that

> it had not "come from" anywhere, since it did not necessarily move through physical space and in any case its previous environment had not been, strictly speaking, a "where," being without spatial location or co-ordinates. It was not, for that matter, an "it." It possessed neither form nor mass; its composition included nothing identifiable by the terms of this universe, or subject to any known or unknown laws of physical science. Even the verb "to be" is inappropriate. By any rational and objective standard, *it did not exist.*[23]

Here, Sanders challenges readers to grapple with a concept that he cannot possibly explain and that we cannot possibly imagine. As Billy and Janna confront that Creature, they also have to grapple with their sheer inability to make sense of it. It defies Western knowledge when it fails to adhere to either the "known or unknown laws of physical science" or the very basic building blocks of Western language. If we return to Vine Deloria Jr.'s claims about the Western impulse to frame the world in terms of "what you allow your mind to accept, not what you experience," we can better understand the challenge issued by Sanders's Creature: in addition to falling outside the realm of Western belief, it is almost impossible to integrate the Creature into a Western worldview because there is no clear way to describe or understand it.[24] Given Deloria's argument that an Indigenous worldview is better situated to acknowledge the unknown, it should come as no surprise that the characters who are ultimately able to combat this Creature are Indigenous. Billy and Janna emerge as the heroes of the story because they can accept "what they experienced as true," even when that experience defies all "rational and objective" standards.[25]

From a theoretical standpoint, the Creature staunchly refuses Suvin's claim that science fiction is about establishing metaphors for human experience. Suvin argues that "whether in space or . . . in time, the new framework is correlative to the new inhabitants. The aliens—utopians, monsters, or simply differing strangers—are a mirror to man just as the differing country is a mirror for his world."[26] And yet, this theory clearly fails to encompass the radiation Creature found in *The Ballad of Billy Badass*, where not only metaphors but *all* language fails to convey meaning. Instead, we might better understand the extreme Otherness of the radiation Creature by returning to Pinsky's model of science fiction as ethical encounter with the Other. Sanders's Creature is practically the platonic ideal of the alien Other as described by Pinsky: it completely resists any attempt to assimilate the Other into the Self because, as Sanders establishes from the outset, there is no way to bridge the gap between this Creature and anything in our own world. And yet, this Otherness is also a point of unresolved tension within the novel: in a book about the ethical treatment of the Other, why create an alien Other that must literally be destroyed in order to save humanity?

This unbridgeable Otherness is particularly unusual within a Cherokee context because, as Brian Burkhart suggests, traditional Cherokee monsters, like monsters in many other Indigenous traditions, still exist in relation to kinship. Describing a story in which the Cherokee trickster Jisdu defeats a monster, Burkhart notes that Jisdu first tricks the monster by dressing up as his auntie and paying him a visit. Even the monster is obliged to welcome this auntie, to provide her with a meal and a place to sleep. He points out that a similar relationship exists in other Indigenous literary traditions, as among the Navajo, where both Enemy Way and Blessing Way offer structures for maintaining relationships. As Burkhart puts it, "You can't be out of kinship. Even walking away or shunning, it's a form of kinship."[27] The fact that Sanders's radiation Creature is not metaphorically human, that it *does* exist outside of kinship relations, indicates how radically un-Indigenous it really is. Here, we might draw similarities to accounts of early warfare between European and Indigenous groups, where Native peoples were shocked to realize that the European method of warfare culminated in total annihilation rather than maintaining a balance between traditional enemies. Similarly, a Creature that exists outside of kinship responsibilities, a Creature that threatens to destroy the entire world, is foreign to traditional Cherokee understandings.

Perhaps the Creature resists being brought into relationship precisely because its existence in our universe is predicated on Euro-American behaviors and decisions: it has been accidentally conjured by Magda Simone, proprietor of the New Age Enlightenment Center and Guest Ranch. At expensive New Age retreats, Magda dresses up as a priestess and

> serve[s] up a goulash of Indian mumbo-jumbo—both kinds of Indian, of course—and fake Egyptology and Confucius-say Oriental philosophy, spiked with old-fashioned gypsy fortune telling and topped with a thick layer of Little Men From Outer Space like in the Spielberg movies.[28]

This description of Magda's New Age philosophy could have come straight from Deloria's critique of New Age practices:

> Thus astrology, numerology, flying saucers with heavenly "space brothers," past-life regressions, a variety of martial arts techniques, various brands of shamanism, and modern versions of witchcraft fill the empty hours of the affluent fringe groups who reject Christianity but want to have some hold on religious experiences.[29]

Both Deloria and Sanders are critical of the melting-pot appropriation of religious experiences, which is not only disrespectful to the original practices and cultures but, as Sanders suggests, may also cause serious damage: by appropriating various traditions and combining them at random in order to make a profit, Magda and her customers accidentally open up a portal between dimensions through which the radiation Creature falls.[30] The New Agers are quickly punished for the act of cultural appropriation when the Creature literally rips their heads off, but the damage is already done. Just as Euro-Americans historically refused or abused kinship relations with their Native neighbors, so does the New Agers' refusal to respect other cultures lead to the summoning of a Creature that resists engagement through either metaphor or ethical encounter.

This appropriation and abuse of sacred knowledge also illustrates an important connection between Indigenous and Western scientific knowledge: in much the same way that sf depicts both the benefits and dangers of technology, *The Ballad of Billy Badass* depicts the benefits and dangers inherent in Indigenous knowledge. Through Magda's example, Sanders warns non-Native folks who might be tempted to dabble in a tradition that they fail to understand and that simply does not belong to them. Alternately, Billy and Mickey model the responsible use of sacred knowledge through their careful treatment of ceremonial tobacco. This pair of positive and negative examples parallels the treatment of powerful but dangerous scientific knowledge in *Godzilla*. In the original film, the scientist Serizawa has made a revolutionary discovery: an Oxygen Destroyer that, when detonated, sucks all the oxygen out of the water so that everything living in it dies. The Oxygen Destroyer is the one tool that could kill Godzilla and put a stop to further death and destruction, but Serizawa is reasonably concerned that if his creation is used as a weapon, "it could lead humanity to extinction, just like the H-Bomb."[31] Ultimately, Serizawa agrees to use the Oxygen Destroyer, but he also dismantles his lab and dies by suicide to guarantee that his discovery will not fall into the wrong hands. Drawing an explicit connection between the H-Bomb and the Oxygen Destroyer, Serizawa drives home the dangers of atomic power, intimating that perhaps the scientists who created atomic weapons should also have destroyed their research. In *Godzilla*, the implication is that humans cannot be trusted with such dangerous knowledge: even if scientists try to protect their work and control the application of their discoveries, "the politicians of the world won't stand idly by. They'll inevitably turn it into a weapon."[32]

This attitude is echoed in Walter M. Miller Jr.'s *A Canticle for Leibowitz*, in which the survivors of nuclear war decide to destroy all knowledge and technology in order to prevent humanity from recreating nuclear weapons. The novel is critical of these self-proclaimed "Simpletons," siding instead with the scientist-turned-priest Leibowitz and those who preserve knowledge through the Dark Ages that follow the nuclear holocaust. And yet, Miller envisions a future where humans repeat the same pattern of self-destruction: the novel ends in the year 3781 with a rocket full of monks and schoolchildren headed for human colonies on other planets as Earth once again erupts into nuclear war. Although *A Canticle for Leibowitz* is devoted to the story of the monastic order preserving knowledge at great personal expense, it, like *Godzilla*, implies that humans can never be trusted with the powerful knowledge that inevitably arises from scientific exploration. In *The Ballad of Billy Badass*, on the other hand, sacred knowledge need not be destroyed. It should, however, be possessed only by those who have been properly trained to understand and respect it—unlike both the well-meaning Leibowitzian monks who preserve but wildly misinterpret twentieth-century blueprints and other assorted archives and the exploitative use of Indigenous ceremonies by Magda Simone. In contrast to both the monks and the New Agers, Billy can perform a tobacco ceremony not only because he is Cherokee but also because his grandfather taught him the right way to use this medicine. Both mainstream and Indigenous science fiction explore humanity's relationship to powerful knowledge, but only Indigenous sf models the appropriate way of caring for and thus preserving that knowledge.

While both Indigenous and atomic knowledge must be treated with respect, they have little else in common. Indigenous knowledge has a wide variety of purposes—apparently including protecting humans from radiation Creatures—but Indigenous and mainstream sf seem to agree that nuclear power is primarily a hazard rather than a strength. In *Godzilla*, for instance, nuclear testing is to blame for the Creature's origins. According to the original 1954 film, Godzilla is believed to be "a rare intermediate organism" that evolved during the Cretaceous period. It probably lived in an underwater cave, emerging because "repeated H Bomb tests have completely destroyed its natural habitat." As a result of this exposure, Godzilla itself "is emitting high levels of H Bomb radiation," which means that, in addition to physically destroying boats, villages, and cities, Godzilla also threatens to kill Japanese citizens indirectly through high levels of radiation exposure.[33] Similarly, the American movie *Them!*, also released in 1954, introduces viewers to a colony of gigantic ants exposed to radiation in the New Mexico desert, close to the location of the Trinity nuclear test site. Although Sanders's Creature comes from another universe rather than originating on Earth, it transforms when it feeds on "residual radiation in earth and groundwater," much as Godzilla and the giant ants are also transformed by radiation exposure.[34]

In each instance, the unforeseen and unpredictable results of nuclear testing are clearly to blame for the existence of the Creature (or Creatures)—a point that each film drives home in its final moments. *Godzilla* concludes with Dr. Yamane's solemn proclamation that, "If nuclear testing continues, then someday, somewhere in the world, another Godzilla may appear."[35] *Them!* ends with a strikingly similar claim: "When man entered the atomic age, he opened a door into a new world.

What we eventually find in that new world, nobody can predict."[36] *The Ballad of Billy Badass* can be read as a kind of sequel to these and other Creature films of the 1950s: although the initial fear of nuclear power has dissipated, the "door to a new world" remains open—and new radiation Creatures may emerge from it at any time.

In both *Godzilla* and *Them!*, these final doomsday warnings come from scientists whose earlier predictions have already come true. It is unsettling to hear that the Creatures may return, but viewers may be simultaneously comforted by the circumstances of the pronouncement: in each case, the scientist stands triumphant over a vanquished enemy, surrounded by politicians, other scientists, and members of the national military. We see Godzilla's skeleton at the bottom of the ocean; the camera zooms in on burning giant ants, reassuring us of human triumph. Other threats may emerge in the future, but both Japanese and American films imagine a world where scientists, politicians, and the military collaborate to protect their citizens from Creature danger. As Sobchack notes, Creature films "are less about horror and science than they are about the preservation of social order" because the Creatures "act only as foils to the collective hero (the organized institutions of the society: scientific, military, political)."[37] Perhaps this is why the heroes in *Godzilla* include Ogata, who serves in the Japanese Coast Guard; Dr. Kyohei Yamane, a paleontologist; and his colleague, Dr. Daisuke Serizawa.[38] Similarly, in *Them!*, we follow a father-daughter team of scientists who work for the Department of Agriculture. Throughout the film, they collaborate with the local police, the FBI, and the Marines. The same trope is echoed in later films like *Independence Day*, where the protagonists include a Marine pilot, the American president, and an MIT-educated satellite engineer. All three films depict individual characters who represent institutions that prioritize collaboration in order to protect their own citizens.

This faith in and sympathy for formal institutions is noticeably absent from *The Ballad of Billy Badass*. Sanders's protagonists have all been let down by the structures in which they put their faith: Billy is disillusioned by his experiences as a Green Beret in the First Gulf War; Janna's work with "children suffering from the effects of radiation exposure" led both the KGB and the FBI to interrogate her;[39] Sarah is a doctor who works at the local Indian Health Services clinic but insists upon remaining "strictly independent" so that she can conduct her own research.[40] And Mickey is an ex-Catholic priest who founded his own church—"The Last Church of Naked City"—whose primary purpose is to feed the homeless population of Las Vegas.[41] In each character's case, the institutions on which they once relied supported and enforced policies that either neglected or directly harmed the citizens whom they are ostensibly meant to protect. Indigenous science fiction, then, challenges normative assumptions about the trust we place in social structures and thus disrupts the order that is preserved in mainstream Creature films.

As opposed to the unified front presented in mainstream Creature films, *The Ballad of Billy Badass* ends with Billy and Janna driving off into the sunset, trying to figure out what to do next. Billy worries that they will be blamed for the destruction caused by the radiation Creature and wonders what to say to the police when he and Janna are inevitably questioned.[42] Because authority figures are a threat rather than a source of protection, Billy and his friends are in an unfamiliar position within the genre: they must focus on building individual relationships among themselves rather than relying on social institutions for protection. Sanders devotes a significant portion of *The Ballad of Billy Badass* to establishing such a relationship between Billy and Janna, one instigated and cemented by their shared experiences of settler colonialism. Their early courtship consists largely of sharing the stories of oppression that have shaped both their lives, and the space within the novel that Sanders gives over to that courtship encourages readers to take their critiques seriously. The couple's careful analysis allows them to form a genuine logical and emotional alliance, as opposed to the tokenizing representations found in weak cosmopolitan texts such as *Star Trek* or *Independence Day*, which threaten to erase both cultural specificity and personal difference.

For instance, when Billy tells Janna about the Trail of Tears, she quickly draws a connection to her own people's experiences: "'I know about deportations,' she said. 'Kazakhstan is full of people who were deported from other parts of the Soviet Union.'"[43] When Billy explains that a third of the Cherokee people died during removal, Janna tells him "Stalin killed a third of our people in the nineteen-thirties."[44] And the similarities in Cherokee and Kazakh experience extend beyond the history of removal: like many American Indians, the nomadic Kazakh people "were forcibly resettled on collective farms—usually on land that was hopeless for farming—and the traditional chiefs and elders were replaced by Stalinist bureaucrats and secret-police bullies."[45] This description is reminiscent of the experiences of many Plains tribes, who regularly moved as they hunted buffalo. When they were contained on reservations and encouraged to become "civilized" farmers, many starved or were punished for leaving the reservation in search of food. As in the case of the Kazakhs, traditional tribal leaders were often replaced by governmental representatives, whether Indian agents or members of the tribe more likely to cooperate.

Janna goes on to explain that after the Indigenous peoples of Kazakhstan had been contained, "great numbers of Russian colonists were brought in to settle and farm the so-called Virgin Lands, evicting such few bands of traditional herders as still remained."[46] This part of Janna's story mirrors multiple events in American Indian history: in the South, Cherokee removal led to the expansion of the southern plantation economy, while across the country, the Dawes Act broke reservations up into individual rather than communal parcels. Because each family received only 160 acres, a large portion of reservation land suddenly became "available," and the federal government encouraged U.S. citizens to move to these new farms.[47] Indigenous peoples residing in the United States were thus dispossessed of much of their remaining land by encroaching settlers, as happened in Janna's home country.

Beyond these clear similarities between the Cherokee and the Kazakhs, Billy further extends the connections among Indigenous nations as he reflects on the relationship between the Cherokee and the Kurdish rebels whom he encountered when he served in the U.S. army. He explains to Janna that he worked with these rebels until "the United States just backed off, once their usefulness was finished, and left them to starve or be massacred."[48] As he watches the rebels struggle, it occurs to Billy that

> this is what the Trail of Tears must have looked like. Another bunch of people, like us, who made the mistake of counting on the honor of the American government. . . . Because we made the same mistake, you know. The Cherokees helped Andrew Jackson fight the Creeks, figured that would get us better treatment, and the son of a bitch double-crossed us the same way.[49]

Billy's comparison suggests that a similar relationship between Indigenous peoples and colonizers recurs in a variety of situations, extending to locations beyond the United States and Kazakhstan. Moreover, the simile establishes connections across time, drawing attention to the fact that colonial practices employed in the early days of settling the United States and strengthening the South have continued in various forms into the late twentieth century. Contemporary U.S. citizens may be tempted to separate themselves from men like Andrew Jackson by pointing out how much has changed since the 1830s. But, given that the experience of the Kurdish rebels is so similar to that of the Cherokee, the distinction—like the ostensible distinctions between the histories of the Cherokee and the Kazakhs—becomes increasingly unclear. As Billy observes, the practices and patterns of the past continue into the present. Although we might not initially recognize them in their new forms, drawing these connections among discrete events reveals the structures of settler colonialism that undergird so many interactions between the United States and other nations.[50]

Billy's observation also highlights the messy realities left in the wake of imperialism and genocide. As settler colonialism has reshuffled political boundaries, initiated diaspora, and recalibrated identity categories to suit itself, it has also, though perhaps incidentally, restructured—and sometimes created—relationships among disparate groups. Historically, the Cherokee and the Kurds had little in common and may not even have been aware of one another's existence. But, thanks to the interference of U.S. imperialism, an unexpected alliance has emerged. This is not to suggest that such alliances can undo or offset any of the ills of colonialism, but it *is* to say that forced removal, much like the creation of nuclear weapons, has unexpected consequences. In each case, the groups remain distinct entities, but their identities become reframed. Through the interference of first England and then the United States, the Cherokee, for instance, became part of "the South," the "Five Civilized Tribes," the larger category of "Native Americans," and, larger still, of "Indigenous peoples." Those new identities, problematic as they often are, may nonetheless offer new ways of resisting the settler colonialism at the root of the problem.

Such relationships appear across tribal nations, regions, and nation-states. They are predicated upon the shared experiences of colonialism, but they also combine to create larger patterns, such as those that Silko depicts in *Ceremony* or the ones that Awiakta speaks into being when, "at the end of every public speaking or reading engagement, [she] routinely invites the audience to come forward to receive a seed of corn that she places reverently in the palm of each hand as a reminder of our common human bond and task."[51] Removal, like the invention and proliferation of atomic energy, represents the ongoing work of Euro-American settler colonialism. Each occurs in a specific place—or, perhaps, in multiple and discreet places—but the effects nonetheless radiate outward. The individual pinpoints on the map remain distinct, but as they reach across time and space, they build community among the affected.

Sanders models this distinctive balance of local specificity and global alliance as Billy and Janna attend both a powwow and a Cherokee stomp dance. Janna mistakenly describes the powwow dances as "Ceremonial. Sacred"—an assumption that non-Native readers might also make.[52] Billy explains that "nowadays the average powwow's just a social event, and some of the big ones are as commercial and phony as Buffalo Bill's Wild West Show."[53] To help Janna understand the wide variety of Native cultures in the United States, Billy teaches her about the different styles of dancing, such as "Southern Plains style" and the "Northern traditional dancer."[54] He takes the opportunity to emphasize the distinctions between tribes and cultures, which are important even in a pan-Indian space like the powwow. When Janna wants to learn more about Billy's own traditions, he takes her to the Keetowah Society's ceremonial grounds to watch a Cherokee stomp dance.[55] While the novel does not critique the space of the powwow, it does insist on the importance of maintaining individual tribal traditions alongside newer cultural developments. Ultimately, the novel demonstrates that tribal specificity does not have to result in political isolation, since there is space for both the powwow and the ceremonial dance.

Sanders demonstrates his own commitment to both the sacred and the tribally specific in the author's note at the beginning of the book, where he explains that "many of the details of Cherokee tradition, especially concerning ritual matters, have been deliberately altered. . . . The traditions described are valid in general outline but not necessarily so in all details" because "for the author to give an accurate and specific description of, for example, a tobacco-remaking procedure would be sacrilegious."[56] This note demonstrates Sanders's deep regard for such rituals, and by stepping outside the space of the novel to give this explanation, he also sets a respectful tone for his readers that indicates how seriously he takes Cherokee rituals and implies that audiences ought to do the same. In this note, Sanders also discusses the issues of radioactive waste and nuclear weapons, further emphasizing that he considers both Cherokee rituals and nuclear technology equally real. The structure of the note sets up a discussion of science and religion that foreshadows their intersection and models a way that these two kinds of knowledge can coexist in the world.

Within the novel itself, the Cherokee tobacco ceremony is the first line of defense against the radiation Creature. To prepare for that ceremony, Grandfather guides Billy through the process of "remaking" or "programming" tobacco "for the desired effect."[57] Notably, there is room for adaptation in Grandfather's ritual: since Billy does not have access to any specifically Cherokee tobacco in Nevada, he uses

Mickey's instead. Adaptation is a key part of many Indigenous worldviews, including Cherokee traditions, so the act of improvising further reinforces Billy's Cherokee approach to the world. He explains that "in Cherokee medicine, the tobacco itself was not of absolute importance. In a pinch, even cigarette tobacco could be 'remade' for ritual purposes with the proper *igawesdi*. Still, it was better to do things right."[58] So, although Mickey is Mohawk rather than Cherokee, and although he has been a Catholic priest as well as a medicine man, his tobacco works for Billy's ceremony. In fact, this tobacco is closer to "doing things right" than cigarette tobacco, suggesting that sacred objects from other traditions have power and should be honored. Here again, the novel emphasizes the importance of following tribally specific practices, but it also suggests that alliances across cultures can be beneficial. As opposed to the New Agers who dabble in a multitude of traditions without committing seriously to any of them, Billy is grounded in a tradition of his own, but he is also able to incorporate other traditions, as long as he does so thoughtfully, respectfully, and with permission.

After he has "programmed" the tobacco, Billy and Janna go camping in the desert. Before they settle down for the night, Billy places the tobacco in a pipe, lights it, and makes four circles around their campground, blowing smoke in each of the four directions as he goes.[59] Sanders explains these actions precisely, noting that Billy "did not offer the pipe to the four directions in the way of the plains tribes," and that he also "did not sing or make any sound at all" because "the *igawesdi* was already contained in the tobacco, stored and now released by the act of smoking."[60] Although Sanders has already explained that he will not describe a real tobacco ceremony, he nonetheless gives readers a sense of the precise structure and logic of the ritual and its grounding in a Cherokee worldview. By devoting several paragraphs to this description, the novel emphasizes the weight of such a ceremony, and a few pages later, that serious attitude is justified when the tobacco protects Billy and Janna.

The Creature appears after they have fallen asleep. Billy and Janna are awoken by a Creature "at least as big as a six-story office building" making its way toward them.[61] When the Creature reaches the edges of Billy's protective circle, it stops "as if it had suddenly run into an invisible barbed-wire fence."[62] Although the Creature circles the perimeter of the medicine circle, it is unable to come any closer. When it tries to push through, Billy relights the pipe, takes a deep drag, and blows "smoke straight at the thing."[63] He repeats the process seven times, until, "all at once, the roaring stopped, the lights died, and the monstrous form ceased to press forward."[64] Although Sanders does not draw attention to it, it is important that Billy goes through the process seven times given the number's importance for the Cherokee. According to ethnographer James Mooney, "the two sacred numbers of the Cherokee are four and seven, the latter being the actual number of the tribal clans, the formulistic number of upper worlds or heavens, and the ceremonial number of paragraphs or repetitions in the principal formulas."[65] By incorporating real elements of Cherokee belief, as well as by distinguishing between ceremonies that belong to tribes from the Plains or the Southwest, Sanders once again emphasizes that Billy is grounded in a tribally specific approach. Moreover, this scene demonstrates that Indigenous knowledge can be effective where Western science fails—a fact especially true in a work of science fiction, where, by the nature of the genre, the characters will confront the unknown. Because the novel invites readers to sympathize with Billy and Janna as they learn more about each other's cultures, we are encouraged to approach the unknown of Indigenous cultures in a similarly respectful way. As readers of Indigenous science fiction, we learn the value of accepting what we see rather than refusing to acknowledge anything that does not fit with what we believe. Because Billy's Cherokee approach is the only successful one, the novel reinforces the value of Indigenous ceremonies and worldviews, even when confronting issues that have been caused directly by Euro-American scientific experiments like nuclear testing.

At first, Cherokee ceremony alone is enough to stop the Creature. But as it grows, Billy and Janna must draw on stronger forces, and the Creature is ultimately destroyed by an unlikely source: the power of all the children around the world who have been harmed by radiation exposure.[66] Though the novel does not give a detailed explanation of how the children are able to defeat the Creature, they seem to have harnessed the power imparted by the radiation that has so affected them. The children are led by Sammy, a severely disabled Native child whom Sarah has been treating at the Blacktail Springs clinic. In the final confrontation, Sammy points an eagle feather at the approaching radiation Creature as thousands of children materialize all around them.[67] Billy sees American Indian children, children from "the Asian heartland," Japanese children, Indigenous Australians, and Pacific islanders. He also notes that "not one was whole in body"; each of these children has been somehow affected by exposure to radiation, whether directly or through genetic mutations passed down by their parents and grandparents.[68] Just as the Creature itself is the physical embodiment of that exposure, so are the children the physical embodiment of the harm that has been done.

The children might typically be seen simply as victims because of their disabilities, but here, they actually have immense power: they have the agency necessary to confront and destroy the Creature that represents the source of the damage done to both themselves and their communities. In some ways, the children are also the literal manifestation of the alliances formed in the wake of colonialism. Their lives would surely be better if they had never been affected by it, but they have found new power and agency in the very thing that disrupted those lives. Moreover, because these children come from all over the globe, the novel once again points to the ways that the regional and the tribally specific are yoked to the national and the global. Although two Indigenous characters lead the way, they are victorious only because they are supported by allies from a variety of other cultures and nations.

Once again illustrating the careful balance of the local and the global, the novel's resolution also reflects traditional Cherokee stories like the creation story, in which the smallest beings are able to effect the most change. The story describes various animals diving to the bottom of the ocean in search of land. In some versions, such as in Joseph Erb's short film, "The Beginning They Told," the animal who finally succeeds is the tiny water beetle, who is therefore responsible for building the earth itself.[69] In the same way, the children that Sammy summons are able to save the world by collaborating to solve a seemingly overwhelming problem. In order to achieve their goal, they draw on individual strengths, but they also recognize their similarities and agree to work together. Just as Billy, Janna, Mickey, and Sarah form cross-cultural alliances, these children draw on one another to mount their resistance.

But before Sammy can summon these children and defeat the radiation Creature, he has to be cared for by Sarah. When the radiation Creature attacks, he has to be rescued from the clinic by Janna and Billy. And before that, he had to be cared for by his biological family. Despite the fact that Sammy's disabilities make it quite challenging to care for him, a number of people have worked together to keep him healthy. These people all accept responsibility for Sammy without knowing that he will save the world. As we see in many works of Indigenous science fiction, an ethical response to the Other means protecting and caring for those who are weaker or have less privilege than oneself.

The ethical treatment of Sammy is especially important here because, as Sanders repeatedly emphasizes, Indigenous peoples have so often been treated as less than human. Billy and Janna's discussions of the Cherokee and Kazakh people refer to many examples of such treatment, but Mickey addresses the issue more directly. When Sarah explains her research into the long-term effects of radiation on humans, Mickey sarcastically responds, "Humans. . . . That's the key word. Indians aren't human, don't you know that? It's in the Constitution or something."[70] This refusal to recognize the demand of the Other, beginning with the sixteenth-century debate in the Catholic Church over whether or not Indians were actually human beings, has justified a great many violent and negligent acts, both in reality and within the world of the novel. Billy and Janna have each been harassed and abused because of their Indigeneity, but they are able to break the cycle by caring for Sammy and each other. According to *The Ballad of Billy Badass*, the best way to respond to the monstrosity of colonialism is to treat the Other as human, to accept that Other into one's own community, and to acknowledge the individual's responsibility toward all members of that community, both human and non.

This approach is echoed in Niigaanwewidam Sinclair's definition of ethics as "a responsible curiosity," a responsibility that we all share to build a "mutually beneficial home."[71] Sinclair's model of ethics as a round dance echoes the act of alliance building that we see throughout *The Ballad of Billy Badass*. To behave ethically in the face of an impending apocalypse—whether it comes in the form of removal, nuclear threat, or radiation Creature—we must acknowledge our shared responsibility to both the Other and the world around us, as well as the importance of reframing the ethical encounter: not as a threat to the self, but as a process of building community. As a work of science fiction, *The Ballad of Billy Badass* is able to embody settler colonial nations' repeated refusal to recognize members of ethnic or national minorities as human beings, instead devaluing both their lands and their lives. Although the resulting damage has not yet spawned a radiation Creature in the real world, it is just as pervasive, extending far beyond arbitrary regional and political boundaries. Ultimately, Sanders proposes that by acting for the good of the community rather than the individual—that is, by following an Indigenous model of ethics—it becomes possible to combat the monstrous effects of colonialism and, finally, to save the world.

CHAPTER TWO

Radioactive Rabbits and "Illegal Aliens"

Border Crossing in It Came from Del Rio

Few authors have contributed so much to the field of Indigenous science fiction—and experimental genre fiction overall—as Stephen Graham Jones, whose diverse body of work raises many questions about the role and responsibilities of Native writers in the twenty-first century. The 2008 novel *Ledfeather* was among the first of Jones's works to attract critical notice, largely because of its experimental retelling of a historical event, the Blackfeet Starvation Winter of 1883–84. Many of his other novels and stories received more widespread attention after the publication of two books: Theodore Van Alst's edited collection *The Faster Redder Road* in 2015 and Billy Stratton's *The Fictions of Stephen Graham Jones: A Critical Companion* in 2016. As opposed to the "literary" tone of *Ledfeather*, novels with titles like *The Last Final Girl* and *Zombie Sharks with Metal Teeth* gleefully embrace the tropes of pure genre fiction. Some of Jones's most interesting work strikes a balance between these two approaches, experimenting with high and low literature and questioning the utility of drawing such rigid boundaries.

Jones's 2010 novel *It Came from Del Rio* is a perfect case study for exploring the issues of both genre and identity politics. The novel draws on elements of science fiction and horror to tell the story of Dodd Raines, a U.S. citizen who flees to Mexico after a botched bank robbery. He now makes a living smuggling illegal goods across the border, and the novel opens as Dodd accepts a job delivering a mysterious package that his employer simply describes as "moon rocks."[1] He later discovers that these rocks are highly radioactive, and even brief exposure is deadly. After carrying the "moon rocks" for several days, Dodd is doomed to die, so his employer speeds the process up by shooting him. Because the novel toes the line between horror and science fiction, it makes perfect sense that the same radiation exposure that nearly kills Dodd eventually brings him back to life. Reincarnated but disfigured, he hides his mangled face by wearing a large, decomposing rabbit head as a mask. The new Dodd also glows in the dark and is accompanied by a pack of wild jackals that witnesses mistake for chupacabras. Thus outfitted, he sets out to get revenge on his mysterious employers. Wild as this plot sounds, Jones's choice to situate the novel at the U.S.-Mexico border, as well as to draw on particularly Latinx and Indigenous concerns, allows him to use science fiction and horror conventions to explore the relationship between empire and humanity, between border crossing and genre crossing, in a novel that examines both formal and political marginalization and the importance of recognizing the Other—whether in the guise of an "illegal alien" or a radioactive zombie smuggler—as human.

Like much of Jones's work, *It Came from Del Rio* challenges the definition of a term like "Indigenous science fiction." Must such texts tell specifically Indigenous stories? Do they qualify so long as they have been written by Native authors? To what degree must Indigenous science fiction (sf) feature Native characters, cultures, and plots? Van Alst argues that in Jones's work, "unless I'm told otherwise, all of the characters are Indian. But best of all, very best of all, they're incidentally Indian."[2] The "incidental" nature of "Indianness" in Jones's work is key, emphasizing the idea that while Indigeneity should not be ignored, neither should it become the single defining quality of either authors or their characters. This argument comes up again in *The Fictions of Stephen Graham Jones*, in which Van Alst returns to the idea that Indigeneity is both present and incidental throughout Jones's work—and especially in *It Came from Del Rio*. Here, he calls out those readers who might demand a specifically Indigenous reading of the novel:

> Some of you might be reading this for a class. A Native lit class, say. And you're going, wait, isn't Jones a *Native* writer? Shouldn't we be attending to *Indian* things? Turn down those "miner lights" and maybe you'll see that we already are, but that

question is also why Jones says he "started writing about zombies and aliens" in the first place.[3]

The quotation, and the metaphorical "miner lights," refer to Jones's interview with Billy Stratton, included in the same collection. As Jones explains:

> People are always asking me, "What's Indian about this?" So I started writing about zombies and aliens to stop getting that question because I hate that question. That question means people are going into this book with their miner lights turned up too bright, looking for just one thing.[4]

Or, as Jones says in his "Letter to a Just-Starting-Out Indian Writer—and Maybe to Myself,"

> *You don't have to be able to define what an Indian is in order to write "Indian."* Putting a definition on us, that's playing their game, that's submitting to being an entry in an encyclopedia. That's saying yes, you drew the boundaries well, I will live just in this little block of text. Instead, just, you know, *write*. If you are Indian, whatever "Indian" might be, then whatever you do, that's Indian as well.[5]

From both Van Alst and Jones himself, then, we receive the clear message that it would be a mistake to comb through Jones's novels looking for their "Indian" content, in much the same way that if critics focus only on *Ledfeather* because it most obviously meets the definition of "Native literature," they may find themselves in the position of the border patrol in *It Came from Del Rio*: policing identity by relying on inaccurate markers to enforce imagined boundaries. In his discussion of Jones's work as potentially postmodern, A. Robert Lee acknowledges many of the same concerns. He notes that although the phrase "Native postmodern . . . risks sounding like contrivance, an Atlantic fashioning foisted upon Native authorship . . . [it] actually does aptest service in holding Native experience to light."[6] Although Lee ultimately chooses to focus on *Ledfeather* and *Bleed into Me*, he refers to a wide swath of Jones's work to support his argument, suggesting that all of Jones's texts, not only those with a "Native focus," fit within the category of the Native postmodern.[7]

As part of a larger discussion about the controversy surrounding the term, Lee also offers a useful overview of the debates, both historical and ongoing, over what should or should not be included in the category of "Native literature":

> The controversies over "authenticity" go on circling as to texts that do or do not do
> justice to the Native-real, authors who do or do not pass muster in the way of Native
> credential. . . . Do spy or detective novels meet the prescribed Native bar, Martin
> Cruz Smith's post-Soviet *Red Square* or Mardi Oakley Medawar's Cherokee-written
> but Kiowa-centered *Death at Rainy Mountain*?[8]

Lee's questions, especially when paired with Jones's own critique and Van Alst's suggestion that Indigeneity runs throughout Jones's work, combine to establish a framework for discussing *It Came from Del Rio* as a work of Indigenous science fiction. To divide Jones's stories and novels into two categories—those that are "Native" and those that are not—is to miss the point, just as it is beside the point to debate whether his work should be considered high-brow literature or mere popular fiction. Jones deconstructs such distinctions through formal experimentation and the content of each story. In the case of *It Came from Del Rio*, the novel deals explicitly with border crossings and the blurry distinctions between the natural and the supernatural; readers are invited—and sometimes explicitly encouraged—to challenge received notions of race, ethnicity, and nationality, as well as our understanding of genre as a whole and of "Native literature" in particular.

Although both of the novel's protagonists appear to be Euro-American, *It Came from Del Rio* depicts the kind of ethical encounter with the Other that is key to Indigenous sf. Jones explores this concept on a philosophical level, troubling Euro-American and settler colonial responses to the Other even without offering an explicitly Indigenous model as an alternative. Both Dodd, who narrates the first half of the novel, and his daughter Laurie, who narrates the second, self-identify as "white" at various points, and both rely on their racial and national privilege on numerous occasions. Before becoming a radiation Monster, Dodd is a successful smuggler primarily because he does not draw suspicion at the U.S.-Mexico border, a fact that he acknowledges when he explains that "what I had working for me, too, was that this was America, and I was white under my Mexico tan, a sunbeaten kind of look that was characteristic of all the veterans-turned-hippies who lived along the border."[9] Comments like this one point to the inconsistent relationship between race and nationality in a context where border patrol officers are tasked with identifying "illegal aliens" based on their presumed nationality. Because there are no reliable visual indicators of citizenship, the officers rely instead on racial profiling to determine whether someone "belongs" in the United States. Such a practice misidentifies not only Dodd, but also those Latinx and Chicanx folks who are U.S. citizens, and it further fails to consider the presence of Native peoples living on either side of an artificially imposed border. Indeed, given the complicated history of Texas and the Indigenous peoples residing in that area, the novel raises implicit questions about the constructed nature of race and citizenship, as well as the creation of "Indigenous," "Mestizo," and "Mexican" as discrete categories within the space of the borderlands.

Further challenging the functionality of such tidy categories, Jones asks readers to sympathize with a narrator who transforms into both a literal and figurative alien after prolonged exposure to the radioactive rocks that he is carrying across the border. Like so many undocumented immigrants, Dodd finds himself crossing the desert on foot and being harassed by a corrupt border patrol officer, who takes his water, backpack, and boots before stranding him in the desert. Dodd ends up sleeping in a water trough in an open field, where he is discovered by a Mexican cowboy. As he wakes up, Dodd realizes "why the situation was funny to [the cowboy]. It was a reversal—the white guy was the wet. Dripping, even."[10] As Dodd literally becomes a "wetback," the derogatory term used to refer to undocumented Latinx immigrants, Jones reminds readers of the arbitrariness of privilege based on skin color and nationality, since such boundaries can so easily be crossed and reversed. The presence of the cowboy is also a nod to Indigeneity, since it is difficult to separate cowboys from Indians—especially in the writing of an Indigenous author whose work draws on the genre conventions of the Western. The trope of "cowboys and Indians" recurs throughout Native literature: in just one example, Thomas King recalls playing "cowboys and Indians with the rest of the kids."[11] After describing his own cowboy costume, King reflects, "I don't remember anyone who wanted to be an Indian."[12] When juxtaposed against the Mexican cowboy, then, Dodd finds himself in two unpopular positions simultaneously: he has stepped into the position of both the "wetback" and the "Indian," labels that estrange him from mainstream American society. In moments like these, the novel reminds readers of the racial hierarchy that has always informed popular discourse in the United States.

Dodd's transformation into an "illegal alien" is not yet complete; although he has lost much of his privilege by the time he confronts the Mexican cowboy, he continues to wield whatever power is available to him. To maintain control of this particular situation, he invokes the specter of Sebby Walker, a white man who smuggles immigrants into the United States and sells them into slavery after they cross the border.[13] Dodd disapproves of Sebby's business for both moral and practical reasons, but he nonetheless regains authority by telling the Mexican cowboy that he is "the new Sebby."[14] Dodd continues to take advantage of any privilege he can, no matter how unfairly he might obtain it or how problematic it might be. He does not relinquish his unearned privilege until, having become a radioactive zombie wearing a rabbit head, Dodd truly has no other choice. In losing his ability to pass as a white American, Dodd also loses the ability to blend in—and thus, to remain invisible.

Dodd attempts to maintain his privilege by envisioning himself as a hero despite his long criminal career. In fact, once Dodd accepts this particular job, for which he believes that he is transporting "stellar geology" rather than narcotics, he admits, "I kind of liked it."[15] The representative who hires him plays on Dodd's fantasy by asking, "didn't you want to be an astronaut, Dodd?"[16] This is a tempting narrative, and Dodd buys into it wholeheartedly: he soon finds himself imagining that his limited rations are "like the astronauts ate, yeah."[17] Further reinforcing his embrace of Western heroism, Dodd compares himself to "the old time cowboys," who, like astronauts, are imagined as fighting for a noble cause.[18] Because cowboys in the Wild West are typically depicted as being above the law, Dodd can imagine that he, too, is a strong, masculine protector, at odds with corrupt border patrol officers as he embarks on his noble quest.

Of course, cowboys and astronauts have more in common than their reputation as heroes in popular culture: they also serve as figures of western expansion and colonialism. Astronauts, like other explorers in the Euro-American tradition, strike out to discover—and claim—new territory for the nations that fund their expeditions. We need look no further than the opening statement of the original *Star Trek* series to hear echoes of the settler colonial mission often associated with space travel: "Space: the final frontier. These are the voyages of the starship *Enterprise*. Its five-year mission: to explore strange new worlds, to seek out new life and new civilizations, to boldly go where no man has gone before."[19] More recent (as well as more scientific) sources have drawn similar parallels between astronauts and settler colonialism. For instance, in a 2016 article about NASA's Office of Planetary Protection, Kevin Carey explains that, among its other purposes, the "office serves to prevent NASA from doing to Martians what European explorers did to Native Americans with smallpox."[20] The existence of such an office emphasizes NASA's awareness of the ethical implications of space exploration and the dangers inherent in potential encounters with the Other—a responsibility that Dodd is slow to acknowledge.

Lost in his fantasy, it is already too late when Dodd realizes that "what I'd been muling north, then, was the first shipment of the new empire. They'd given me the new world in a case, and paid me to carry it into America."[21] This description reinforces his connection to both the history of colonization and contemporary black-market operations in the borderlands. His word choice conflates "the new world" and "the new empire," troubling an idealistic depiction of settler colonialism and reminding readers that a new world is always built on the foundations of an older one. The Europeans who settled "the new world" in the fifteenth century established their empires with both weapons and disease; in the twenty-first, Dodd carries a deadly disease across the border and infects anyone with whom he comes in contact. As in Carey's metaphorical connection between NASA and smallpox, Dodd becomes an unintentional mobile biological weapon.

In addition to smuggling radioactive rocks across the border, Dodd also attempts to die by suicide by jumping into a well—which, unbeknownst to him, connects to the water supply of Austin, Texas. Albeit accidentally, Dodd threatens the lives of all the citizens of Austin, regardless of race, class, or nationality. Jones suggests that when nuclear technology is used to wage wars, it has unforeseen consequences and affects a wider population than just the targeted "enemy." Having been literally contaminated by "the new empire," Dodd becomes an embodiment of settler colonialism, which in turn means his actions have the potential to devastate contemporary communities as effectively as smallpox decimated Indigenous populations five hundred years ago. Once again, *It Came from Del Rio* reminds readers that racial and national boundaries are permeable and artificial, easily crossed no matter how humans try to reinforce them. Such a reminder not only echoes the rhetoric of the borderlands, it also underlines an Indigenous perspective that portrays people as dependent upon and responsible to one another, as well as to the world around us.

Jones reinforces the specter of colonialism through the presence of a pack of supposed chupacabras who trail Dodd across the borderlands. In his book-length study, Benjamin Radford describes the chupacabra as a supernatural creature, often resembling a wild dog and first widely reported in Puerto Rico in 1995.[22] Since then, the chupacabra has appeared almost exclusively in Spanish-speaking communities across the Americas.[23] According to Radford, many people believe that "the U.S. government specifically ... created the chupacabra in an evil, clandestine genetics experiment gone horribly wrong."[24] He attributes this belief to the history of colonialism in the Americas, noting that "Latin America, like many postcolonial societies, also endured a very real historical vampirism as Europeans took what they wanted and left the rest."[25] Thus, "the perception and resentment of having native resources taken by outsiders are very much a part of the Latin American cultural and social fabric."[26] In a novel set in the borderlands that highlights issues of racial, socioeconomic, and national inequality, Dodd's faithful chupacabras draw further attention to the ways that Euro-Americans have mistreated the Indigenous inhabitants of the continent in the past, as well as the ways that they continue to do so in the present. As Radford notes, the presence of the chupacabras reminds readers that while "the vampires may be metaphorical . . . they are no less real."[27]

Although the chupacabra is a modern creature, born out of radiation exposure and conspiracy theories, its genesis in Jones's novel is connected to much older stories: the radioactive material to which the animals have been exposed is itself ancient. As Dodd explains, "Two years before, some graduate anthropology student had uncovered a mass of molten metal and rock deep underneath a Mayan ruin of some sort. Not a pyramid, like for worship, but more like the way you cap off a well."[28] The graduate student thinks that it might be "an old meteorite," which suggests that the metal actually *does* come from space, and thus that "moon rock" is a relatively accurate description of what Dodd is carrying.[29] Later, Dodd compares the rabbits watching the jackals invade their territory to "the way the Mayans watched a fireball burrow through their sky five or ten thousand years ago," suggesting the rocks' genesis.[30] What is most important about this explanation is that it highlights the efficacy of Indigenous knowledge, especially in contrast to Euro-American responses. The Mayans had the good sense to bury this material—and they did so quite effectively, given that it remained undiscovered in the intervening years. The moon rocks' origin story rejects stereotypical depictions of Indigenous peoples as primitive savages who blindly worshipped empty sources of power; rather, the Mayans in Jones's narrative are fully capable of recognizing the inherent danger of the rocks. Unlike the clients who employ Dodd, they resist the temptation to use that power. They further succeed in finding the necessary blend of metal and rock to cap off the source and protect their people from exposure. Dodd's clients, on the other hand, appear to have a minimal grasp of that technology, as evidenced by the fact that they can only reduce his exposure enough to keep him alive for a few days.

Jones also draws on the history of colonialism in the story of Lem Marsh, the man who controls the cartel. Dodd tells us that Lem made his money in South America, where he "lucked into enough cash . . . to scrub his record clean. It wasn't drug money, either, but something to do with mines. He had a silver cartel, I don't know. Or Aztec gold."[31] What slowly emerges is that Lem, who once partnered with Dodd in the botched bank robbery that caused them both to flee the country, has been running the mining operation responsible for unearthing Dodd's "moon rocks." The vague description of Lem's business as being somehow related to silver cartels and Aztec gold suggests connections between the science fictional moon rocks and the very real valuable metals that have historically been mined and sold for a great profit. Such materials are usually extracted by enslaved peoples who are treated as commodities, exploited for their labor and discarded when they are no longer useful. In the Americas, whether in fifteenth-century Spanish silver mines or twentieth-century American uranium mines,[32] Indigenous laborers were literally worked to death or left to die of exposure to radiation in much the same way that Dodd is discarded after delivering the rocks to his client. In each instance, the results are the same: Europeans and Euro-Americans make a considerable profit while Indigenous peoples sacrifice their bodies and lives. Moreover, these resources, whether uranium or "Aztec gold," were originally stolen from lands belonging to Indigenous peoples. Whatever the particulars of Lem's crimes, he has made his fortune by exploiting and dehumanizing others.

This discussion of dehumanization brings us back to Pinsky's argument that science fiction is ultimately about ethical encounters with the alien Other, both metaphorically and literally. Such encounters are common in the borderlands, where colonizers have historically emphasized difference rather than commonality and insisted on maintaining strict borders between races, ethnicities, and nations. While Dodd is aware that these acts of dehumanization occur, he remains personally unaffected by them so long as he presents as a white American. His transformation into a glow-in-the-dark zombie means he experiences the process firsthand. Even before he becomes a literal alien, Dodd is figuratively dehumanized by the men who hire him to carry the "moon rocks" into the United States. As one smuggler explains just before shooting Dodd, "If we could use you again—if anybody could—we would, in a heartbeat. But, as you can see, man, I think you're just about all used up here."[33] And once he is "used up," once Dodd's employers can no longer benefit from his labor, he is disposed of. With this declaration, Dodd becomes an alien Other whose worth is measured by his capacity for productivity.

The dehumanization of the oppressed and the alienation of the Other are themes that echo throughout *It Came from Del Rio*—in the smugglers' treatment of Dodd, but also in the way that the border patrol officers treat people of color and in the way that both Dodd and Laurie have been complicit in that treatment. At first, these activities happen in the background, where a casual reader might not even notice them. It is only after Dodd's transformation, as he begins to draw public attention, that the theme of alienation comes to the forefront. When a Texas convenience store records footage of Dodd shoplifting, the film plays over and over on the local news. Laurie describes it as "just the kind of comedy segment the news always wants, as, in comparison, it makes them look more human, I suppose."[34] Her assessment is key to the fascination with the monstrous in this novel: Jones's characters are reassured and united against any Other they can find—from undocumented immigrants to radiation Monsters. As Judith Butler suggests,

> the operation of repulsion can consolidate "identities" founded on the instituting of the "Other" or a set of Others through exclusion and domination. What constitutes through division the "inner" and "outer" worlds of the subject is a border and boundary tenuously maintained for the purposes of social regulation and control.[35]

In other words, humans construct our own identities by establishing boundaries, a process that requires us to identify an Other against which we can define ourselves. Through this process, we identify "the 'abject,' designat[ing] that which has been expelled from the body, discharged as excrement, literally rendered 'Other.' This appears as an expulsion of alien elements, but the alien is effectively established through this expulsion."[36] In Dodd's case, the media depicts him as a monster in order to affirm its own humanity, but it creates the very category of the monstrous through this act of alienation, much as Refugio and other border patrol officers create and maintain sociopolitical borders in the targeting and deporting of undocumented immigrants. This process of Othering also has a long history in Indigenous/Euro-American relations. Native peoples have been Othered and treated as subhuman since the European "discovery" of the Americas. Beginning with the doctrine of discovery and extending through claims of manifest destiny and on into the present, Euro-American society has repeatedly defined and constructed itself in opposition to Black, Indigenous, and other peoples of color.

A similar impulse to define and expel the Other appears in *The Ballad of Billy Badass*, but there is a key difference in the portrayal of the monsters in each story: as Sobchack would argue, *The Ballad of Billy Badass* is a Creature story, while *It Came from Del Rio* is a Monster story, told from the perspective of the dehumanized Other. Monsters are more closely associated with horror than science fiction, but there is nonetheless considerable overlap between the two categories. Sobchack tells us that "the Creatures and Monsters of certain SF films seem to roam the earth almost by accident," as in the case of Sanders's radiation Creature, while "in the horror film . . . the Monster seems less accidental; he seems to arise inevitably out of a personal Faustian obsession or the inherent animal nature of Man."[37] In *It Came from Del Rio*, Dodd's monstrous existence could be blamed on either his own obsession with accepting "one last job," which ultimately leads to his transformation, or on his clients' greed and their willingness to commit murder—that is, their "animal nature" and lack of compassion. While Sanders is not interested in presenting the world from the radiation Creature's perspective, Jones paints a sympathetic portrait of his Monster by telling half the story from Dodd's point of view—further reinforcing Sobchack's argument that "in the horror film there is always something sympathetic about the Monster, something which gives us—however briefly—a sense of seeing the world through his eyes, from his point of view. He is not other than Man; he is the dark side of Man and therefore comprehensible."[38] Because Dodd is a compelling and sympathetic narrator—and because, when the novel opens, he is a social outcast but still quite human—readers are encouraged to see the world through his perspective. Like other Monsters, he "is a *human being*" who "is through a great portion of the [novel] at least semirational."[39] In such stories, "good" and "evil" become more difficult to map. Just as the boundaries between the United States and Mexico or between the hero and the villain are blurrier in this novel than in *The Ballad of Billy Badass*, so too is our understanding of what constitutes monstrosity and humanity. We repeatedly see atrocious human behavior, while Dodd, the ostensible Monster, claims to be driven by love. Instead of delineating between binary categories of good/evil, *It Came from Del Rio* suggests that such boundaries are almost always both arbitrary and permeable.

Recognizing the humanity of the monstrous Other may be part of the ethical imperative in Jones's novel, but he simultaneously asks whether humans are actually ethical beings and whether "humanity" is even a virtue worth striving toward. Because he focuses this question through Dodd's experience, we might understand the novel as an exploration of what can go wrong when a person follows settler colonial values to their logical end. As in the case of Pinsky's argument about the human tendency toward assimilation, it is useful to remember that Dodd is an example, not of all humanity, but of a single cultural perspective. Take, for instance, Dodd's return from the dead. After he has been shot and killed, his murderers roll his body up in wire fencing and leave it in a warehouse storage yard to decompose. He stays there for fourteen years, in a kind of dreamlike state, before fully reawakening and crawling out of his makeshift coffin.[40] When he finally emerges, Dodd discovers that he has been sharing the warehouse yard with a colony of rabbits, and at first, he believes that he is a rabbit, too. During this time, he has no "human thoughts" and "the days smear together into one single kind of ideal day."[41]

From a Euro-American perspective, Dodd's transformation appears to be pure science fiction: like many superheroes before him, he survived a freak accident involving exposure to radiation, and as a result, he takes on the qualities of the animal that was present at the time of the accident. The most famous example of this trope is probably Spider-Man, who gained his superpowers when he was "bitten on the hand by a radioactive spider and accidentally irradiated by a particle beam."[42] But Spider-Man is just one of many superheroes created by Marvel Comics in the early 1960s, when the company used its platform to publish stories that "were commentaries on Cold War politics, reflecting a vision of American global dominance."[43] Matthew J. Costello notes that "the fear of atomic war looms" in these comics:

> created under the mushroom cloud of nuclear war, Marvel heroes' origins derive mostly from radiation, whether direct exposure (The Fantastic Four and Hulk), indirect exposure through radioactive waste (Daredevil), spiders (Spider-Man), or through a general increase in radiation in the atmosphere due to the testing of nuclear weapons (X-Men).[44]

Similarly, Dodd's origin story is one of direct exposure, while the stories of Daredevil and the X-Men echo themes that are also at play in *The Ballad of Billy Badass*. Costello goes on to argue that the Marvel superheroes from this time period "are often antiheroes, outsiders . . . ugly monsters that are shunned." Ultimately, they are "victims of nuclear technologies" who "skirt moral boundaries" as they represent a "nascent questioning of the triumphal American global role, pointing to a concern with the costs of empire."[45] In addition to sharing a similar origin story, Dodd is also a "victim" who lives in a moral gray area, his behavior raising real questions about the consequences of American imperialism.

In superhero comics, these critiques have become more pointed over time until, by the early 2000s, "American superhero narratives cast America as culpable in [terrorist] attacks and portray such displays of power as hubristic and threatening."[46] *It Came from Del Rio*, published in 2010, offers a similar critique. Though Dodd becomes a threat to the safety of U.S. citizens, he only arrives in this position after being mistreated and neglected throughout his interactions with various systems of

American power. Economic desperation leads him to rob a bank; fear of his daughter growing up in the foster care system, like her mother before her, leads him to flee the country; an inability to provide for his family leads him to accept smuggling jobs. If America took better care of its citizens—if its social programs were more expansive and its law enforcement focused greater attention on rehabilitation rather than imprisonment—Dodd would have been far less likely to become a radiation Monster who poisoned Austin's drinking water.

But we can also read Dodd's transformation through an Indigenous lens: from this perspective, his experience of leaving behind his "human thoughts" to live as a rabbit might be understood quite differently. In many Indigenous storytelling traditions, humans and animals are viewed as relatives who exist in relationship with one another, as opposed to the Christian tradition that asserts Man's dominion over the Earth and its creatures.[47] While it is important to avoid generalizing or essentializing Indigenous cultures, it is worth noting that in many traditions, Rabbit plays a prominent role as a trickster figure—a point that Van Alst also alludes to briefly.[48] Moreover, Dodd's ability to transform into a rabbit, to literally become an alien Other, echoes an Indigenous approach to ethics and a worldview that is grounded in what is experienced rather than what is believed, as per Deloria's argument. By recalling Sinclair's metaphor of ethics as a round dance, through which participants work together to find a common rhythm, we can also understand Dodd's transformation as an example of an Indigenous ethical approach—a willingness to adapt to the rhythms of life among the rabbits in order to join the Other on their own terms.

It is not surprising, then, when Dodd acknowledges that he was happiest during this time. He confesses that "in my calm moments, now, I sometimes go back there still."[49] He later describes the rabbits as his community and his family, explaining that he lived "as one of them," that he "was a rabbit."[50] This emphasis on community, on the role one plays within a family and an individual's responsibility to others, further reflects Indigenous values. When Dodd adheres to these values, he is most at peace. The relationship is one of balance rather than conquest: not only does he accept the rabbits, but despite his differences, they also accept him. They do not treat him like a monster; instead, they adapt to his presence and include him in their community. For instance, Dodd describes an intimate exchange with a female rabbit: "I'd watched her give birth a few weeks ago. She'd even let me touch her once, with the side of my hand, but then had hopped off, as if pretending this had never happened."[51] This vaguely unsettling encounter emphasizes Dodd's unique role within the community, suggesting that he has formed an emotional relationship with the rabbits, while his observation of the birthing process gestures to his desire to become more completely involved in their life cycles and community.

Dodd remains with the rabbits until they are attacked by a pack of jackals, an experience that triggers his memories of life as a human. As the jackals devour the rabbits, Dodd realizes that "the carnage before me—it wasn't as unfamiliar as it should have been. Instead, it was like a stencil laid on old memories. It was giving the random images in my head form, shape, structure."[52] This scene suggests that violence is what ultimately defines humanity—or, at least, settler colonial humanity. Only after he has witnessed the fight between the jackals and the rabbits does Dodd stand on two legs for the first time since his near death and resurrection. Leaning on the fence for balance, he inadvertently touches a dead rabbit, the one "who had let me touch her once."[53] Although he recognizes this rabbit and remembers his connection with her, it is telling that, in his first action as a human, Dodd "pick[s] the [rabbit] meat from the fence with my teeth."[54] Dodd's act of cannibalism separates him irrevocably from what had been his community. He eats not just any rabbit, but the one with whom he had the most developed relationship, and he looks up to realize that the other rabbits "were watching me, as if disappointed."[55] In the very act of embracing his identity as a human and a settler colonist, Dodd becomes a Monster, willing to betray and devour his family.

It can be rather difficult to feel sympathy for Dodd, not only in this moment but throughout the novel. After all, he chose to rob a bank, abandon his dying wife, flee the country, smuggle drugs across the U.S.-Mexico border, and leave his young daughter on her own. Even before the gruesome scene in which he eats the rabbit, it is hard to imagine him as a hero. But, in keeping with Pinsky's theory that science fiction is about the ethical encounter with the Other, Jones challenges readers to recognize the potential for good in Dodd despite his monstrous appearance and behavior. Dodd makes no excuses, but he does offer a theory as to why he has survived: "If you think it was any black rock from space that brought me back to this world, then—I don't know. You haven't been listening, I don't think. It was [Laurie]."[56] Dodd believes that he came back to life to protect his daughter because she "was telling me to keep her safe. That she trusted me to keep her safe."[57] He failed to protect her when he was shot and left for dead for fourteen years, leaving Laurie to be raised by Refugio, a corrupt border patrol officer who convinces Laurie to follow his career path. But his failure does not indicate a lack of love. Despite all the ways that Dodd has been alienated and estranged, his loyalty to and love for his daughter continue to humanize him. In return, although Dodd has been treated like a monster by every human he encounters, Laurie still recognizes her father beneath his hideous appearance. Narrating their first meeting, Laurie says that "for a moment he seemed to forget what he looked like, I think, what he'd become. For a moment he was just Dodd, smiling a confused smile behind his mask, his off-hand rising as if to cup the side of my face."[58] In this moment, as he comes face-to-face with his daughter for the first time in fourteen years, Dodd is briefly able to forget about getting revenge, about his appearance and his self-awareness, and the power of this moment allows the novel to argue that human beings have the potential to be more than just violence and carnage. We are also capable of responding to the Other with love. As in *The Ballad of Billy Badass*, this radical love is both humanity's defining feature and our ethical responsibility.

The novel concludes by suggesting that we must establish and prioritize such ethical relationships in order to survive as a species: as an FBI agent investigating Dodd's case observes, "Every track is the right track down here. . . . It's all connected!"[59] The agent goes on to describe the situation as "an international investigation with truly global implications."[60] Depending on who gains access to the "moon rocks" and how effectively those people can contain the radiation, it is easy to imagine various scenarios that would lead to the development of additional nuclear arms or the widespread use of biological weapons. Jones suggests one particularly nightmarish possibility: having realized that he is effectively undead and toxic, Dodd attempts to isolate himself in order to avoid harming others. He goes "to the one place he knew would take him, Jacob's Well," which, so far as he knows, "has no bottom."[61] Here, Jones plays with the generic conventions of the horror film, in which the Monster "is almost always a misfit in the sense that he does not conform with accepted modes of social behavior, or does not obey orders, and thus places himself in isolation, away from society, so that he alone is contaminated."[62] Although this is Dodd's intention, he fails because Jacob's Well actually connects to Edward Aquifer, which flows into the drinking water of Austin.[63] Thus, even when Dodd tries to minimize the damage, his actions ultimately reinforce the connection between the local and the global and the responsibility that all humans owe to their larger community. Isolation is simply not possible. Instead, both Dodd and those with whom he interacts must acknowledge that they exist inescapably within their relationships, which extend beyond any political borders.

The novel ends without resolving this final crisis, though it turns to Laurie to offer a potential solution. Just as she is capable of an ethical response to the Other when she first encounters undead Dodd, so does she offer a positive example to counteract Dodd's negative one. As the narrator of the final chapters of the book, Laurie explains that she has been arrested for her role in helping Dodd escape the FBI and then reveals that her part of the story is "draft number one of my allocution," a legal document that exists "in that little cranny of the law called 'attorney-client privilege,' [which] should be invisible to you [the reader]."[64] In other words, if Laurie's story is shared with anyone other than her attorney, her case will be declared a mistrial.[65] The ostensibly private story ends with the revelation that Dodd has infected Austin's water supply, and the only way to alert the citizens to the "rabbit content of their drinking water" would be to share this legally private information.[66] If Laurie's allocution is publicly released, the judge will have to throw out the case. As she says, "after reading this, no honest judge in his right mind could ever send me to Huntsville."[67] Laurie and her attorney are thus betting that the judge will prioritize the ethical over the legal, saving the lives of thousands of Austin's residents while allowing Laurie to go free.

Although readers of the novel are not actually in a position to judge Laurie's case, we are nonetheless implicated in the judge's decision. As it becomes clear that the entire second half of the novel has been Laurie's allocution, we realize that we have been breaking the law by reading her private documents. In the last pages, Laurie speaks directly to the audience, encouraging us to act out and alert the public. She assumes that we, like the judge, would make an ethical decision and choose to value thousands of human lives over upholding the letter of the law. In this conclusion, Jones challenges readers to recognize our responsibility to our own communities, both local and global. The ease with which Dodd infects the water supply reminds us of our simultaneous control over and dependence upon natural resources. Artificially imposed political borders fail to depict the reality of our situation: if we destroy our land or water or air, whether intentionally or accidentally, political boundaries—between the United States and Mexico or between the United States and tribal nations—will do nothing to stop the spread of death and disease. Rather than isolating ourselves, we must recognize the ethical demand of the Other and form transnational alliances that acknowledge our responsibility to a global community.

The Ballad of Billy Badass and the Rose of Turkestan and *It Came from Del Rio* use the related sf tropes of the radiation Creature or Monster as an entry point to discuss questions of alienation and the ethical encounter. Jones humanizes the Monster by telling the story from his perspective while simultaneously critiquing his actions, while Sanders's Creature remains a truly inaccessible, and even unimaginable, alien. Ultimately, both authors place not only the blame but also the responsibility on the humans who have created, tested, and manipulated nuclear power for political and economic gain. When people are motivated entirely by self-interest, they fail to recognize the ethical demand of the Other—especially when that Other includes already marginalized groups. In *It Came from Del Rio*, Dodd recognizes the abuse that takes place at the U.S. border, but he disregards it in order to manipulate the system for his own profit. In *The Ballad of Billy Badass*, both the United States and Russia fail to recognize members of ethnic or national minority groups as human beings, instead using their land to test nuclear weapons and dispose of toxic waste. In both novels, the damage is pervasive, extending far beyond the arbitrary political boundaries established by federal governments. The only way to prevent or address such contamination is for people to treat radiation itself as the enemy. By acting for the good of the community instead of the individual—a value that is inherent to many Indigenous cultures—it becomes possible to combat the effects of imperialism and, ultimately, to save the world.

PART TWO

Reimagining Resistance

Alternate reality and virtual reality are two closely related generic tropes that allow Indigenous authors to depict "history and the contemporary intersecting at the ground zero of tribal identity."[1] In these stories, as opposed to stories of actual time travel, characters may revisit and reinterpret the past, but they cannot change events that have already taken place. Locating the subgenre of alternate reality firmly within science fiction, Philip K. Dick argues that science fiction (sf) cannot be defined as "a story (or novel or play) set in the future" because there is also science fiction "set in the present: the alternate-world story or novel."[2] Where Dick only mentions the trope in passing, Karen Hellekson offers a more complete definition of alternate history as "that branch of nonrealistic literature that concerns itself with history turning out differently than we know to be the case."[3]

For one of the most famous examples of this subgenre, we can look to Dick's 1962 novel, *The Man in the High Castle*, which imagines a world in which the Axis won World War II. The novel is set in 1962—also the year in which it was originally published—and many historical details establish a similarity between its world and our own. For instance, when Germany's Reichskanzler dies, several actual historical figures are identified as potential future leaders of the Nazi party—Joseph

Goebbels and Hermann Göring among them.[4] There is also a brief reference to Joe Zangara, who really did attempt to assassinate Franklin Roosevelt in 1933. In Dick's version, however, Zangara was successful, and the United States struggled during the war because it lacked FDR's strong leadership. Another major storyline focuses on Robert Childan, an American antiques dealer whose collection runs the gamut from butter churns to Mickey Mouse watches to Colt .44s used during the Civil War. In each of these examples, we see enough recognizable details to understand that the world of Dick's novel mirrors our own up to the point at which the Allies lost the war. That fact serves as a catalyst for everything else, shaping both the characters' daily lives and the events that make up the plot.

As Hellekson suggests, the primary function of alternate history is to "ask questions about time, linearity, determinism, and the implicit link between past and present."[5] In *The Man in the High Castle*, Dick explores these themes by telling several seemingly discrete stories that are ultimately connected to one another as well as the world at large. One of the novel's protagonists, Frank Frink, addresses these questions directly when he consults the *I Ching*. Based on his reading, he believes that the oracle is warning him about the potential for a "Third World War! All frigging two billion of us killed, our civilization wiped out. Hydrogen bombs falling like hail."[6] Upon contemplating how such events might have been set in motion, Frink suggests that "it's the fault of those physicists and that synchronicity theory, every particle being connected with every other; you can't fart without changing the balance of the universe."[7] That notion of synchronicity is borne out in the novel's complex relationships, which often remain unknown to the characters themselves. For instance, Frink is primarily interested in finding a new way to make a living after losing his factory job. He and a friend open their own business creating jewelry. In a roundabout, haphazard way, one of Frink's pieces ends up in the hands of Mr. Tagomi, a high-ranking Japanese official who ultimately saves Frink's life without ever meeting him or learning that he made the jewelry that has so strongly affected Tagomi. Complex, seemingly random connections like this one abound throughout the novel.

Dick's concatenation of events such as these reinforces Hellekson's claim that "parallel worlds stories assume that history can change at almost any point, even if seemingly insignificant, with every choice resulting in a new universe splitting off."[8] She goes on to argue that this realization "provides great power to the individual while simultaneously indicating that because everything literally happens, there is no moral imperative."[9] In *The Man in the High Castle*, for instance, Mr. Tagomi comes to this realization when he concludes that "there is no answer. No understanding. Even in the oracle. Yet I must go on living day to day anyhow."[10] He reaches this conclusion after experiencing a truly surreal series of events: his much-anticipated business meeting turns out to be a ruse when Tagomi's colleague, the ostensibly Swedish businessman Mr. Baynes, explains that he is actually an undercover German Nazi whose real purpose is to arrange a meeting with a high-ranking Japanese official, General Tedeki. At that meeting, Baynes warns Tedeki that Germany is making plans for a nuclear attack against Japan. The meeting ends dramatically when Sicherheitsdienst officers break into the office and Tagomi shoots them with a gun he keeps in his desk, a "Colt .44 ancient collector's item."[11] When the danger has passed, Baynes realizes "how deep [Tagomi's] distress was. For him, Mr. Baynes thought, this event, his having had to kill and mutilate these two men, is not only dreadful; it is inexplicable."[12] Tagomi's feeling that there is no ultimate truth or purpose echoes a belief repeated in other postmodernist texts, where characters are often overwhelmed by the seemingly pointless chaos, bureaucracy, and potential for total annihilation that characterize the modern world. In mainstream sf novels like *The Man in the High Castle*, the trope of alternate reality allows writers to examine the inexplicable and illogical way that historical events unfold while also considering the larger implications of that randomness on individuals' lives.

The genre's ability to contemplate the ways that humans shape historical events makes alternate history an especially useful tool for Indigenous writers, who use the subgenre to revisit and resist the history of colonialism and genocide against Native peoples. In the texts that I examine here, D. L. Birchfield (Choctaw) and Blake M. Hausman (Cherokee) write alternate histories in order to reimagine the forced removal of southeastern tribes that took place in the 1830s. By focusing on this particular historical moment, Hausman and Birchfield bring attention to a series of events that are often glossed over in American history, but they also examine the ways that those events are framed and retold in the present. As Hellekson notes, alternate reality is "concerned with questions particularly relevant to the historian: who brings about history? Is the historian a transcriber of facts or a site of synthesis? Can anyone involved with making history be disinterested? What can be inferred from information?"[13] By setting their stories in the twentieth and twenty-first centuries, rather than simply writing historical fiction set in the nineteenth century, both Birchfield and Hausman create a space to explore such questions.

But Indigenous science fiction also challenges these mainstream definitions, using the same tropes to reach different conclusions and thus expanding the possibilities of the genre. As Rebecca Roanhorse argues, Indigenous sf "fold[s] the past into our present" in order to "writ[e] a future that is decidedly Indigenous."[14] Where mainstream alternate histories typically "conclude that humans have no individual essential nature but rather are beings constructed by the forces of their world," Indigenous sf takes a different view.[15] Just as postmodernist literature written by Black or Indigenous authors insists on an ethical approach often missing from Euro-American texts, so does Indigenous alternate history continue to insist that humans have both an "essential nature" and a "moral imperative."[16] "Custer Under the Baobab" is Cherokee author William Sanders's alternate history of George Armstrong Custer, though the conclusion is much the same: even as he escapes death at the Battle of the Little Bighorn and begins a new life in the imagined African country of Drakia, Custer remains a virulent white supremacist who joins other white men in violently and pointlessly killing the native inhabitants of the land. As in our own history, Custer is ultimately killed by the Indigenous peoples that he has terrorized.

In Sanders's version of history, Custer is ousted from the U.S. military after his shameful retreat at Little Bighorn. To get a fresh start, he moves to Drakia and becomes a militant police officer whose job is primarily to murder the "Bushmen" who live in that region. Sanders's gruesome story imagines Custer's death at the hands of these indigenous Africans, who retaliate after Custer and his men massacre a local village in a scene reminiscent of Indian massacres in the United States. Here, as during the very real massacres at Sand Creek and Wounded Knee,[17] the Euro-American soldiers kill "the slower ones, the elders and the women who paused to snatch up children."[18] In Sanders's alternate history, the message seems to be that even in a parallel universe, nothing changes: white supremacist colonizers who enforce dominance through violence will behave the same way in any place, in any political circumstances, when they come face-to-face with a group of people different from them. As opposed to the postmodern bent of mainstream alternate histories, where there is no essential human nature and "no moral imperative,"[19] Indigenous alternate histories like Sanders's demonstrate a clear need for an ethical response to the Other, even as Euro-American colonizers like Custer refuse to acknowledge that demand.

Birchfield's *Field of Honor* and Hausman's *Riding the Trail of Tears* explore this idea of the ethical imperative at greater length. Like Sanders, Birchfield and Hausman take the unethical behavior of Euro-Americans for granted. Rather than dwelling on that behavior, both authors focus instead on their Native protagonists' ethical responsibilities and obligations. This move highlights the agency and sovereignty of Indigenous peoples rather than continuing to cast them as the helpless victims of colonialism. Furthering this strategy, each novel also focuses on a contemporary Native protagonist in order to consider the ways that Native people today continue to be influenced by and respond to the traumatic history of removal.

Hausman and Birchfield are both citizens of southeastern tribes—Cherokee and Choctaw, respectively—and they both turn their attention to the forced removal of their peoples to Oklahoma in the nineteenth century. Hausman situates the trope of virtual reality in a decidedly Indigenous novel, a maneuver that allows him to reimagine the trauma of the Cherokee Trail of Tears while also acknowledging the ongoing influence of historical narratives in the present day. Birchfield's novel takes place in an alternate reality similar to our own, but for one rather large difference: in this world, some Choctaw have responded to the United States' demand for removal by literally going underground, so that the Choctaw language, culture, and people have survived into the twenty-first century intact and with little outside influence, protected by an elaborate series of caves beneath Oklahoma. If, as Thomas King has argued, "the truth about stories is that that's all we are," then the stories that we tell about the past—and especially about a catastrophic event like removal—will continue to shape our lives in the present.[20] Thus, the science fictional trope of virtual and alternate realities that Hausman and Birchfield employ is important primarily because of its narrative approach, which defies a linear, Euro-American understanding of history and suggests that we might more appropriately confront the trauma of Cherokee and Choctaw removal by examining its effects, not only on the particular time of the mid-nineteenth century, but also within the particular space of Cherokee and Choctaw territories as they continue to exist in both the past and the present.

Instead of trying to erase or reverse this history of removal, Hausman and Birchfield employ alternate realities to focus on the ways that contemporary Native peoples might understand and respond to that history. If the texts had simply introduced a plot device that allowed the characters to go back in time and undo the past, both would become works of fantasy, problematically erasing the very real history of Native people who died during removal as well as those who survived and learned to navigate an unfamiliar political and geographical landscape. Moreover, such stories would be less useful to contemporary Indigenous peoples, who have no such time machine to change their own lives. Instead, by telling the stories of the

Cherokee and the Choctaw in the early twenty-first century, Hausman and Birchfield offer new models of resistance and empowerment in the face of historical trauma.

CHAPTER THREE

Until the Danger Passes

Dystopian Sovereignty in *Field of Honor*

D. L. Birchfield's *Field of Honor* refuses to be analyzed through a single framework; even more than the other texts I discuss here, it challenges readers to reconsider popular definitions of generic categories. At first, the novel appears to be a work of science fiction primarily because it takes place in an alternate reality. But that term alone is insufficient to describe Birchfield's story, which reviewer Scott Andrews calls "nearly manic."[1] Given the importance of considering the novel from a Native perspective, we might also read *Field of Honor* through Dean Rader's concept of the Indian invention novel, one that can be paired with the tribally specific lens of *shukha anumpa*, or Choctaw "hogwash."[2] Each of these frameworks addresses some aspects of the novel, but they both still fall short of encompassing the whole. Ultimately, *Field of Honor* straddles two distinct discourses, appropriating generic conventions from mainstream science fiction as well as relying on traditional Choctaw storytelling methods. As a result, the novel is able to challenge internalized colonization while advocating for Choctaw epistemology and sovereignty.

Field of Honor tells the story of Patrick Pushmataha McDaniel, a paranoid veteran of the Vietnam War who believes he is being hunted as a deserter. When

McDaniel stumbles into a secret training exercise and finds himself captured by the army, he witnesses the murder of an officer and learns that the U.S. military has been infiltrated by what appear to be glow-in-the-dark aliens. Suddenly, a hundred pages into the book, the plot takes an even sharper turn: while fleeing from the apparent alien murderer, McDaniel stumbles into an underground Choctaw community called Ishtaboli. Here we learn that in the alternate reality of the novel, a group of Choctaw resisted removal to Oklahoma in the 1830s by moving into a series of underground caves beneath a tract of land that they received in the 1820 Treaty of Doak's Stand. One hundred fifty years later, Ishtaboli is still organized according to traditional Choctaw political divisions. All its citizens speak Choctaw, and the children attend the Academy of the Little Choctaws, where they study such subjects as Elementary Choctology, English spelling, and "German" history.[3] The Choctaws of Ishtaboli refer to all Europeans and Americans as "Germans"—much as many Americans refer to all Indigenous people as "Indians"—and the children's classes have a decidedly anti-German sentiment. The culture has also been heavily influenced by Choctaw game theory, with the end result that ball players and *alikchi* doctors are the most respected members of the society.[4] Over the next hundred pages, McDaniel finds himself caught up in political intrigue, a whirlwind romance, and intense immersion into Choctaw culture. McDaniel then flees the Choctaw city, returns to the army's secret headquarters, and learns about yet another secret plot, this one involving the U.S. military's deliberate plan to stage a botched war in Vietnam. And before readers can ascertain whether the third plot is a delusion or yet another alternate universe, McDaniel once again flees and the novel ends abruptly.

While readers try to keep up with these twists and turns of plot, *Field of Honor* also cycles through a variety of genres and narrative styles, illustrating Birchfield's deft codeswitching between the conventions of mainstream science fiction (sf) and traditional Choctaw storytelling. The first time that the novel draws direct attention to these shifts comes early on, as McDaniel runs through the woods to escape half a dozen men who have begun shooting at him for no apparent reason. In an instant, the narrative's tone switches from colloquial storytelling to scientific overdrive:

> the sudden intake of Stockholm Cowardice Syndrome sensory stimuli triggered [McDaniel's] Involuntary Instantaneous Overriding Psychomotor Overdrive Dysfunction, rotating his body 180 degrees in a lightning-quick hop, while activating the muscles in his legs in conjunction with a massive discharge of adrenaline into

his bloodstream, and he shot across the clearing as if he had been spring-loaded and trip-released.[5]

This is a very long-winded way of saying that McDaniel experiences a surge of energy and runs away—at, apparently, an almost superhuman speed. The language Birchfield uses to describe the moment suggests satirical echoes of scientific discourse: the precise biological cause of McDaniel's motion comes before his physical movement, and Birchfield also diagnoses his hero with both a syndrome and a dysfunction, each of which has a lengthy and confusing name. The description marks a distinct shift from the more straightforward language of the rest of the novel. For instance, earlier in the same scene, Birchfield includes such mundane descriptions as "a big puddle of blood marked the spot where he'd hit the dirt" and "they all had rifles."[6] Precise language, complex sentences, and polysyllabic jargon clearly distinguish this passage from those around it.

But in the next sentence, the novel employs yet another kind of discourse. The new paragraph suggests that we set aside "Western medical science."[7] Drawing self-conscious attention to his own language, Birchfield reiterates his disdain for scientific writing, raising the question of why such jargon has been included in the first place. Given the way that the novel flouts most other generic conventions, it seems unlikely that Birchfield is interested in satisfying Suvin's theoretical requirements for a work of science fiction by including a cognitive explanation here. Clunky though it may be, however, science writing does play a useful role in this scene: it is one way of understanding McDaniel's behavior, of appealing to a Euro-American audience that insists on rationalizing an absurd series of events. Such an explanation grounds the rest of the novel in a reasonable, logical world, though readers may struggle to see it that way.

Field of Honor reaffirms the necessity of Western medical science in other ways, too. Most notably, part one of the novel is called "Stockholm Cowardice Syndrome Dysfunction." This title is simultaneously a reference to the field of Western medicine and another joke at its expense: adding several words to a recognized medical condition makes it difficult to connect McDaniel's diagnosis to a real-world condition. The extra words also mask the nature of McDaniel's problem: Is it his syndrome that is dysfunctional, or are "Syndrome" and "Dysfunction" just repetitive terms? Is Cowardice the cause or the effect? The term purposely obscures the nature of the condition, and Birchfield's use of Euro-American medical terminology ultimately serves to criticize that language.

Nonetheless, the diluted reference to Stockholm Syndrome invites readers to see McDaniel as a hostage who has become sympathetic to his captors. As a veteran of the Vietnam War, McDaniel has been "captured" by the Marines. Even though he has returned home safely, he continues to live as though he were at war, and in this way remains captive. In fact, when the novel opens, McDaniel has spent the past eleven years preparing for the moment when the Marines will arrive to punish him for desertion. He has devoted all his energy and resources to a needlessly complicated scheme that involves such activities as taking apart and reassembling an experimental prototype of a naval cannon, bending a ninety-foot pine tree to create a giant slingshot, and building a series of entrenched positions armed with fifty-caliber machine guns stolen from National Guard armories throughout Oklahoma.[8] Birchfield also reveals that because McDaniel suffers from something like Stockholm Syndrome, he has only built these complicated booby traps in order to help the Marines uphold their reputation. As he sees it, the Marines might be embarrassed by the fact that they have been unable to capture a single deserter. Thus, McDaniel strives to "become a man worthy of holding the Corps at bay for so long."[9] So, rather than simply being grateful to have survived his time in Vietnam, rather than moving on with his life, McDaniel continues to be held hostage by his loyalty to and obsession with the Marines.[10]

Birchfield exaggerates to an absurd extent McDaniel's concern for the very military that asked him to risk his life in a notoriously unnecessary and unwinnable war, but his satirical approach invites readers to extend the metaphor to its logical conclusion: McDaniel, along with all other citizens of the Choctaw nation, has been taken hostage by the United States itself. According to this reading, the Choctaw were "captured" in the early nineteenth century, both when they agreed to ally themselves with the United States and when they signed a series of treaties agreeing to removal. Like McDaniel, they have since become sympathetic to their captors as they have adapted to Euro-America culturally, linguistically, and politically. It is important to note, however, that both McDaniel in particular and the Choctaw more generally have only given their consent "in a context of coercion,"[11] as Scott Richard Lyons would call it. Birchfield's use of faux medical terminology to describe McDaniel's situation creates a kind of shorthand to draw attention to and summarize the complicated relationship that has evolved between the Choctaw and the United States over more than two centuries.

But Birchfield's use of medical jargon also distances readers from the novel's protagonist. The diagnosis of "Stockholm Cowardice Syndrome Dysfunction" invites audiences to question the reliability of McDaniel's perspective. Although the story is told in the third person, much of it takes place inside McDaniel's head. Birchfield transcribes many of McDaniel's thoughts and reactions for readers, and this imposed critical distance is key in understanding the novel. It is not unusual in Native literature to encounter a protagonist dealing with post–traumatic stress disorder (PTSD), but McDaniel's situation is unique. Where veterans like William Sanders's Billy Badass or Tayo in Leslie Marmon Silko's *Ceremony* suffer from depression and PTSD as a result of their experiences on active duty, these characters understand—as do those around them—that something is wrong. They might not have a cure or even a way to describe it, but the illness itself is evident.

McDaniel, on the other hand, fails to recognize his own "Dysfunction." He has spent the past eleven years living alone in the woods, hiding out because he believes himself to be a Marine Corps deserter.[12] In fact, it is later revealed that he is a military hero who blacked out during the stress of battle. Because he was no longer with his troops when he came to, McDaniel assumes that he must have run away. Rather than questioning why he was sent to Vietnam or recognizing the damage that has been unjustly inflicted upon him, as so many other soldiers and veterans have done, McDaniel's entire life remains centered on the shame he feels for having abandoned his position. Thus, even though he imagines that the Marines are dedicating serious resources to hunting him down and punishing him, he remains desperately loyal to the U.S. military.

The novel's appropriation of medical terminology is further complicated by yet another tonal shift—one that occurs in the very next paragraph. After employing and promptly discarding official medical discourse, the novel reinterprets the same moment through a very different perspective:

> there might be a hint of revelation to a discerning Choctaw eye that McDaniel might possibly be what Choctaws call—in their fullest and oldest and most reverent sense of the word—*chufki* (Rabbit), who has become partly known to non-Choctaws as ole Br'er Rabbit, a trickster as old as the ole mighty *misha sipokni* (Mississippi)—with both the ole trickster and the ole river being as Choctaw as Choctaw can be.[13]

This response to "Western medical science" introduces the inherently Choctaw themes of the novel, which come back to play a much larger role in part two. Birchfield also uses this moment to appeal to an audience with a "discerning

Choctaw eye," immediately establishing his credibility as a Choctaw author writing a distinctly Choctaw story. Other than the initial introduction of McDaniel as a "half-blood Choctaw Indian," this is the first time that Choctaw identity has played a role in the novel, and Birchfield takes advantage of the moment to speak directly to a knowledgeable Choctaw audience.[14] For the uninitiated reader, on the other hand, this passage provides some quick definitions and context. The reference to Br'er Rabbit offers a non-Choctaw audience a point of entry into the story, but it simultaneously reminds those readers that their perspective is now secondary. By privileging Choctaw terms like "*chufki*" and "*misha sipokni*" and placing their English translations in parentheses, as well as by claiming the Mississippi as Choctaw rather than American,[15] Birchfield insists on the primacy of a Choctaw worldview rather than a Euro-American one.

The juxtaposition of these two paragraphs is representative of the way that Birchfield weaves in and out of the two perspectives throughout the novel. Even McDaniel's name reinforces the novel's rejection of black-and-white categories and its inclination to tell chaotic, paradoxical stories that cross cultural and national boundaries in complex ways. The protagonist's full name is Patrick Pushmataha McDaniel, a blending of an Irish-American name and the name of one of the most famous—and most controversial—Choctaw leaders. As McDaniel explains, he was named after Patrick Henry, a "Founding Father" of the United States who is most famous for the phrase "Give me liberty or give me death!"—a sentence that McDaniel cites when declaring his own loyalty to the Marines.[16] Pushmataha, on the other hand, was one of three district chiefs of the Choctaw in the early nineteenth century. He is a complicated figure, considered "the great man of the nation and of the age," but also a man who, as southeastern Indians tried to defend themselves from an influx of American settlers, seems to have gone to great lengths to side with the United States.[17] According to Birchfield, however, "the Choctaw story is the story of America's betrayal of its most loyal Indian military ally, a story that American historians have never quite figured out how to give the right kind of spin."[18] Thus, at least from Birchfield's perspective, Pushmataha should be considered a great military leader who deserves to be rewarded for his continued loyalty to his American allies, a man who is framed as a hero rather than a traitor.

Given that McDaniel seems similarly intent on maintaining loyalty to the United States at all costs, it is worth exploring his Choctaw namesake's biography in greater detail. Gideon Lincecum, "a self-taught physician, naturalist, ethnologist, folklorist, and philosopher" who settled in Mississippi in 1818 and lived in the region until 1848, wrote "the closest to a firsthand account" of Pushmataha's life currently available.[19] In *Pushmataha: A Choctaw Leader and His People*, Lincecum writes about how he befriended several Choctaws, including both the principal chief, Mushulatubi, and Pushmataha, who was chief of the Okla Hannali district.[20] Notably, when McDaniel stumbles upon the underground Choctaw community, he finds himself in the "Okla Hannali part of Ishtaboli,"[21] in a community whose leader is named Moshulatubbee. Gideon Lincecum seems to have been far more receptive to learning about his Indigenous neighbors than many Americans of his time: he learned to speak and write the Choctaw language, studied with a Choctaw "doctor of great reputation" named Eliccha Chito, and visited regularly with a Choctaw elder, Chahta Immataha, to learn more about Choctaw history.[22] According to Lincecum, Pushmataha was a great warrior and a talented orator, and he possessed "the strongest and best balanced intellect of any man I had ever heard speak."[23] While Lincecum, as a white American moving into Choctaw territory in the early nineteenth century, might be expected to praise a leader who welcomed his white neighbors, his views also seem to reflect popular opinion among the Choctaw. Lincecum collected quite a few stories about Pushmataha's impressive feats as a warrior and orator, and he notes that the Okla Hannali leader was frequently chosen to represent his district in negotiations.

And yet, some of Pushmataha's actions seem, particularly in hindsight, to be counterproductive for the Choctaw people. In perhaps the most perplexing example, the famous Shawnee leader Tecumseh sent his brother, Tenskwatawa, "the Prophet," "on a visit to all southern tribes" in 1812.[24] The brothers advocated for the formation of a "permanent Indian state," and when political negotiations failed, they formed "a huge pan-Indian coalition which, by remaining resolutely united and only striking when the time was right, would finally succeed where [earlier Native leaders] had failed."[25] As Lincecum describes it, Tecumseh and Tenskwatawa were "predicting the downfall of the government of the United States" and the "repossession of the whole continent by the red people," but Pushmataha "told [Tenskwatawa] that he was a hireling, that his predictions were false, and that he must absent himself from the Chahta country."[26] Although James Wilson points out that most southeastern tribes hesitated to join Tecumseh because they were "aware of their own vulnerability," Pushmataha's loyalty to the Americans rather than a pan-Indian alliance that advocated for Native sovereignty makes him an odd choice for a twenty-first-century Choctaw hero.[27] Not only did Pushmataha refuse to join Tecumseh; he also served under Andrew Jackson in that war, although other

Choctaws chose to fight against the Americans. Taking his loyalties a step further, after the war ended, he "hunted up and put to the sword all he could of his traitor countrymen."[28] Pushmataha's clear demonstration of his loyalty to the United States, even at the expense of other Choctaws, emphasizes the complexity of the Choctaw–U.S. relationship over the past two hundred years.

With Pushmataha as a namesake—and a role model—McDaniel's fervent loyalty to the United States in general and the military in particular begins to make more sense. McDaniel is "acutely aware of his Choctaw military heritage, of how his people, generations ago, under the leadership of his namesake . . . had set their feet firmly on the course that had made them the most loyal military allies the Americans had ever had."[29] Because he views himself within this tradition, he is deeply ashamed that he apparently deserted during battle. He also worries that because the Marine Corps has failed to locate him in the intervening years, "he must surely be an embarrassment to the Corps."[30] Afraid of causing any more problems for his allies, McDaniel actually begins helping the Corps locate him, imagining that his capture will bring great glory to the Marines.[31] Such a response is certainly exaggerated for the sake of satire, but it nonetheless demonstrates that McDaniel, like Pushmataha, continues to maintain a deep loyalty to the United States even when it goes against his own interest.

Through this complicated positioning, Birchfield seems to suggest that Pushmataha, like McDaniel, had only the best intentions when he negotiated treaties with the United States and fought under Andrew Jackson. Offering a more generous interpretation of Pushmataha's refusal to join Tecumseh, he paints a picture of the two men going through fourteen rounds of public debate, each trying to persuade the Choctaw "military muscle" to support his side in the coming war.[32] In Birchfield's version of history, Pushmataha could see that "Tecumseh had been successful in swaying about half of the Choctaws to his side, and raised the horrific specter of a Choctaw civil war."[33] And so, Pushmataha "threatened them that he would lead the roughly one-half of the Choctaws who adhered to his view in a Choctaw civil-war slaughter against the other half of the Choctaws, to make sure that they were not able to do anything to help further Tecumseh's vision."[34] Birchfield suggests that Pushmataha made this threat, not because he genuinely planned to kill anyone, but in order "to shock his own Choctaw people into contemplating the gravity of what they were deciding."[35] Moreover, by persuading the Choctaw to side with the United States, Birchfield argues that Pushmataha was directly responsible for the U.S. victory over the British and Tecumseh.[36] It is somewhat difficult to determine, given Birchfield's tongue-in-cheek style, just how proud Pushmataha should be of this dubious honor. However, as Birchfield demonstrates, it is at least possible to read Pushmataha—and, by extension, McDaniel—as American heroes whose loyal intentions should be applauded rather than criticized.

In case there was any doubt of Pushmataha's loyalty, he again sided with the United States "during the war of 1818 against the Creeks, Mikisukies, and Alocheway Indians," where he again served under Andrew Jackson.[37] Two years later, in 1820, Pushmataha reencountered Jackson when he negotiated and signed the Treaty of Doak's Stand, in which the Choctaw ceded a portion of their lands to the United States in exchange for some territory beyond the Mississippi River, "where all, who live by hunting and will not work, may be collected and settled together."[38] In *Field of Honor*, McDaniel's guide, Little Elroy, explains that, without Pushmataha's work to negotiate that treaty, "the Choctaws might not have been in a position to return to their old homeland in the West, the land above us."[39] In Birchfield's work, then, Pushmataha is framed as a hero, someone whose willingness to negotiate and work with the United States has allowed for the continuance of Choctaw land and culture well into the twentieth century. Drawing on the tropes of alternate reality, Birchfield reinforces that perspective by suggesting that the underground Choctaw nation that is at the heart of the novel could not exist without his contributions.

In his account of the treaty negotiations in 1820, Lincecum notes that "another great benefit to be derived from this arrangement would be the removal from among the people at home who are already inclined to progress and civilization of the bad example of those who, in their wild, wandering propensities, do not care for improvement."[40] Lincecum's bias as an American shines through quite clearly here, but at least he acknowledges that when the Choctaw chiefs and headmen discussed the offer in private, "they considered it a wise and benevolent proposition" while also recognizing that General Jackson "had been guilty of misrepresentations which he knew were such, and others which he was not perhaps apprised of."[41] The Choctaws, according to Lincecum, chose to "adopt the white man's rules in the transaction and get all they could from them."[42] This account, much like Birchfield's, resists worn-out narratives about Europeans taking advantage of tribal nations that were too naïve or too powerless to resist. Instead, Lincecum paints Pushmataha as a savvy negotiator who sized up the situation and understood how to manipulate the American legal system in his own favor.

As Scott Richard Lyons has argued, an Indian's signature on a treaty "signifies power and a lack of power, agency and a lack of agency. It is a decision one makes when something has already been decided for you, but it is still a decision."[43] In other words, rather than simply reading treaty signers as traitors to their people, both Birchfield and Lyons argue that we must recognize their agency in the treaty-making process, including their ability to make the best out of a difficult situation. If we read Pushmataha in this way, as Birchfield and Lincecum do, we might acknowledge that negotiating with the United States probably saved more lives than joining Tecumseh's fight would have done. As Lyons suggests, an x-mark "symbolize[s] Native assent to things (concepts, policies, technologies, ideas) that, while not necessarily traditional in origin, can sometimes turn out all right and occasionally even good."[44] Whether or not one agrees with this interpretation of Pushmataha in the real world, his actions are clearly justified within the alternate reality of the novel, where his treaty negotiations have allowed the Choctaw access to the underground caves where they have not only survived but even flourished since the time of removal. If "the alternate history asks questions about time, linearity, determinism, and the implicit link between past and present,"[45] then Birchfield uses this subgenre to illustrate the same point he makes in his nonfiction discussion of Pushmataha: that he is a hero whose strategic negotiations in the past preserved Choctaw civilization in the present.

The fact that Birchfield feels the need to make this argument is a reminder of the difficulty of maintaining a relationship between those who were forced to leave their homelands and those who risked their lives by staying behind. Although most Choctaw were forced to relocate to Oklahoma in the 1820s and 1830s, some were able to stay in Mississippi. Another Choctaw author, LeAnne Howe, depicts the strained relationship between the descendants of these two groups in her novel *Shell Shaker* when a group of Choctaws from Oklahoma, Louisiana, Texas, Alabama, and Mississippi come together to bury a chief in Mississippi. As they walk around the sacred mound of Nanih Waiya, Delores, an Oklahoma Choctaw, explains that "before the Choctaws left Mississippi, they came here and grabbed a little bit of the Nanih Waiya to take with them on the long walk," to which her Mississippian companion notes that "there are those of us who never left."[46] Delores is ashamed to have said "such a callous thing, as if the only true Choctaw went to Oklahoma," but the woman from Mississippi graciously forgives the slight as she observes that "we've been separated for so long, it's hard for us to remember that we once thought of ourselves as one body with different parts, but with one heart."[47] Through this exchange, Howe acknowledges the complexities of the relationship between

Choctaw communities scattered across the southeast, simultaneously encouraging members of various communities to rebuild their relationships.

Where Howe's characters vow to be more inclusive in the future, the Choctaw in *Field of Honor* are able to model that inclusivity thanks to the imagined space of Ishtaboli. As Little Elroy explains, "The Choctaw origin story tells of a time when most—but not all—of the Choctaws emerged from beneath the earth. They say they came from this place down here [Ishtaboli]. . . . Now, they say they've simply returned to the womb, to their place of origin, to join the old ones down here, until the danger passes."[48] The relationship between the Choctaw who emerged from the earth and those who stayed behind is strong enough that those who wished to could simply return home. Little Elroy also notes that, although it was a dangerous journey, there were Choctaws who would "come out here from Mississippi to visit the Choctaws who still lived down here in Ishtaboli."[49] This version of the story differs significantly from most versions of the Choctaw creation story, in which all the Choctaw people (not just "most of them") emerged from belowground. Moreover, those stories do not generally mention any return visits.[50] *Field of Honor* accepts the Choctaw origin story as reality rather than a kind of cognitive estrangement, but it also reimagines that narrative, adding the concept of the aboveground Choctaws visiting their belowground relatives, in order to craft the novum that serves as the catalyst for the rest of the novel.

In Birchfield's version of history, the Choctaw not only accepted their relatives from above, they also made space for other peoples, including members of the Natchez and Catawba tribes who were displaced by American expansion.[51] Little Elroy explains that "we few Natchez are well treated, even privileged. We're allowed our ancient customs, even though the behavior of our unmarried females is a scandal among the Choctaws."[52] This willingness to accept others into the Choctaw community while also allowing them to live according to their own rules and traditions is a clear example of Indigenous knowledge and ethics in action. As opposed to the Euro-American push toward assimilation that Pinsky assumes to be part of any ethical encounter, Birchfield depicts an Indigenous response to the Other: the Choctaw acknowledge the ethical demand of their fellow humans by making space for members of other tribes who have been threatened by Euro-American colonization. But rather than insisting that the Natchez and Catawba assimilate to Choctaw traditions within the space of the Choctaw community, they are each allowed to maintain their own cultures. Each group has adapted in some practical ways: they are able to speak the Choctaw language, and their children, like Little

Elroy and his sister Little Ejay, attend Choctaw schools, but space is also reserved for them to maintain their traditions within the larger community.

This space is most evident in the story of Elena, Little Elroy and Little Ejay's aunt, who becomes romantically involved with McDaniel. Following a complicated set of social mores, Elena offers herself to McDaniel as a potential wife. As part of the process, she must be judged by the community, who will either vindicate her or label her a "slut."[53] When this process first begins, Little Elroy believes that Elena will be "judged a slut" because "the Choctaws think Natchez girls are sluts anyway."[54] In fact, the community responds in exactly the opposite way. As Little Elroy reports, "Elena not being Choctaw seems to be making quite a difference. The Choctaws are going out of their way to make allowances for her being a Natchez girl."[55] Thus, even as the Choctaw apply their complex courtship rules to Elena and McDaniel, they also make allowances for cultural difference.

McDaniel receives the same kinds of adjustments upon his arrival in Ishtaboli. Because he unexpectedly (and unintentionally) wins a ball game for the Okla Hannali, McDaniel is immediately given the honored title of Lighthorseman, which reflects the community's respect for his athletic prowess. And yet, because he is ignorant of Choctaw language and culture, the council feels that McDaniel has not quite earned the title. Therefore, they create a new category for him: "Lighthorseman, A.B.E.," which stands for "All But Examination."[56] Although Birchfield, who was a professor at the University of Lethbridge until his death in 2012,[57] clearly intends to poke fun at the hierarchical structure of academia, this compromise solution also reflects a flexibility and willingness to establish new rules as appropriate, particularly in the case of an outsider to the community. Because McDaniel is Choctaw but unfamiliar with the culture, the council decides to send him to the Academy for Little Choctaws, where he will have the opportunity to learn more about his people before taking the examination that would make him a full-fledged Lighthorseman. Here, as with Elena, the Choctaws' ability to uphold their own laws and values while simultaneously offering a flexible framework for those who do not share their perspective or experiences is a key example of how Indigenous ethics can function to resolve conflict and form relationships with the Other in a work of science fiction.

Although *Field of Honor* offers this uplifting model of ethical relationships, it also offers several negative examples that can serve to warn readers against the dangers of demonizing or oversimplifying the Other. We first see this negative response presented satirically at the Academy for Little Choctaws, where McDaniel and Little Elroy peek in on classes that include Elementary Choctology, German History, and English Spelling. Although Birchfield gives readers a relatively brief glimpse into each classroom, it is easy to see why he has described the novel as "anthropological satire."[58] In Elementary Choctology, a teacher helps students to translate Choctaw sentences into several dialects of English, including "Missionary Choctaw" and "Enlightened Missionary Choctaw."[59] Across the hall, in history class, we learn more about the Choctaws' decision to refer to all people of western European descent as "Germans," including the "European Germans," "English-Island Germans," and "North American Germans."[60] What most Americans would refer to as the Revolutionary War is thus considered "The First North American German Civil War," the War of 1812 is referred to as "The Second North American German Civil War," and so on.[61] As the history teacher explains, "It is our misfortune that our continent is being invaded by such a barbarous, warlike people and that there is no way to escape their incessant and bloody civil wars, which now threaten all life on the planet."[62]

The Choctaws' decision to refer to all Europeans and their North American descendants as "Germans" satirizes the Euro-American tendency to lump all "Indians" together—an unfortunate assumption that McDaniel also encounters. Before his trip to Ishtaboli, the local sheriff delivers a letter from Marine headquarters to McDaniel. As he does so, he complains about the "goddamn Indians" who refuse to use mailboxes.[63] Even his best friend from his military days addresses him as "Injun" in their correspondence.[64] During his brief time in Vietnam, McDaniel, "being an Indian, was given the point."[65] Like many other American Indian soldiers, McDaniel was assigned to the most dangerous position because the superior officers genuinely believed that as an Indian, he had supernatural scouting skills. When the Choctaw take the same kind of reductionist approach to Euro-Americans in these scenes, non-Native readers may find themselves slightly offended—and, hopefully, reflecting on the importance of cultural specificity and a sympathetic perspective in telling their own stories.

Similar oversimplifications and misunderstandings are applied in each class-room at the Academy for Little Choctaws: the spelling teacher relies on misspelled English words to draw conclusions about how English speakers are disrespectful and likely to steal. She describes Christianity as the "cult of the dead Jew," noting that "it is beyond comprehension why anyone but a German would willingly adopt such depraved superstitions."[66] Her use of the word "superstitions" is especially pointed, given the long history of Americans discounting—and even outlawing—Indigenous religions. The Choctaw version of American culture is not entirely inaccurate, as the teacher points to Christianity as the motivation for "German" missionizing, and especially for the creation of Indian boarding schools, "where they will force you to practice the cult of the dead Jew, force you to give up your language, your culture, your religion."[67] Here, again, non-Native readers are likely to experience a "shock of dysrecognition" as their culture is described from an outsider's perspective. In this case, both McDaniel and Moshulatubbee, the current leader of Ishtaboli, resist these depictions. Just as William Sanders relies on Billy and Janna's comparisons between the United States and the USSR to critique American Indian policy, so does Birchfield rely on this inversion to invite non-Native readers to reflect on what they may have learned about "Indian" cultures and how that information has been presented, even in formal and ostensibly unbiased academic settings.

As the material taught at the Academy for Little Choctaws suggests, Ishtaboli is not quite a utopia. Although it has developed without direct Euro-American influence, shaped instead by Choctaw traditions and beliefs, Birchfield is careful not to idealize the place.[68] In one of Little Elroy's explanations of how Ishtaboli operates, he casually mentions that "it's all pretty much run by slave labor, mostly by unemployed 'Germans' who get kidnapped and brought down here from the surface."[69] Historically, some Choctaws, like members of other southeastern tribes, owned slaves of African descent until the mid-nineteenth century. Like all others who had been enslaved in the United States, those people who had been enslaved in the Choctaw nation were emancipated, and according to *The Freedmen Bill*, the Choctaw Freedmen were accepted as "citizens of the Choctaw Nation" in 1880.[70] Given the actual history, the suggestion that the Choctaw of Ishtaboli have restarted or perhaps never stopped this long defunct practice is especially troubling.

At McDaniel's prompting, Little Elroy explains that these "unemployed Germans" are largely scientists or engineers, who can be caught simply by "put[ting] a job ad in the right publication" because "a German without a job, without work to be doing for nearly every waking moment, can never feel like his life is complete."[71] Although Birchfield uses this moment to satirize the Protestant work ethic—particularly as it appears in American academe—it is nonetheless important to examine the role of slavery in the novel in greater depth. Little Elroy says that "we hardly ever see any of the slaves,"[72] a statement that is also true within the confines of the text: we never meet any of these enslaved Germans, but their presence nonetheless creeps around the edges of the story. For instance, when the Choctaws fear that an intruder has managed to find Ishtaboli, Colonel McGee's second command—even before he sends out search parties to locate the intruder—is to "get all the slaves back in their quarters. Put them in lockdown."[73] The enslaved community must pose a fairly significant threat to Ishtaboli if McGee prioritizes their containment during a crisis.

By marginalizing the enslaved Germans, both within Ishtaboli and within the novel itself, Birchfield allows the reader, like the average Choctaw citizen, to forget the presence of slavery, and the community's dependence upon it, most of the time. However, as David T. Fortin points out, "despite the Choctaw desire to dissociate themselves from the inferior religious and economic systems of the 'Germans,' . . . they remain utterly dependent on them for the technology that structures their built environment."[74] The citizens of Ishtaboli both engage in the ethically reprehensible behavior of enslaving other humans and hypocritically rely on that culture to keep their society running smoothly and help them to make technological advances.

In addition to the burdens already placed upon the enslaved Germans, Birchfield suggests that they have been tasked with developing nuclear technology for Choctaw use—presumably against their fellow "Germans." Moshulatubbee warns that the Choctaw will "lose everything . . . if McGee gets his way. You've seen what he thinks he can get the German slave scientists to produce. All he will need then will be a delivery system. The man is mad."[75] McGee is at work on an educational experiment that will indoctrinate students at the Academy of the Little Choctaws to believe anti-German propaganda. His project has been presented to the children as "some new kind of teaching method" for learning "Indian history."[76] During the first lesson, the children are given glasses of milk spiked with drugs and forced to watch films that depict the Choctaw "as the sweetest, most angelic creatures who ever lived" and the Germans as monsters who hack children to pieces in "scene after scene . . . of terror and carnage."[77] Although Europeans and Euro-Americans have certainly been guilty of some of the acts depicted in the film, even the Choctaw leader Moshulatubbee complains that the lesson plans are false, noting that "the Germans are bad enough as it is. There's no need to lie about them."[78] In other words, although the Choctaw clearly have legitimate grievances against the Germans, Birchfield warns of the danger of clinging too closely to and amplifying those grievances. Efforts to preserve and honor the past must be balanced with plans for the future: if education and politics revolve around resentment and hatred of the Germans rather than continuing to develop and embrace Choctaw culture for its own sake, then the people of Ishtaboli will, as Moshulatubbee fears, "lose everything."[79] In *Field of Honor*, then, the mad scientist trope treats narrative itself is a dangerous weapon: although McGee's goal is to protect Ishtaboli by educating the Choctaw children and preparing them for future interactions with the Germans, he uses ethically problematic methods to tell a story that is primarily grounded in hatred and revenge. If the children grow up believing this narrative, they, like McGee himself, may become obsessed with history and unable to create a future for their community.

This combination of indoctrination and obsession with the past is also what has shaped McDaniel's life for the past eleven years: because he continues to interpret his life through an incorrect and often harmful narrative, he—like many veterans suffering from PTSD—is trapped in the past and unable to build a life for himself in the present. For instance, McDaniel gives away a check for $327,464.35 worth of "back pay" because he believes that it is a Marine trap. He ignores the offer of a full college scholarship. He refuses to obtain psychiatric treatment, which might have helped him readjust to daily life after the war. Even when he is granted an honorable discharge, McDaniel becomes upset that he has been "kicked out" of the Marines. Because he clings to a problematic and downright mistaken narrative about the trajectory of his life, McDaniel continues to act defensively, responding to past events rather than adapting to the present or planning for the future.

Similarly, the Choctaws of Ishtaboli, at least under the pending leadership of McGee, threaten to become single-mindedly obsessed with the wrongs committed against them in the past. They may become trapped in a narrative that simply repeats the same cycle of violence again and again, rather than dealing directly with the trauma of removal and beginning to move past it. Birchfield suggests that obsessing over the past, which can lead to breeding hatred and starting wars, is not an appropriate response to the evils of colonialism. While this does not mean that the actions of the Germans should be forgiven, neither does it suggest that the Choctaw should initiate nuclear warfare, which would threaten the entire Earth rather than just the Germans in question. Instead, Birchfield advocates a return to the model of past Choctaw leaders, as invoked by McDaniel's implicit reference to Pushmataha.

When he learns about McGee's plans, McDaniel immediately devises a strategy to stop him while staying within the carefully delineated rules of Ishtaboli. He follows a rather intricate series of steps that ultimately allows him to challenge McGee to a duel. Although this response may seem counterintuitive, it is actually an effective way of handling the problem because, as Little Elroy explains, the Choctaws of Ishtaboli rely on duels as a way of avoiding "serious disharmony within the community. . . . In a Choctaw duel, both people die. . . . Each one appoints an assistant, called a second, usually his best friend, and, on signal, at the same time, each assistant chops his friend in the head with an axe."[80] In this way, a duel guarantees the death of one's opponent, but it also requires the sacrifice of oneself. By challenging McGee, McDaniel follows the example of Pushmataha, who made the sacrifice of agreeing to removal rather than initiating another civil war. In the same way, McDaniel prioritizes peace over war despite the fact that he relies on an act of aggression to do so. By invoking Pushmataha as McDaniel's namesake and role model, Birchfield returns to the old Choctaw values—among them a steadfast loyalty and the maintenance of alliances—as well as the ability to adapt to a crisis through careful strategizing and manipulation of an obtuse set of rules. Above all, the novel emphasizes the importance of avoiding serious conflict and disharmony at all costs, suggesting that compromise and sacrifice are always preferable to outright warfare.

With such a reading in mind, we can return to the initial question of how *Field of Honor* fits into various generic categories. At first, as Birchfield describes his protagonist's behavior in terms of the Choctaw trickster *chufki*, the novel seems to match Rader's definition of the Indian invention novel, which specifically includes the trickster tradition. However, it is not only a trickster story; it is also an example of *shukha anumpa*, a phrase that translates loosely to "hogwash."[81] In *Choctaw Tales*, folklorist Tom Mould describes *shukha anumpa* as "make-up stories."[82] As he explains,

> There is double meaning here: as an adjective—fictional—as well as a verb—making up stories. There is no belief that Henry Williams or any of his ancestors could have wandered through the woods and stumbled across talking animals burning their tails. *Shukha anumpa* are made-up stories, not literally true. . . . The demand of *shukha anumpa* is, above all else, to be funny, and consequently to provoke the audience to laughter. Narrators are expected to adapt the stories creatively, to invent not merely recite.[83]

Reading *Field of Honor* according to these generic expectations allows us to make more sense of the chaos inherent in the novel while also highlighting the satire at the heart of the text. For instance, in the final chapters of the book, after McDaniel has fled Ishtaboli, we learn that the Vietnam War began when Lyndon Johnson simply "looked around the map and picked Vietnam" as a good place to start a war, and the army "responded by thinking up ways to bungle the war, to make him look bad."[84] Stories like this one "provoke the audience to laughter" and demonstrate Birchfield's ability to creatively adapt Choctaw trickster tales. On the other hand, when Birchfield describes his protagonist's behavior according to "Western medical science," he is reading through a Euro-American lens, which relies primarily on a logical or scientific worldview—what Suvin would refer to as a cognitive explanation of events.[85]

Because *Field of Honor* borrows from both traditions, it is able to criticize and satirize the incompetency of the U.S. military and their historical treatment of the Choctaw while simultaneously poking fun at the Choctaw themselves. This critical response is a feature of both genres: *shukha anumpa* encourages laughter, while science fiction "has moved into the sphere of anthropological and cosmological thought, becoming a diagnosis, a warning, a call to understanding and action, and—most important—a mapping of possible alternatives."[86] And that is precisely what Birchfield does: he maps an alternate reality. By employing this trope, he not only encourages laughter and criticism: he also offers readers a picture of a truly sovereign Choctaw nation and warns against the dangers that might threaten such a nation. In *Field of Honor,* Birchfield presents a rich and complex Choctaw community instead of dwelling on the stereotypical stories of poverty, assimilation, and victimhood frequently associated with Native American literature. He contains and reshapes the Choctaws' historical traumas in a different kind of narrative, encouraging both readers and his own characters to footnote the events that are often treated as the main text.

CHAPTER FOUR

The Stories Began to Change

Rewriting Removal in *Riding the Trail of Tears*

I n Blake M. Hausman's 2011 novel *Riding the Trail of Tears*, scientists use a new technology called Surround Vision to create a virtual reality window into the past. This technology attracts attention primarily for its money-making potential; it is used to develop a tourist trap in northeast Georgia called the TREPP, or "Tsalagi Removal Exodus Point Park."[1] The coupling of bureaucratic language and the word "Tsalagi" hides the violent history inherent in both the ride and north Georgia itself; behind the catchy name, customers are actually paying to experience Cherokee removal by riding a virtual Trail of Tears.[2]

Hausman relies on the conventions of two subgenres to tell this story: alternate and virtual reality. The novel can first be classified as alternate reality because it takes place in a present very similar to our own, with one major distinction: the existence of the TREPP. To reinforce this similarity, Hausman includes specific and accurate descriptions of the world outside the game, such as its precise location in northeast Georgia and an accurate history of European contact with Native peoples. Like his protagonist, Hausman is a graduate of the University of Georgia in Athens, and he provides a variety of concrete details, such as the "fries and feta cheese dip" available at a well-known diner and the "three rackety flights of stairs" leading to the balcony of the Hunter-Holmes Academic Building on North Campus, that reflect real-world Athens in highly recognizable ways.[3] The novel's protagonist, Tallulah, is a virtual tour guide who tells her tourists about many actual events, ranging from Hernando De Soto's trip through Cherokee territory in 1540 to the looting and pillaging of Cherokee homes after their occupants were forcibly removed in 1838.[4] Such details confirm that the world of the novel corresponds directly to the one with which readers are already familiar.

Hausman's alteration of the world is relatively minor—he does not change the outcome of any wars or imagine entire nations hiding below ground, as Philip K. Dick and D. L. Birchfield do. Nonetheless, *Riding the Trail of Tears* asks similar questions about "the implicit link between past and present . . . the individual's role in making history, and . . . the constructedness and narrativity of history."[5] In order to answer those questions, Hausman turns to a secondary trope, employed alongside alternate reality: virtuality. Rather than actually rewriting the history of Cherokee removal as part of an alternate timeline, *Riding the Trail of Tears* imagines a virtual world where both digital characters and actual humans can explore, question, and challenge the historical record. Because the TREPP has been created by a team of researchers and programmers, the novel is able to explore the ways in which the history of removal has been constructed and narrated. By placing contemporary characters in Cherokee territory in 1838, the text also creates a space where it can contemplate the relationship between past and present. As opposed to simply writing a historical novel, Hausman's use of two science fiction (sf) subgenres allows for a far more complex investigation of these themes.

Alternate reality is well suited to inquiries into the nature of history, while, in contrast, "the virtual is the space of emergence of the new, the unthought, the unrealized, which at every moment loads the presence of the present with supplementarity, redoubling a world through parallel universes, universes that might have been."[6] Because virtual reality is not bound by the physical limitations of the "real world," stories in this subgenre are often even more surreal, with even more radical novums, than the ideas encountered in other types of sf. Or, as Thomas Foster argues, "'Virtual' often seems to function primarily to designate the ungrounding of various phenomena from any empirical base, their denaturalization or deterritorialization, imagined as the precondition for greater openness, mutability, and availability to change and becoming."[7] We see this mutability in one of the more famous examples of the subgenre, the Wachowski Sisters' 1999 film *The Matrix*. The film follows Neo, a computer programmer and gifted hacker who learns that the "real world" is actually a simulation called the matrix. In reality, Earth has been conquered by a species of A.I. that grows and harvests humans as its energy source. To keep them subdued, humans are placed in individual pods and plugged into the matrix. Neo learns that, because the world he lives in is only a simulation created by the A.I., it is possible to manipulate the laws of that world. His mentor, Morpheus, famously urges him to "free your mind,"[8] advice that allows Neo to jump across rooftops, master multiple martial arts in a single day, and even stop bullets in midair. By realizing that the world around him is a construct, Neo ultimately becomes "the One," a superhuman savior who can change the world by disregarding the laws of physics.

As liberating as it might be to learn that "some of [the rules] can be bent, [and] others can be broken,"[9] virtuality also has its drawbacks. As Foster notes,

> Virtual reality technologies can be read as a fantasy of technologically literalizing and intensifying the separation between mind and body and the organization of this dualism into a hierarchy that privileges the mind's ability to transcend the materiality and particularity of embodiment.[10]

This reiteration of Cartesian dualism is present throughout *The Matrix*—not only in the scenes where Neo learns to "free his mind" in order to control the physical world, but even in the film's exploration of the nature of reality. As Neo marvels at a computer program that "seems so real," Morpheus asks, "What is real? How do you define real? If you're talking about what you can feel, what you can smell, what you can taste and see, then real is simply electrical signals interpreted by your brain." Or, to put it more simply, "Your mind makes it real. . . . The body cannot live without the mind."[11]

Although it is not so explicitly stated, a similar theme runs through the 1982 film *TRON*, among the first cinematic examples of virtuality. The movie tells the story of Flynn, a software programmer who is kidnapped into a corporate computer system by the Master Control Program (MCP), which has defied its human programmer and begun to think for itself. Although the MCP's ultimate goal remains unclear, it has threatened to access the Pentagon and the Kremlin, and it consolidates its power by assimilating other programs into itself. Flynn must work with the human avatars of threatened programs to defeat the MCP. Like Neo, he learns that as a talented programmer and a human "User," he can exert an unusual control over the space of virtual reality. Framing Users as gods who shape the world of cyberspace, *TRON* depicts Flynn's superhuman feats, which range from rebuilding a flying ship with his mind to bringing a humanized program back from the brink of death. Both films also lean heavily on the idea of an individual hero who will save the day: Neo and Flynn have teams supporting them, but they each distinguish themselves by manipulating the physical aspects of the virtual world more adeptly than anyone else. As Flynn himself says postkidnapping: "No sweat. I play computer games better than anybody."[12] So, although *TRON* and *The Matrix* are both action movies, they paradoxically prioritize the power of the mind over the body and thus reinforce a problematic Euro-American interpretation of the world.

Indigenous virtuality, on the other hand, employs the same narrative tools to convey drastically different philosophies. As Nalo Hopkinson says, "In my hands, massa's tools don't dismantle massa's house . . . they build me a house of my own."[13] In *Riding the Trail of Tears*, for instance, we encounter some familiar tropes: programs represented by human avatars, players trapped inside a game, programs rebelling against their creators, and the physically impossible made possible within virtual reality. In Hausman's hands, however, these tropes are used to reflect Cherokee values: a return to Indigenous structures of governance rather than a deconstruction of all systems; the importance of collaboration among members of a community rather than an emphasis on individual heroics; the holistic relationship between body and mind; and the undeniable impact of actual historical events, despite the mediation or modification of the historical narrative.

Following a familiar generic convention, *Riding the Trail of Tears* begins when the virtual reality malfunctions and leaves the novel's protagonist, a virtual tour guide named Tallulah, trapped inside the game with a group of disgruntled tourists. When technology malfunctions in works of mainstream virtuality, we might expect to learn a lesson about putting too much faith in machines—a lesson driven home in both *TRON* and *The Matrix*, which tell similar stories of an A.I. that has become sentient, defied its programmers, and attacked its human creators. But Hausman reverses generic expectations by considering a typical science fictional scenario from an Indigenous perspective: in *Riding the Trail of Tears*, the technology behind the TREPP is portrayed as an organic part of the world rather than a threat to humanity. When that technology becomes sentient, it offers its human players an opportunity to reshape the painful history of removal. Thus, by embracing the conventions of sf and then subverting and adapting those conventions to reflect a Cherokee worldview, *Riding the Trail of Tears* alters the parameters of the genre and creates a space of both virtual and real resistance. Within the world of the novel, not only does virtual reality itself become Indigenized, but practically speaking, the presence of the book itself challenges received knowledge about the "Vanishing Indian," insisting that far from having been removed in the nineteenth century, the Cherokee remain in their traditional homelands in the twenty-first.

Despite the difficulty of imagining riding the Trail of Tears as a recreational activity, the novel tells us that the attraction is so popular that the TREPP now rivals Helen, a very real "German-theme-town tourist trap" located in the Georgia mountains.[14] Tourists ride the TREPP for a variety of reasons: teachers schedule educational field trips; college students can earn extra credit by participating; computer programmers take an interest in the technology; and the ride is also considered a family-friendly attraction. On the TREPP, tourists are zipped into virtual reality suits and, in just three hours, they experience several months of life as Cherokee citizens during the process of removal from the traditional Cherokee homelands of north Georgia in 1838. Customers can choose the level of violence that they are prepared to encounter on the tour: groups with young children or the elderly should register for Level One, while, on Level Four, customers risk such gruesome deaths as being shot in the virtual face by U.S. soldiers.[15] The attraction is so successful that it has spawned two restaurants, a gift shop, a bookstore, and a movie theater, all located on a road called Tsalagi Boulevard.[16]

The novel provides a clear cognitive explanation for the presence of the TREPP, which Suvin would identify as the book's primary novum. Hausman details the creation of the machine, beginning with a rough prototype Tallulah's grandfather created in his basement. This prototype was later purchased and developed by a large corporation, which initially hired Tallulah to provide both Cherokee history and a general sense of authenticity. Through her recollections, we learn how the machine evolved into a large-scale virtual reality program. Because she has been involved with the TREPP from its inception, Tallulah is able to recall developing and editing the stock characters within the game. As far as she and the rest of the TREPP staff are concerned, those characters are merely computer programs, nonsentient beings capable of being altered and rewritten as necessary. Tallulah also relies heavily on the TREPP's tech crew to answer questions about discrepancies and malfunctions in the game, even when it becomes evident that the crew are no longer in control. These details all confirm that the TREPP has, up to this point, operated according to the logic of computer science and is therefore a clearly recognizable novum, the source of "cognitive estrangement" that becomes the catalyst for later events. This organizational structure mimics the depiction of programs in mainstream works of virtuality like *TRON*: individual programs are represented by their human avatars, and viewers may even feel some sympathy for those programs, but ultimately, they can be erased or rewritten as necessary for the plot.

When the novel opens, something has gone wrong with the Surround Vision technology, and Tour Group 5709 is stuck inside the game. This scenario is staunchly situated within at least two familiar sf conventions. First, as Everett F. Bleiler notes, early science fiction stories are often "concerned with processes, inventions, actions, or social matters that bear their own inner destruction or malfunction: Things go wrong."[17] Although Bleiler is focused on sf published in the 1920s and 1930s, the website TV Tropes suggests that this theme is also present in many contemporary texts. The site notes that "Gone Horribly Wrong" is a

> stock phrase used whenever that nasty old "science" inevitably messes up royally. The basic setup is simple: You have a . . . facility dedicated to the research and production of technological marvels, staffed with . . . ambitious persons pursuing a goal with the aims of profit, peace, or other potential applications. . . . In the course of their reasonable, maybe even noble quest to advance scientific knowledge, make a profit, help humanity . . . or otherwise undertake a high risk/high reward venture, *something* will have gone horribly wrong.[18]

The theme appears in countless sf stories: in the film *Jurassic Park*, for instance, the scientists who recreate dinosaurs fill in the missing DNA with frog DNA, overlooking the fact that some species of frogs can change sex in order to reproduce.[19] The geneticists have decided to create only female dinosaurs in order to limit reproduction but fail to anticipate that their dinosaurs, like their frog forebears, will be able to change sex as needed. Similarly, in *The Matrix*, we learn that humans scorched the sky to destroy the solar-powered A.I., but their plan backfired when the machines realized that humans make an excellent alternate energy source. In both of these texts, as well as in *Riding the Trail of Tears*, scientists assume that they are in control of their creations—be they dinosaurs, artificial intelligence, or a virtual reality game—and realize their mistake only when things go wrong.

Riding the Trail of Tears also relies on a second familiar convention, which appears just after Tour Group 5709 realizes that the game has malfunctioned. One tourist asks if they can just reboot the game, but Tallulah explains that "the Trail has begun, and we can't stop it now. We have to see it through."[20] The trope of the unending game echoes a video game trope called the "Point of No Return," which was originally a "term used in air travel where after a certain point it becomes impossible to turn around and return to the point of origin (for example, not enough fuel); even if there is a sudden emergency, the plane *must* continue toward its destination."[21] Although the trek has just begun, it is already too late to change course—a feeling that was probably shared by many Cherokee in 1838. Outside of video games, we see this idea at play in the award-winning children's picture book *Jumanji*, in which two children find a board game at a local park. In the instructions, they encounter an unusual warning: "ONCE A GAME OF JUMANJI IS STARTED IT WILL NOT BE OVER UNTIL ONE PLAYER REACHES THE GOLDEN CITY."[22] *Jumanji* is perhaps closer to fantasy than science fiction, as no explanation is provided for the fact that whatever happens in the world of the game also happens in the children's home: a lion in the bedroom, monkeys in the kitchen, and a monsoon in the living room, for instance. As stated in the rules, each scenario continues until someone wins the game; as in *Riding the Trail of Tears*, the point of no return and the beginning of the game are in the same spot.

An example that is more clearly grounded in the realm of science fiction comes from an episode of *Star Trek: The Next Generation* called "The Big Goodbye." Here, Captain Picard and three members of his crew decide to enjoy a short vacation in the holodeck, a virtual reality simulator located on the ship. The holodeck can be programmed to mimic any setting, real or fictional, so the captain asks it to recreate the world of his favorite series of detective novels. While Picard and three other officers are inside the game, a probe from an alien ship disrupts the program, causing it to malfunction. When the ship's chief engineer goes to investigate, he reports—aptly enough—that "something's gone wrong."[23] In this case, that "something" is the holodeck's refusal to follow verbal commands, which makes it impossible to find an exit within the game. Whereas escape from *Jumanji* depends on the children reading the instructions and completing the game, the *Star Trek* crew relies on outside assistance to escape the simulation: an engineering crew is stationed outside the holodeck door, scanning the system for inconsistencies that must be physically repaired. Within the game, Picard and his colleagues are not necessarily required to reach the end of the story; however, given that they have been cornered by fictional gangsters with very real guns, they are also under pressure to successfully resolve their in-game adventure.

In stories like *Jumanji* and "The Big Goodbye," the inability to exit the game advances the plot by forcing the characters to confront an unrealistic situation. In each case, the protagonists also learn to take the game more seriously: at first, they imagine that it will be fun to enter a 1940s detective novel or go on a jungle adventure, but in each case, they change their minds as it becomes clear that their lives are actually in danger. In "The Big Goodbye," for instance, Dr. Crusher initially applauds when a fellow crew member is shot by a gangster. Only when she realizes that there is real blood coming from his wound does she begin to take the situation more seriously. In addition to forcing the characters to work through unlikely scenarios, this trope also creates a perfect opportunity for a deus ex machina: when a situation becomes particularly dire, the writers can extract their characters from danger by abruptly ending the game. At the key moment, the holodeck doors suddenly open or one of the players finally rolls the number necessary to get to the end of the board game.

In *Riding the Trail of Tears*, the "Point of No Return" functions similarly in that it forces its characters to engage with a scenario that they would rather not confront—in this case, the historical reality of removal. Tallulah's polite explanation—"if it could be stopped, the realism of the whole enterprise would be lost"[24]—suggests that this is not the first time her tourists have reconsidered their decision to ride the Trail of Tears, though perhaps that regret usually appears later in the game. In addition to forcing her tourists to endure immense suffering on the Trail, the trope of the unending game conveniently forces Tallulah to stay inside the TREPP long enough to confront her recurring dreams and experience catharsis. As with other texts in this genre, it also provides Hausman with a deus ex machina: much like "The Big Goodbye," the game actually ends when the programmers interfere from outside the game rather than when the players achieve a particular goal within the game, though, from a literary standpoint, Tallulah does conveniently achieve some resolution before she is released. After she has forgiven her dead father, the techs are finally able to bring her back to the real world. Thus, in Indigenous sf as in mainstream texts, the trope of the unending game allows the author to play with the structure of the narrative, both expanding and compressing the time spent in the imagined world to suit the story they want to tell.

But *Riding the Trail of Tears* is more than a science fiction story that happens to take place in Cherokee country. Hausman takes advantage of the necessary vagueness in a scientific explanation of the TREPP to introduce a particularly Indigenous perspective, one that challenges both Euro-American worldviews and Suvin's clear-cut distinction between science and religion. The breakdown in technology in this novel cannot be blamed on the technology itself; rather, the TREPP breaks down because the Cherokee Little People, creatures that ethnographer James Mooney describes as "fairies no larger in size than children,"[25] are inexplicably living inside the game. Moreover, because one of these Little People is the narrator of the novel, readers have no choice but to acknowledge their presence. Although the inclusion of these "mythical" creatures in a work of sf might appear to trouble Suvin's theories, his definition of the genre actually establishes a space for cultural difference. Suvin argues that a work of science fiction must contain "an imaginative framework alternative to the author's empirical environment," which means that the reality of the novel is defined by the author's understanding of that term, which does not necessarily have to correspond to a Euro-American scientific worldview.[26] Because Hausman is Cherokee and the Little People fit within the "empirical environment" of a Cherokee worldview, their presence does not mark the novel as a work of fantasy or science fiction. Although some readers, particularly those who are non-Native, may encounter a "shock of dysrecognition" upon encountering the Little People, this moment should be read as an opportunity to learn about Cherokee culture rather than to categorize the novel as genre fiction.[27] If we read the presence of the Little People as a novum, we run the risk of conflating the lived experiences of Cherokee people with science fiction, thus suggesting that a Cherokee worldview is somehow less realistic than a Euro-American one.

However, Hausman's Little People go on to subvert the expectations of a traditional Cherokee worldview, by which act Hausman establishes them as a second novum, in addition to the TREPP itself. Rather than following in the footsteps of traditional Cherokee stories about the Little People, the novel's narrator offers some new definitions:

> First, there are the Nunnehi, the immortals, who are about the same size as average humans. And then, second, there are the Little People, who are naturally smaller than the Nunnehi. And then, there's us. We're the real Nunnehi, the real immortals, and those human-sized creatures who appear from time to time are actually man-ifestations of our labor. . . . For convenience's sake, you can call me the Little Little Person. Or you could call me Nunnehi, because, as I said, we're the real Nunnehi.[28]

Unlike the presence of the Little People, the introduction of "the Little Little People" is a secondary novum because these beings are not included in traditional Cherokee stories or worldviews. It might be tempting to categorize the Little Little People as another piece of mythology, of magic creeping into a work of science fiction, but once again, Hausman provides a cognitive explanation for both their existence and the fact that no one knows about them. Following Mooney, he tells the story of a caste of Cherokee priests who took advantage of their position and sexually assaulted several beautiful young women while the men were away hunting. When the men returned, the people "rose up and killed their leaders, killed them all. Every single priest, dead."[29] One result of the revolution, according to Hausman, was that "the stories began to change."[30] The narrator suggests that "some stories changed so much that everyone—storytellers and listeners—forgot the originals. Our story is one of those stories. When the priests were killed, we were accidentally cut from the people's memory."[31]

While the killing of the priestly class is indeed a story that Mooney recorded, including pointing to several earlier historical accounts that supported his version, he does not mention any description of lost stories—and perhaps he could not, given that the stories were lost to the Cherokee before Mooney met them. Nonetheless, the Little Little People's story is supported by historical accounts, just as Tallulah's stories about De Soto have a historical basis. The emphasis on storytelling as knowledge also reflects an Indigenous worldview, and the idea that lost stories must be recovered echoes similar concerns in many contemporary Native communities where tribal leaders are working to establish language preservation and revitalization programs.[32] This second novum, so clearly grounded in a Cherokee perspective, combines with the TREPP to establish a story that is both science fiction and Native literature.

Although the novel allows for multiple perspectives, the presence of the Little Little People clearly exposes the differences between Euro-American and Cherokee worldviews. Suvin claims that all "mythical" stories are also "static" because he believes that, in a world determined by religion, there is no possibility for real change. But the Little Little People are ostensibly "mythical" beings that also change over time. What we know of their history is connected to adaptation and innovation: they existed in the people's stories before the revolution, but their stories later disappeared. Nonetheless, the Little Little Person narrating the novel has found a way to recover those stories and gain a new audience. He tells readers that "I'm probably more indigenous than you, and the digital earth is where I'm indigenous."[33] It is unclear how the Little Little People, who existed "before the big colonization, before Cristobal Colon, before Hernando De Soto," can be indigenous to a digital environment that has only been developed in the last ten years, but these partial explanations certainly suggest a long history of change rather than stasis.[34] Thus, the narrator's fixed position also fluctuates, as we learn when he explains that "I'm more Nunnehi than you probably thought Nunnehi could be, but I never took such a formal shape until they built their ride."[35] Repeatedly, the Little Little People refuse absolute definitions and defy the strict separation of science and religion inherent to Suvin's argument. This restructuring of categories also echoes Gregory Cajete's definition of Native science as "the entire edifice of Indigenous knowledge."[36] Because a Native worldview does not distinguish between science and religion, the combination of the TREPP and the Little Little People within *Riding the Trail of Tears* empowers the Cherokee by insisting upon the value of Indigenous knowledge as a more appropriate framework for understanding our complex world.

This empowerment of Indigenous traditions is reinforced by the fact that the Little Little People ultimately save the day: they are able to literally rewrite the history of the Trail of Tears without erasing the memory of the original events. As a site of virtual reality, the TREPP provides a space to confront the violent history of removal; the Nunnehi appropriate that space, and with the help of traditional Cherokee figures, they guide both the tourists and Tallulah in a new and more productive direction. According to Mooney, both the Nunnehi and the Little People are kind beings who often take in lost wanderers and lead them back home.[37] This is precisely what the Nunnehi in the novel are able to do as they redirect Tour Group 5709. Within the virtual space of the game, they lead Tallulah and her tourists away from the Trail of Tears and back to a portion of the Cherokee homelands in present-day North Carolina, where some Cherokee people who were able to evade removal in the 1830s took refuge. Today, the Eastern Band of Cherokee Indians is a sovereign nation located on land called The Qualla Boundary, which is part of "The Original Home of the Cherokee."[38] Eastern Band citizens include descendants of those who "hid during the Trail of Tears," alongside the descendants of some Cherokee who "made it to Oklahoma and then walked back home," as well as others who "managed to keep land they owned and did not march West."[39] Fittingly, the virtual version of the North Carolina mountains is also where Tallulah reconciles with her dead father.

As proven by the actions of the Nunnehi, the TREPP has the potential to create positive change within the world of the novel. Despite the fact that it capitalizes on the attempted genocide of the Cherokee people by the United States, it could instead offer an educational experience, using virtual reality as a new medium through which to present Cherokee history and worldviews to a mainstream audience. This goal seems close to what the original creator—Tallulah's grandfather—might have had in mind. In his prototype, passengers rode inside a Jeep Cherokee whose windows were converted to television monitors. Each screen displayed scenes from the Trail of Tears, so as the car drove virtually, it accompanied the digital Cherokee on their walk "from the stockades in Georgia to the hills and lakes in northeastern Oklahoma."[40] Tallulah remembers her first ride in Grandpa Art's invention, describing the digital Indians as "a mass of bent and broken bodies that stretched up to ten miles long at the beginning of the trip" as they appeared to "stare right through her."[41] In this early incarnation, Tallulah sees the historical, digital Cherokee as real human beings, and she shares their suffering despite the fact that she is relatively isolated as a passenger inside the Jeep. To understand her experience in the context of sf, we might return to Pinsky's argument that "we exist already in the world, and any understanding of ourselves must go hand-in-hand with an understanding of ethics and our relationship to others."[42] In Grandpa Art's prototype, passengers are encouraged to consider their relationship to both the digital and the actual historical Cherokee people, even though those virtual Cherokee were much less convincingly real than the programs tourists interact with in the final version of the TREPP. When Grandpa Art's digital Cherokee stare at Tallulah, she experiences an encounter with alterity, a moment in which the arrival of the Other results in "a disruption of time and space" that "destabilize[s] the ordered Self."[43] This unsettling confrontation is missing from the commercialized version of the game, which goes out of its way to avoid disrupting or destabilizing its paying customers.

The form of the TREPP could also hypothetically provide a space to revitalize Indigenous oral storytelling traditions, as opposed to the Euro-American written form that we commonly rely on to learn about Native literature in the twenty-first century. Tallulah notes that "today Cherokees around the world learn about their culture from the Mooney book."[44] As many scholars and storytellers have pointed out, oral stories often lose something when they are translated into text. Within the virtual reality space of the TREPP, the digital Cherokee could be programmed to tell both traditional and contemporary stories, which would then become more accessible to tourists, while allowing Cherokee cultural consultants like Tallulah to maintain control of those stories. Because the digital Cherokee are programmed to "react to [tourists'] reactions," they might be able to reflect the traditional practice of telling particular stories only within the appropriate contexts. The digital Cherokee can also be programmed to share certain stories when they are most applicable to the listeners' experiences, providing a kind of personal connection difficult to reproduce through written texts.[45]

In addition to the possibilities of oral storytelling, the program also has the potential to bring traditional characters to life for new audiences. Rather than constantly reenacting the violence of the Trail of Tears, Hausman hints at the ways the virtual world could allow tourists to learn about, and even participate in, these traditional stories. Because there are often multiple versions of such stories, tourists could influence a flexible narrative rather than being forced into a strict script. Although no traditional stories are reenacted in the novel, characters from these stories do exist inside the game. Among the characters who have evolved with the help of the Nunnehi rather than being created by the programmers, we meet Ish and Fish, twin boys employed in the kitchen with their father, Chef, who is responsible for feeding all the digital renegades. The family is reminiscent of the traditional story of Kana'ti and Selu and their sons, the Good Boy and the Wild Boy.

In fact, Tallulah refers directly to this story, which she presumably learned about by reading James Mooney.[46] In Mooney's version, Kana'ti provides game for the family, and his wife, Selu, provides vegetables. When their two sons get curious about where their mother gets corn and beans every day, they follow her to the storehouse and watch her produce corn by rubbing her stomach and beans by rubbing under her armpits.[47] Convinced that their mother is a witch, they kill her. This murder might explain the strange absence of the boys' mother—or any elder women—within the TREPP.[48] After killing Selu, the boys follow her directions to "clear a large piece of ground in front of the house and drag my body seven times around the circle."[49] Corn begins to grow along the path where they drag her body, and her story explains the origin of corn for the Cherokee. Similarly, the boys follow Kana'ti and watch him release game from a large pen in order to provide meat for his family. Because the story of Kana'ti and Selu explains how the first Cherokee obtained staple foods, it makes sense that their corresponding digital versions would be responsible for feeding the Cherokee people within the game. When Tallulah first meets the boys and wonders whether they are twins, she quickly answers her own question: "Of course they are. . . . How could they not be? It's all part of the mythology."[50] Later, when she refers to Fish as "the Wild Boy," Tallulah confirms their identities.[51] Their presence throughout the novel suggests that the TREPP could be an excellent place for tourists to learn about traditional Cherokee stories by interacting directly with them.

While Ish and Fish are clearly connected to these traditional Cherokee characters, it is important to note that Tallulah and the programmers did not actually

create them. Ish, Fish, and Chef only emerge when the TREPP begins to "malfunction." In fact, Tallulah is frustrated by these characters and initially believes that
Chef and his sons are part of the problem. She is eager to finish her last tour before
vacation, so Tallulah is unhappy to encounter characters outside the virtual Trail's
fixed narrative. Even when Ish and Fish interact pleasantly with one of Tallulah's
tourists, she remains suspicious of their friendship. Rather than these traditional
Cherokee figures, who introduce an element of near-chaos into the world of the
TREPP, Tallulah prefers the reliable stock characters—the ones who, by design, never
"destabilize the ordered Self" or force the tourists to reflect on their responsibility
to the virtual, historical, or contemporary Cherokee.

One of the best examples of these stagnant, programmed characters is the
Wise Old Medicine Man, whom Tallulah created in collaboration with the TREPP
technicians. "Old Medicine," as Tallulah refers to him, is one of the main attractions
of the tour. He greets each tourist who dies on the Trail, but those who survive also
get to visit him before returning to reality. As the narrator explains, Old Medicine's
"program ensures customer satisfaction on the Trail of Tears."[52] He is a mishmash
of popular stereotypes, a wise old man who "uses your comments and questions to
determine your beliefs. He then reaffirms your personal ideology by showering you
with the kind of aboriginal spirituality that only dead people can exude."[53] He is so
popular that tourists sometimes contemplate in-game suicide in order to speed his
arrival.[54] In Tour Group 5709, a tourist who dies when a soldier shoots her in the
face later exclaims that "that whole Trail of Tears was totally worth it," because she
had the opportunity to meet Old Medicine at the end.[55]

The tourists love Old Medicine despite—or more likely because of—the fact
that he reinforces stereotypes and perpetuates the romanticization of Native
peoples. He is not tribally specific, nor does he share any actual Indigenous
beliefs. Rather, he simply reinforces whatever tourists already believe rather than
challenging guests to recognize the demand of the Other. Because Old Medicine
is the last thing people experience before the game ends, he encourages them to
disregard the very real suffering they have witnessed, focusing instead on what a
great time they had—an impulse that may encourage repeat customers, but that
undermines any educational or ethical goals of the tour. Ultimately, this exaggerated
character depicts Indigenous peoples as, to borrow Suvin's language, "mythical and
static" rather than constantly changing or evolving, and it enables tourists' desire
to remain "static," secure in their own identities and beliefs.

Within the world of the novel, Hausman emphasizes the ways that the TREPP inflicts direct harm on Cherokee peoples as the owners of the company and the tourists who travel the Trail consistently deny their ethical relationship to both Tallulah and the digital Cherokee. Rather than confronting, responding to, and attempting to process the genocide committed against her ancestors, Tallulah is forced to relive the trauma every time she goes to work. As the narrator explains, "Tallulah's stomach grinds while telling her tourists that it will all be over soon. For her it never ends. This is her one thousand one hundred and third trip through the Trail of Tears."[56] While the tourists get to end the game with a restorative visit to Old Medicine, Tallulah receives no such reassurance. In addition to reliving the original trauma of the Trail, Tallulah's experience of violence is exaggerated by the TREPP's commercial exploitation of the past, which emphasizes the importance of customer service rather than historical accuracy: Tallulah must be polite and professional, and she must not upset her tourists, because she must encourage repeat customers and think about the reviews and tips that she will receive at the end of the game. Even before the trip begins, Tallulah reminds herself that "it's never a good idea to alienate a tourist. . . . An alienated tourist is a tourist who doesn't tip."[57] With this motto in mind, Tallulah must somehow, impossibly, walk her tourists through historical trauma while keeping them happy enough that they will want to visit again. Ironically, when Tallulah succeeds at her job, she does so by shielding the tourists from ethical encounters, discouraging them from pondering their own relationship with and responsibilities to the Other.

Like Tallulah, the digital Cherokee experience violence as they relive the Trail for each new group of tourists. While Tallulah has only ever thought of these stock characters as computer programs, she learns that some of them have gained self-awareness and, as a result, retain their memories of each trip. If Tallulah has ridden the Trail of Tears over a thousand times, that number can be multiplied for the digital characters, who ride the Trail with every tour guide at the TREPP. The Nunnehi narrator explains that these characters "have all bled to death thousands of times, and they feel it each time. They feel every drop of everyone's blood, their own blood and the blood of their young ones. They remember every moment."[58] Awful as this description is, it reinforces the importance of community for the Cherokee; they share everything with one another, even the pain and death that accompany the Trail. They keep repeating this experience over and over because they have been "made to belong" to a place that "is not our home."[59] They have been "made" to live in this place by the programmers who "programmed [them] to be killed, then brought back to life."[60] They have been forced into this violent narrative in much the way that the real-world Cherokee, both historically and in the present, have been "made to belong" in Oklahoma rather than in their eastern homelands. Like Tallulah, they must relive, on a daily basis, the historical violence done to their people. Each experience adds another layer of trauma. For both the real tour guide and the virtual Indians, the act of reliving this experience simply perpetuates the cycle of violence against the Cherokee people.

Nonetheless, the digital Indians also seem to be imbued with Indigenous knowledge that includes the Cherokee homeland. They know that they belong in the mountains of North Carolina,[61] not the artificial stockade where they live in between games. Without ever having been to the motherland, the digital Cherokee know "how nice" North Carolina is.[62] When asked how they can know about a place they've never been, one of the Cherokee leaders simply responds that "we *know*. . . . We *all* know."[63] Similarly, they explain that they know what is going to happen in the game because "we know things" and "we are part of this machine."[64] Their information seems to be tied up in both Indigenous knowledge—like knowing about the Cherokee homeland—and Euro-American technical, scientific knowledge, because they are indigenous to the machine itself. As in Suvin's definition of science fiction, which includes "intrinsic, culturally acquired cognitive logic" as well as "scientifically methodical cognition,"[65] this combination of different kinds of knowing allows the digital Cherokee to resist their programming, ultimately empowering them to resist further assimilation and colonization. By giving equal weight to Euro-American science and Indigenous knowledge, *Riding the Trail of Tears* expands the possibilities of the genre and models the importance of cultural knowledge in the twenty-first century.

Hausman's decision to recognize the digital Cherokee as real people further reinforces an Indigenous perspective in which nonhuman creatures are recognized as peoples who are deserving of respect and compassion. As opposed to Pinsky's description of Euro-Americans who alienate or assimilate the Other, Indigenous epistemologies encourage people to recognize and respect alterity. This impulse appears in several other works of Native sf, as when the protagonist of *The Ballad of Billy Badass and the Rose of Turkestan* must recognize Sammy as human despite his extreme disabilities or when, in *It Came from Del Rio*, Laurie recognizes Dodd as her father despite his hideous and terrifying appearance. Here again, a Native author encourages readers to acknowledge the humanity of the Other and respond ethically to the Other's demand. In this case, the digital Other demands that Tallulah try to end the characters' suffering by breaking the cycle, leading them back to North Carolina rather than continuing to follow the preordained historical narrative.

Responding ethically to the Other is understandably difficult, especially within the context of a traumatic event like the Trail of Tears. It is not surprising that tourists would rather spend time with the Wise Old Medicine Man, who plays into long-standing U.S. fantasies about Native Americans. This trend has been discussed at length by Philip J. Deloria, who argues that early twentieth-century U.S. citizens, often distrustful of modernity, "imagined a radical break in history and posited a desirable Indian on the far side of societal, racial, and temporal boundaries."[66] This imagined Indian became the symbolic representation of a nostalgic past, which eventually led to the early twentieth-century popularity of summer camps and youth organizations such as the Woodcraft Indians, the Boy Scouts, and the Camp Fire Girls. Through such experiences, children could "gain *access* to the authentic" without sacrificing their own modern identities.[67] As Deloria explains,

> The mutually constitutive nature of modern/antimodern practices—becoming an Indian-child in order eventually to become a clerk, banker, broker, or housewife and mother—typified the many touristic escapes that defined modern life. Through purchase and travel, upper- and middle-class Americans made a series of moves back and forth from the city to the country, from work to leisure, from industrial production to handcrafted souvenirs, from the anonymous crowd to the ethnic community, from the insincere contemporary to a more authentic primitive past.[68]

Although this antimodernist rhetoric originates in the early twentieth century, Deloria argues that the "modernist search for authenticity . . . has reverberated throughout the twentieth" century.[69] Thus, it is also possible to trace the American quest for authenticity through a twenty-first-century novel like *Riding the Trail of Tears*, where both Tallulah and her tourists continue to struggle with similar anxieties. The TREPP tourists, like their modernist counterparts, have sought out a "touristic escape," which Hausman reveals to be a blatant tourist trap. As with summer camps and youth organizations, upper- and middle-class Americans rely on vacations to escape the reality of modern life, even when that vacation somehow involves spending three hours living through the experience of nineteenth-century genocide. Four of Tallulah's tourists are college students in search of extra credit for a history class, but there are also two families on vacation in Tour Group 5709.

While the Trail of Tears seems unlikely to offer relaxed family bonding, its popularity speaks to the strength of the desire to escape one's own life by "playing Indian."

As a contemporary touristic escape, the TREPP is also more convenient than summer camps or scouting groups. Rather than devoting the entire summer to "playing Indian" and making a trek into the actual wilderness, customers can fit the tour into a single afternoon. Although time expands within the game, only three hours will pass in the real world, a perk that many of the tourists allude to in the novel: the college students are eager to attend a Georgia football game later that day, while the Rosenberg family is anxious to get home in time for a pot roast dinner. Because of the fixed amount of time that tourists spend in the TREPP, Tallulah can guarantee that each group will be able to keep their plans. Moreover, while only children can attend summer camp, the TREPP is accessible to the whole family. Even families without children, like the Rosenbergs, can participate. In fact, because each group can choose the level of violence with which they are comfortable, the TREPP can be tailored to adults as well as children. So, where twentieth-century campers might have spent the summer in an "authentic" space before growing up into bankers and housewives, busy adults who are dissatisfied with modern life can shrink two or three months into the more convenient three-hour escape into "Indianness" offered by the TREPP.

In Hausman's world, virtual reality offers an improved solution to the American dilemma of modernity: as far as tourists are concerned, the Trail of Tears that they experience is a perfectly authentic representation of the past. In fact, "authenticity" is a common criterion for an educational experience. Twentieth-century tourists, who only had access to the real world, worried about "contaminating the authenticity of the primitive" through their own presence, but this problem has been resolved in virtual reality, as the TREPP tourists are conveniently transformed into Indians themselves in order to enter a virtual world where only their guide is "authentically" Native.[70] It is no surprise that Tallulah—one of only two Cherokee employees—serves as the poster child of the company and its most popular tour guide. In order to read Tallulah's presence as a mark of authenticity, we must overlook quite a few related issues, but within the world of the novel, only Tallulah herself seems to be aware of those inconsistencies. She has become a token minority, expected to speak for all Native peoples and all tribal nations in both the present and the past. Such expectations are, of course, impossible, but they are especially unrealistic for Tallulah, who feels profoundly disconnected from Cherokee culture and community.

The tourists are not the only ones who tokenize Tallulah; they are simply following the example set forth by the TREPP's business plan and promotional literature. The programmers treat her like a bridge between Native and Euro-American cultures. While developing the Wise Old Medicine Man, they tried to "inject authenticity into Old Medicine" by doing "what all good TREPP employees do—they asked Tallulah for guidance."[71] It becomes her responsibility to share cultural knowledge—most of which comes directly from reading James Mooney—with the developers, and that knowledge becomes the basis for all representations of the Cherokee in the TREPP. As a result, Tallulah becomes a bridge not only between cultures, but also between the past and the present. Her customers have similar expectations: they ask Tallulah to interpret Cherokee culture, language, and history, both the traditional and the contemporary. Because she is Cherokee, they assume that she is an expert on all things "Indian." They also assume that it is Tallulah's job to help them gain "access to organic Indian purity," which has been the goal of cultural tourists throughout the twentieth and twenty-first centuries.[72] By paying for the experience of riding the TREPP and being guided by Tallulah, the tourists believe that they have "preserve[d] the integrity of the boundaries that marked exterior and authentic Indians" while simultaneously gaining access to that world for themselves.[73]

Tallulah's role within the TREPP, much like the Little Little People's, is vexed by the complex and contradictory definitions of this virtual Indigenous space. Although the building that houses the TREPP theme park is built on historic Cherokee territory in northeast Georgia, that space is today more frequently seen as part of the American South. Tallulah certainly understands that the Cherokee were illegally removed from this space, but most of her tourists are only vaguely aware of that history. The multiple understandings of the land are further complicated by the existence of the virtual space itself, which is ostensibly Cherokee rather than American. Within the game, Tallulah spends her time in "Indian country," but that country has been created by programmers, none of whom are Cherokee themselves. Although Tallulah is a cultural consultant, she does not ultimately have control over the landscape or the characters in the TREPP. Thus, the Indian country of the TREPP can only be an imperfect, simulated version of the real space.

On the other hand, because the game focuses on the experiences of the Cherokee, the majority of the characters who populate the virtual world are Cherokee citizens themselves, despite the fact that their creators are largely non-Native. In fact, even the tourists *appear* Cherokee within the game, leading to the illusion of a Native majority within the virtual space. But "authentic" Native identity is a much thornier concept than either the tourists or the programmers acknowledge, and the tourists' Indigenous appearance further problematizes that question of identity: Is it enough to "look" Cherokee, to have physical characteristics that will be interpreted as "Indian"? Tallulah "looks" Cherokee, in large part thanks to her braids, which are "the most Indian of her features," but she often worries about her own authenticity.[74] Through Tallulah's uncertainty, Hausman insists that Native identity requires more than biology, and certainly more than physiognomy; having braids or even meeting blood quantum requirements is less important than cultural identifiers, which are much more difficult to establish, especially within the virtual world of the TREPP.

Even if we accept that the digital Indians are "authentically" Cherokee—and at least those created by the Little Little People seem to be—the TREPP is still a contested territory because it is located in time as well as space. As long as the TREPP is stuck in 1838, it can never be a purely Cherokee space; it will always be defined by the American soldiers whose goal is to force the Cherokee to move west. Indeed, those characters who fully embrace Cherokee identity are most likely to suffer during the game. When American soldiers round up Tour Group 5709, Tallulah "instructs her tourists to do as they're told and follow the soldiers' orders."[75] If they try to resist, if they try to protect the Cherokee homelands, culture, and people, they will be attacked and perhaps even killed early in the game. So, although the goal of the TREPP is ostensibly to teach tourists about lived Cherokee experience, to allow them to identify with an unfamiliar group of people, it actually encourages them to surrender that identity in order to survive.

The characters whom the tourists encounter in the game have also been programmed as perpetual victims, repeatedly suffering at the hands of the American soldiers. For instance, Tallulah's tourists always spend the first night inside the game with a digital Cherokee couple, Deer Cooker and Corn Grinder. Every time, the tourists wake up to American soldiers invading the house, and so, every time, the digital family must walk the Trail of Tears with the tourists. Tallulah compares their reaction to her own, noting that the family "walks with similar stoicism. They are professionals too."[76] Later, after Corn Grinder's inevitable death at the hands of the soldiers, Tallulah considers that

> Deer Cooker is programmed to grieve. Traumatized and suddenly weary, Deer Cooker plays the role of a model American Indian—he does not fight back, he does

not harbor lasting resentment toward the soldier who killed his wife, and he does not protest when another soldier grabs his arm and hoists him back onto the Trail.[77]

So long as the digital Cherokee are programmed to give in, and so long as the tourists are encouraged to follow their lead, the ostensibly Cherokee space of the TREPP will never be truly Indigenous. Instead, Deer Cooker's experience indicates that a certain amount of internal colonization is built into the game. This is quite literally true for the digital characters, who have been "programmed to grieve"—or, worse, programmed to die—and Tallulah, the only "real" Native American whom the tourists encounter in the TREPP, shares this assimilated mindset. Ultimately, although tourists may feel that they are getting an "authentic" experience, the TREPP is always already a contested and problematic space.

These issues are reflected in the creation story of the TREPP itself, which began as a collaboration between Tallulah and the programmers. Over time, however, Tallulah has become critical of other people's contributions: she complains about the "historical inaccuracy" of the tourists' slightly enlarged breasts and penises within the game, and also about a stock character called The Drawl, whose thick southern accent is "offensively overstated."[78] Valid as her criticisms might be, they are also indicative of Tallulah's desire to maintain exclusive control over the world of the TREPP. Similarly, in her own life, Tallulah believes that she "didn't need anyone's help."[79] Even the design of the TREPP reflects this stereotypically Euro-American desire for independence and individuality; rather than several passengers riding together in a Jeep Cherokee, as in Grandpa Art's original prototype, "the Chairsuit Visor is totally individualized. It is the single-occupancy realization of [Tallulah's] grandfather's dream."[80] In other words, tourists embark upon the difficult experience of riding the Trail of Tears by themselves, despite the fact that communal support might help them cope with and survive removal. Tallulah's desire for control and independence, reflected in her game design as well as in her own life, goes against a Cherokee emphasis on community and, once again, reflects the Euro-American epistemologies that inform the game.

This juxtaposition is exemplified by Tallulah's walkie-talkie, which she uses to communicate with the tech crew from inside the game. The walkie-talkie is shaped like a water beetle, a tiny creature who plays a prominent role in some versions of the Cherokee creation story. In that story, First Woman falls through a hole in the sky and lands on earth, which is completely covered in water. She perches on

Turtle's back while the animals try to create land for her. Several animals dive to the bottom of the ocean in search of mud, and Water Beetle is the first to succeed. As Tallulah explains, he "spent years diving down to the bottom of the ocean and swimming back up with little bits of earth" until he had enough to cover Turtle's back and create the land.[81] The water beetle, and the earth diver story in general, serves as a reminder that the Cherokee world was created collaboratively and required the efforts of even the smallest creatures.

The walkie-talkie connects Tallulah back to the material world, but it is also a symbol of world creation, a reminder that Tallulah is part of a community that worked together to create the TREPP. As one of the digital Indians reiterates, "You must remember, the whole of the community is more important than any single individual."[82] Unfortunately, Tallulah seems to have lost sight of those communal values and shared experiences: she takes on too much individual responsibility for both her tourists and the TREPP. By trying to make and sustain the world alone, Tallulah overworks herself and, ironically, fails her community. She has forgotten to be flexible, to adapt, to turn to others for assistance. Because she has ridden the TREPP so many times, she believes that she can rely on the same script and the same standard responses on each journey, overlooking the fact that the world—even the virtual world—is subject to change. Relying on a standardized script leaves her vulnerable when change actually does occur; she realizes that her stories have become stagnant, and the process of reliving the Trail of Tears over and over has worn her down. The limits of this approach are illustrated as soon as the game begins to malfunction; when one of her tourists disappears without explanation, Tallulah realizes that "she has fumbled the lines. Her words are escaping from her. This is unprecedented."[83] Because her standard script does not address this scenario, she finds herself lost, unable to adapt. Later, when her tour group encounters the Nunnehi and digital Indians who have decided to go to North Carolina rather than follow the Trail of Tears, Tallulah is similarly lost. Although she acknowledges that going to North Carolina would be much better than going to Oklahoma, she still insists that "we're supposed to go west. We need to go west."[84] In this moment, as when she encourages her tourists to give in to the soldiers without a fight, Tallulah actually encourages everyone to keep acting out the process of removal, even when other options present themselves. She has repeated these patterns many times, retelling the same stories in the same language until she has become both dehumanized and colonized by continuing to rely on this single, inflexible, and violent narrative.

The Little Little People intervene in the TREPP in order to resist precisely the kind of pressures that Tallulah faces. By introducing Indigenous knowledge into the machine, they challenge the fixed boundaries between genres and cultures and establish a new form of resistance and survival for the Cherokee. Like the Little Little People, who became indigenous to the digital environment after being lost from a much older oral tradition, the Cherokee have also migrated from one homeland to another. And, while Tallulah struggles to reconcile her Cherokee identity with this sense of displacement, the narrator simply announces that he is indigenous to the digital earth.[85] His confidence despite such a paradox serves as an example for Tallulah and other Cherokee, including those inside the TREPP. Like the Little Little People, Tallulah has the opportunity to reclaim her own story despite the fact that it remains incomplete. At the end of the virtual tour, rather than continuing to reenact the Trail of Tears and reinforcing stereotypes about Native peoples for new audiences on a daily basis, Tallulah ultimately chooses to quit working for the TREPP and return to North Carolina. Although the novel ends without telling us what happens to Tallulah next, she has clearly broken the cycle of violence and begun to tell a new story about her own life.

Because of the intervention of the Nunnehi, Tallulah also begins to resist and even reverse some of the violence that has been done to her people. Rather than leading her tourists, as well as the digital Cherokee, on to Oklahoma as she has done eleven hundred times before, Tallulah agrees to lead this group east, into the virtual mountains of North Carolina. The virtual journey corresponds to her real-life plans for the coming weekend: after finishing this tour, Tallulah will drive to her grandparents' home, which is located in Cherokee territory in the same state. Throughout the novel, she has viewed this particular tour as the last obstacle before her vacation can begin. By changing her plans inside the game, she takes responsibility for both her own life and the lives of the digital Cherokee rather than continuing to ignore the problem by following the same pattern. Instead of enacting yet another painful death, Tallulah contributes to a story of survival and reclamation.

In addition to challenging the Trail of Tears itself, the Nunnehi create a space where Tallulah can confront her own identity issues inside the TREPP. This is possible not because of any program that Tallulah or the tech staff consciously create, but because the Little Little Person who narrates the novel has experienced Tallulah's dreams with her. Because he is also indigenous to the digital earth, the material of Tallulah's dreams becomes part of the TREPP, creating a virtual space where she can encounter and resolve a recurring dream about her dead father. In that dream, Tallulah finds herself in a dark cave with a black bear. She knows that the bear is her father's spirit, but she is unable to have a conversation with him.[86] She compares the experience to a vision quest but worries that she is inadequate, wondering "what was so wrong with [her] that she couldn't even experience a vision properly?"[87] Inside the TREPP, however, Tallulah finally finds her voice: she shares her insecurities, as well as her anger at her father for leaving her, and "for the first time in four years, Tallulah Wilson cried inside the Trail of Tears."[88] In this moment of catharsis, her father comforts her and says that he loves her. Her dream has finally reached a resolution, thanks to the digital space that serves as an intermediary between the physical world and the world of dreams. Such a space is only possible at the intersection of religious and scientific contexts—or, more accurately, by viewing the world holistically, as Cajete suggests.[89] Rather than analyzing the world from a Euro-American perspective, which insists that we divide knowledge into discrete—and often artificial—categories, *Riding the Trail of Tears* demonstrates the individual and communal benefits of interpreting experiences through the lens of Indigenous knowledge.

Although the TREPP does not allow for actual time travel and is thus incapable of changing the course of history, it nonetheless causes real harm by repeating earlier traumas. It is only when the Little Little People interfere that the TREPP becomes a tool of resistance rather than colonization. By creating the digital Cherokee, who rebel against the soldiers and lead Tallulah's tourists to North Carolina, the Nunnehi are able to tell a new story. This story does not undo or erase historical events—but it does challenge the tourists to rethink their assumptions about those events. In a more concrete way, the Nunnehi also encourage Tallulah and the digital Cherokee to disrupt the pattern of violence in which they are trapped. With the assistance of the Nunnehi, Tallulah learns to recognize the digital Cherokee as an Other, as real beings that deserve to be treated ethically. This response also fits with a Cherokee worldview, which recognizes that nonhuman allies are still beings worthy of our respect. And Tallulah also comes to see herself as a being worthy of respect, as opposed to a salesperson who must keep smiling while her tourists treat her—and other Native peoples—as less than human. Finally, by allowing Tallulah to confront her father and sort through her own emotions, the TREPP helps her understand her personal history from a new perspective. She may not be able to change the historic Trail of Tears—in fact, it would be inappropriate to try—but, working as part of a community inside the TREPP, Tallulah can create a new, more hopeful narrative for herself, her tourists, and both real and virtual Cherokee people.

By employing and adapting the science fictional tropes of virtual and alternate realities, Hausman and Birchfield offer a new perspective on the historical removal that affected southeastern tribes in the nineteenth century. Through their focus on contemporary protagonists, both novels draw connections between events in the past and their effects in the present, counteracting a popular narrative that insists that the 1830s are impossibly far away and therefore no longer relevant. Nonetheless, both novels warn against the dangers of becoming trapped in the past, obsessed with removal and unable to imagine a path forward. In emphasizing the stories inherent to a place rather than focusing on the passage of time, both novels reinforce an Indigenous epistemology that serves to collapse the distance between the past and the present, reminding us of the importance of the spatial over the temporal, as Vine Deloria would argue. Birchfield points to patterns in the relationship between the United States and the Choctaw that extend into the twenty-first century in order to highlight both Choctaw loyalty and American unreliability. Similarly, Hausman highlights the ways that the ongoing insistence on romanticizing Native peoples perpetuates earlier historical traumas. Rather than trying to erase the past, the novels suggest ways for contemporary Indigenous peoples to confront and respond to that trauma without succumbing to internal colonization or losing their tribal identities.

Coda

ndigenous science fiction does considerably more than just adding diversity to the genre. It challenges mainstream readers to reconsider their own perspectives and definitions of reality while emphasizing the value of Indigenous knowledge and worldviews in the past, present, and future. By defining Native science fiction (sf) as a specific body of literature, one that depends on the interactions between Indigenous perspectives and science fiction tropes, we can avoid relegating texts that simply reflect Native worldviews to the category of science fiction, which would effectively ghettoize Indigenous texts, cultures, and peoples. Under the definition I propose here, Native sf comprises a relatively small number of texts, but its ranks are growing steadily. Much of the recent discussion of Indigenous science fiction has focused on Indigenous futurism, the term originally coined by Grace Dillon and adopted by a multitude of artists and critics. In "The Space NDN's Star Map," Lou Cornum (Navajo) points to Dillon's *Walking the Clouds*, alongside the release of the short film *The 6th World*, which I discuss in more detail below, as "the official inauguration of indigenous futurism."[1] Like other proponents of this specific subgenre, they argue that placing "the seemingly contrasting symbolic systems of indigeneity and high-tech modernity . . . in dialogue" allows Native writers to challenge the belief that "indigenous life is not only separate from the present time but also out of place in the future."[2] Cornum is one of several authors to refute that stereotype, pointing out instead the real necessity of imagining the future in order to shape it and, thus, of the political imperative inherent to Indigenous futurism as a genre. As William Lempert observes, "While we cannot have a future we do not imagine, we also consciously or unconsciously *create* the future based on what we assume to be possible, desirable, and even inevitable."[3]

Both Cornum and Lempert devote considerable attention to the medium of film: partially because so many short films have been produced in the past ten years and often shared openly online, but also because film so effectively illustrates survivance in both the present and the future. If one of your goals is to demonstrate that Indigenous peoples are alive and well, a film featuring Native actors, voiceover, and languages makes a fairly persuasive argument. As Denise K. Cummings argues, "The visual has become a primary means of mediating identities."[4] This process takes place, first of all, simply through the representation of Indigenous worldviews on screen. Relying on earlier work by Steven Leuthold, Cummings notes that "as the new millennium approached . . . the traditional concepts of connection to place, to the sacred, and to the cycles of nature were finding new expression through westernized media, such as Native filmmaking."[5] Michelle H. Raheja extends this idea by proposing that "film and the forms of new media operate as a space of the virtual reservation, a space where Native American filmmakers put the long, vexed history of indigenous representations into dialogue with epistemic indigenous knowledges."[6] Film is not simply a medium that can reflect Native perspectives—it establishes an entirely new space. In her introduction to Raheja's essay, Cummings neatly sums up this larger argument: "Raheja seeks to help us understand how the filmmakers demonstrate that film itself, as a virtual reservation, is an expressive site that can evoke and enact indigenous knowledges. . . . This view of film, Raheja maintains, presents the screen not as a representative window on the putative 'real' world, but as a world in and of itself."[7] Such an understanding of the power of film explains some of the possibilities inherent in Indigenous futurist films.

As a genre, science fiction is similarly invested in the creation of its own world. And Indigenous futurism, in particular, strives to imagine a world populated with Native peoples in order to enact change in the contemporary real world. To cite Raheja again: "Twentieth-century mass-mediated images of Native Americans, as inaccurate and offensive as they sometimes are, create the possibility of a virtual reservation where indigenous people can creatively reterritorialize physical and imagined sites that have been lost, that are in the process of renegotiation, or have been retained."[8] Although she focuses on films that depict Indigenous spiritualities, not science fictions, her argument nonetheless highlights the importance of maintaining and reclaiming Native territory both physically and metaphorically, an idea that appears often in discussions of Indigenous futurism.

The emphasis on claiming Indigenous territory in the future is thus echoed in many short films. As Cornum notes in their discussion of the independent short film *The 6th World*, Navajo filmmaker "Nanobah Becker shot the Mars scenes . . . in Monument Valley, one of the sacred territories of the Diné. . . . Just because the Diné have not lived on Mars since time immemorial, it does not mean our plants and teachings cannot take root there."[9] *The 6th World* tells the story of a partnership between the Navajo nation and a large corporation, with the two groups working together to send a manned shuttle to Mars and build the first Martian colony.[10] They rely heavily on corn as a source of both food and oxygen during the long voyage, and when the corporation's genetically modified corn fails to thrive in space, the mission is saved by Indigenous knowledge and practices. Pilot Tazbah Redhouse (Jenada Benally) performs a ceremony involving two ears of corn given to her by a Navajo elder, effectively creating new life from a traditional food source. Diné knowledge saves not only the mission, but also an entire future world on Mars.

As Stacy Thacker explains, the film's title refers to the Navajo belief "that there are a number of worlds in which the Navajo people emerged."[11] Earth is the Fifth World, so the title of the film suggests that the Diné's next home will be located in the Martian colony that Redhouse plans to establish.[12] Reflecting a by-now familiar theme, the emphasis here is on the cultural value of change and adaptability rather than the stereotype of the vanishing Indian who is forever trapped in a premodern world. In *The 6th World*, as in *The Ballad of Billy Badass* and *Riding the Trail of Tears*, Indigenous people's ability to simultaneously maintain and adapt their traditions creates space for both Native and non-Native people to move into the future.

The theme of Indigenous territory in science fiction film also appears in Kiowa-Choctaw artist Steven Paul Judd's animated short film "Neil Discovers the Moon." Although it is set in the past rather than the future, it nonetheless claims new territory for Native peoples. The film opens on the iconic moment of the 1969 moon landing, alongside this explanation: "The following classified footage has never been seen by the public . . . until now."[13] We hear a recording of Neil Armstrong's famous declaration as the camera focuses on a stop-motion astronaut planting an American flag in the soil. As he does so, a small Indigenous girl appears, taps the astronaut on the leg, waves at him, and asks, "Does this mean we have to move again?"[14] In addition to being an excellent punchline,[15] the single sentence abruptly reframes an American narrative of exploration and heroism as just one more example of Euro-American colonialism, which has always been at the heart of "discovery." Moreover, it claims the moon itself as Indigenous territory, suggesting that once again, Euro-Americans were not actually the first to inhabit the land. While the film imagines that the moon was inhabited before 1969, the addition of the word "again" implies that Native peoples traveled to the moon specifically in response to the invasion of their homes on Earth. Just as Birchfield's Choctaws established an underground nation to avoid American expansionism and colonization, so has this group left their North American home in order to live beyond the reach of settler colonialism. Even when Indigenous science fiction is set in the past—or, perhaps, in an alternative reality—it continues to carve out land, both real and imagined, for Native peoples.

The fact that many of these films have been released and widely shared over the Internet points to the ways that twenty-first-century technology has allowed for the rapid expansion of Indigenous futurism as some artists blur the lines between film and other new media. Perhaps the most prominent example of this blurring takes place in the work of Skawennati, a Kahnawake Mohawk artist who "makes art that addresses history, the future, and change."[16] In the nine-part digital film series *TimeTraveller*, Skawennati tells the story of Hunter, a Mohawk man living in the future and interacting with famous events in Indigenous history through the use of a commercially available product called TimeTraveller glasses. Not only does *TimeTraveller* rely on science fictional tropes and tools to tell a particularly Native story; its existence also establishes Indigenous territory in cyberspace.

As with other short films, that territory is partially created through the presence of the *TimeTraveller* website. In a more complicated move, however, it is also connected to a growing Indigenous presence in Second Life, the online game that Skawennati used to create the series. Second Life "is a 3D world where everyone you see is a real person and every place you visit is built by people just like you."[17] By relying on computer graphics from Second Life to create the films, Skawennati stakes an Indigenous land claim within the virtual reality world of Second Life. David Gaertner explores the complex development of cyberspace as an actual territory—including Skawennati's presence in Second Life—in his discussion of Indigenous cyberpunk, which, he argues, "has become a vital part of the contemporary literary landscape and the ways in which Indigeneity is imagined into the future."[18] Further uniting physical and creative spaces, Skawennati also serves as coordinator of the Initiative for Indigenous Futures (IIF) at the Milieux Institute for Art, Culture, and Technology at Concordia University. In collaboration with IIF's director, Jason Edward Lewis, she explains that the organization is "dedicated to developing multiple visions of Indigenous peoples tomorrow in order to better understand where we need to go today. . . . IIF will encourage and enable artists, academics, youth and elders to imagine how we and our communities will look in the future."[19] Skawennati's own art, as well as her academic and outreach work, form one of the most compelling examples of imagined futures intersecting with present realities in order to establish or reclaim Indigenous territories.

The possibilities of cyberspace are promising not only because the space itself is so readily available to artists and critics, but also because it is more easily accessible to their audiences. For instance, the majority of texts cited in this chapter were accessed electronically and publicly, without relying on the exclusive research tools available only to those with an institutional connection to an academic library. (I am particularly indebted to members of the Indigenous Futurisms Facebook group, who brought my attention to many of these sources by sharing them on the group page.)

But publication and sharing of such materials takes place not only online. Increasingly widespread Internet access and the trend toward digital rather than print reading has opened up more democratic publishing processes for those who wish to distribute their work in a form more akin to traditional print media. This is a relatively new trend, as we can see from Louis Owens's 2001 comments about the publishing industry. Only twenty years ago, he argued that because the publishing industry is "controlled by highly educated persons of European and European American descent . . . [it] manufactures a product designed primarily for consumers of European and European American origin."[20] He further predicted that "the voices that tell stories too disturbing or too alien will be kept silenced or at best on the publishing margins represented by small presses and, more than ever today, university presses."[21] It is true that many of the texts I have examined here were published by university presses, and it is also true that online publishing and self-publishing still hover on "the publishing margins," but this balance appears to be changing. In an *Atlantic* article exploring the recent rise of women in science fiction, Rose Eveleth argues that marginalized women writers "can use Twitter and Facebook not just to promote their work, but to connect with one another."[22] She goes on to quote sf writer Kameron Hurley, who points out that women writers are able to speak back to the dominant culture "because there are more channels.

There's incredible profusion of all of these other avenues for us to get our voices out there, and to collaborate right."[23] So, although Owens's predictions are not unfounded, writers whose voices have previously been ignored are more frequently availing themselves of a variety of electronic resources in order to change the tenor of the conversation. Looking more specifically at Indigenous writers, we can point to Karuk author Pamela Rentz, who used the website Smashwords to publish a collection of generically experimental short stories that include elements of both science fiction and horror.[24] Andrea Grant (Coast Salish) created her own press, Copious Amounts, which she used to publish her superhero comics series, *Minx*.[25] Such alternate publishing ventures demonstrate that even when Indigenous sf is not set in the future, it often relies heavily on new technologies.

Beyond the work being done in cyberspace, the content of much Indigenous science fiction likewise leans toward the future. Although an in-depth discussion of that genre is beyond the scope of this project, it is worth noting that the trend even applies to traditional print stories and novels. Where short films like *The 6th World* and *TimeTraveller* offer optimistic visions of Indigenous communities in the future, however, recent novels tend more toward critical dystopia—a term that refers to stories set in a hellish future world in order to draw audiences' attention to current crises. The goal of the critical dystopia is to persuade readers to change their current behavior in order to avoid a nightmarish future.[26] It has become increasingly popular with both Native and non-Native authors in the early twenty-first century as an increasing number of artists turn to the tropes of critical dystopia to reflect growing concerns about climate change, late-stage capitalism, and the rise of extreme right-wing governments. Popular dystopian texts by non-Native writers include Suzanne Collins's *The Hunger Games* (2008–10), N. K. Jemisin's *Broken Earth* series (2015–17), Veronica Roth's *Divergent* trilogy (2011–13), and the ongoing Hulu adaptation of Margaret Atwood's 1985 novel, *The Handmaid's Tale* (2017–present). While Native American and First Nations writers like Stephen Graham Jones, Daniel H. Wilson, Cherie Dimaline, and even Louise Erdrich have contributed to the growing body of critical dystopian literature, their work has also highlighted specifically Indigenous concerns such as the recognition of sovereignty, the dangers of establishing and policing identity based on physical appearance, and the threat—both historical and contemporary—of colonial governments forcibly removing Indigenous children from their communities.

One of the first Native critical dystopian books to be published was Stephen Graham Jones's 2003 novel *The Bird Is Gone: A Manifesto*, which uses genre tropes to interrogate the idea of establishing a new "Indian territory" in the twenty-first century. The novel takes place in a future world where a legal loophole allows Native peoples to reclaim the Dakotas as Indian Territory. Initially, this premise sounds like an ideal way to imagine Native sovereignty in a utopian world, but the novel's vision of a sovereign future turns out to be quite cynical. We learn that busloads of American tourists cross the border each day, many of them eager to stay at the Mayflower casino-resort located just inside the Territories.[27] We also learn that as floods of Native people began the pilgrimage to their sovereign territory, they celebrated by drinking. As a result, the no-man's-land outside the Territories is filled with badly crashed cars, many with corpses still trapped inside. Even fourteen years later, citizens sometimes sneak over the border at night to scavenge whatever they can from these cars—a detail that hints at the immense poverty inside the Territories. Moreover, as a result of the drunken partying that took place in those first months, a dropped cigarette started a fire that eventually consumed the Great Plains, leaving behind a "barren ashen region" now referred to as "Two Burn Flat."[28]

Since identity politics are key to defining this new Indigenous nation, much of the tension within the novel itself relies on the characters' failed attempts to distinguish between Native and non. The new Indian Health Services has even introduced a particular strain of pink eye, one that only Indians can get.[29] Ostensibly, this will allow for the easy identification of "real" Indians, but, as the narrator keeps repeating, "there are ways" around such restrictions.[30] We see various characters get vaccinated, use contacts to hide their eye color, or take irritating drops intended to redden their eyes and allow them to pass. Anyone whose eyes are bloodshot because they are hung over or taking drugs—like the cowdrops that the narrator uses— might also appear "Indian."[31] Thus, not only does the basic premise for identification not work as intended, it means that everyone living in Indian Territory always has pink eye—and they are all supposed to be proud of it. Here, as in *It Came from Del Rio*, Jones points to the fallacy of using visual indicators to determine citizenship.

Beyond the issues apparent in the new IHS, the novel also depicts a variety of corrupt leaders, from the tribal police who find themselves engaged in protecting white tourists by racially profiling Native citizens to members of the tribal council who cheat to win the annual AllSkin bowling tournament. Through these details, as well as larger ethical questions about what it means for Native peoples to displace the white Americans who had lived in the Dakotas for several generations prior to their reclamation, *The Bird Is Gone* highlights many of the practical issues that would have to be resolved before any sovereign utopia could be established in the real world. Although this satirical novel offers primarily negative depictions of a Native nation, it nonetheless asks its audience to resolve the ongoing political and tribal issues that might pose challenges along the path to sovereignty.

Another series that imagines a dystopic future is Cherokee author Daniel Wilson's 2011 novel *Robopocalypse* and its 2015 sequel, *Robogenesis*. These books, written in the style of postapocalyptic summer blockbuster films, take place in an unspecified near future where sentient technology has risen up against humanity. A key pocket of human resistance is located at Gray Horse, an Osage reservation in Oklahoma. When the machines attack, Gray Horse is protected because of its isolation, outdated technology, and the inaccessibility of its unpaved roads. In a world where new cars come with an autopilot setting that allows them to hunt down human victims, Gray Horse's remoteness is an unexpected strength. It becomes a stronghold for Native and non-Native survivors who travel great distances to join the community. Two Osage men, a local police officer and his son, turn out to be heroes in the war to save humanity. Not only are they leaders who contribute to the war effort individually, they also form alliances with people from other cultures and nations. The father, Lonnie Wayne Blanton, persuades tribal elders to accept a young Cherokee man named Lark Iron Horse, the first non-Osage survivor to arrive at Gray Horse. That decision sets a precedent for Gray Horse's treatment of strangers, both Native and non. Moreover, Lark goes on to lead Gray Horse Army into battle against the machines, ultimately sacrificing his life to win the war. Lonnie Wayne's son, Specialist Paul Blanton, collaborates with surviving Afghani forces and, ultimately, is responsible for locating enemy headquarters and relaying those coordinates to survivors around the globe. The 2015 sequel *Robogenesis* depicts the survivance of Native peoples and cultures in greater detail, spending more time with the surviving Osage and Cherokee characters and incorporating elements of traditional knowledge and ceremonies in ways reminiscent of other works of Indigenous sf. And, as Steven Spielberg and Michael Bay negotiate the possibility of creating a *Robopocalypse* film,[32] the series may offer additional visions of Indigenous futures on screen.

Cherie Dimaline's *The Marrow Thieves* and Louise Erdrich's *Future Home of the Living God*, both published in 2017, imagine dystopian futures shaped by a combination of climate change and corrupt government policies. Dimaline's novel takes place in a Canada whose geography has been reshaped by the pollution of the Great Lakes and the ensuing Water Wars,[33] while Erdrich imagines a world where global temperatures have risen so quickly that it no longer snows in Minnesota. In both novels, ecological disasters have unexpected effects on human life: Dimaline describes a world where non-Native people have ceased to dream, while Erdrich describes the way that evolution (both animal and human) starts to regress at an erratic pace. In each case, when non-Native people's lives are threatened, the colonial governments attempt to protect Euro-Americans and Euro-Canadians by enacting new policies that, unsurprisingly, target women, Indigenous people, and members of other minority groups. In *The Marrow Thieves*, the Canadian government resurrects the old residential school model: Recruiters abduct Indigenous people and take them to the schools, where their dreams are forcibly harvested from their bone marrow. In *Future Home*, a conservative Christian government abducts pregnant women—especially those who have "any special ethnicity"[34]—and transports them to birthing centers where they are held captive, their babies taken from them as soon as they give birth. Both governments justify exploitation of Indigenous bodies and violence against Indigenous people as necessary sacrifices for "the greater good"—a term that inevitably excludes Native peoples and refers instead to the communities of colonizers occupying Indigenous lands.

Although Dimaline and Erdrich share many of the anxieties of their non-Native counterparts, they also recognize that global catastrophe will not affect all peoples equally—a fact that has been illuminated in the real world by the COVID-19 pandemic. In the early weeks of the pandemic, there was a common belief that "COVID doesn't discriminate."[35] Within a few months, however, the Centers for Disease Control and Prevention acknowledged that "long-standing systemic health and social inequities have put many people from racial and ethnic minority groups at increased risk of getting sick and dying from COVID-19."[36] Erdrich and Dimaline, writing well before the pandemic, illustrate a fundamental understanding of the concept described by the CDC: even in the case of a global crisis, members of marginalized groups will be more adversely affected than those with greater racial and socioeconomic privilege.

In 2014, when I was just beginning to articulate a theory of Indigenous science fiction, I presented some of my early ideas at the Native American Literature Symposium. Gordon Henry, Carter Meland, Francesco Melfi, and I sought to reconcile Euro-American science and Indigenous knowledge by exploring the ways that stories of strange creatures—including Bigfoot, talking animals, and the monsters of science fiction—challenge us to reconcile cultural paradoxes. We concluded that Indigenous knowledge offers a more productive framework for appreciating and understanding such encounters than does Euro-American science. When we opened the panel up for discussion, an enthusiastic audience member asked a question that caught me off guard. According to this argument, he said, couldn't we reframe the story of White Buffalo Calf Woman, the Lakota culture hero, as a work of science fiction?

I knew right away that the answer was "No, absolutely not," but I could not immediately explain why. The question forced me to stop and reconsider the tricky ground on which Indigenous science fiction rests. Up to that point, I had gleefully embraced the novelty and playfulness of the genre. But I hadn't really considered the ways that it might be misconstrued or the damage that might result from a misunderstanding. The question of White Buffalo Calf Woman brought those dangers into sharp relief. If I categorized her story as science fiction, I would effectively be saying that she is not real—and, by extension, implying that all Indigenous religious figures are fictional. This was certainly not my intent, nor was it the effect of the novels I was writing about.

Continuing to wrestle with this question long after the conference ended, I ultimately identified a key difference: unlike Euro-American science fiction, Indigenous sf leaves a space for the sacred. Even more than that, it draws attention to the distinction between a believable but ultimately imaginary novum and the very real belief systems that undergird Indigenous knowledge and cultures. As illustrated by Suvin's vehement defense of the distinction between science fiction and fantasy, mainstream sf has often been used to break down the barrier between the sacred and the secular, with the goal of proving that the sacred is not real, but merely a superstitious belief held by uneducated humans.

Consider, for instance, the episode of *Star Trek: The Next Generation* called "Who Watches the Watchers."[37] The *Enterprise* has been secretly observing the "progress" of a "primitive" people called the Mintaka. When a Mintakan named Liko accidentally discovers the presence of the crew and observes their advanced technology in action, he becomes convinced that the ship's captain, Picard, must be a god. Intent on disabusing him of that idea, Picard allows Liko to shoot him with an arrow to prove that he, too, will bleed. Picard's willingness to sacrifice himself demonstrates his fidelity to the Prime Directive, which warns against interfering in the development of other cultures. Having made the mistake of revealing the *Enterprise* to the Mintaka, Picard does what he can to reverse the damage. Nonetheless, according to the episode's narrative arc, this encounter will have the effect of propelling Mintakan social evolution: now that they have seen and accepted the presence of Western science, they will abandon their "primitive" religious beliefs.

Positioning White Buffalo Calf Woman as a science fiction story would have the same effect. It would relegate a sacred figure to mere metaphor, implying that the Lakota, like the Mintaka, are a "primitive" people who have simply failed to view their story through a Euro-American scientific lens. To prove their sophistication, according to this argument, the Lakota would need to renounce Indigenous knowledge and traditional beliefs, replacing them wholesale with Euro-American science in order to prove their own evolution, modernity, and relevance.

There is an obvious appeal to this rhetoric, which might be understood as a way to make Indigenous stories "cool" and "relevant" while also bringing Native people into the twenty-first century. But ultimately, the idea is neither new nor helpful. Rather, it is just another name for the same old colonial imperative to assimilate. Examples of that imperative abound in both history and literature, but perhaps one of the most famous can be found in Leslie Marmon Silko's *Ceremony*, where Tayo faces immense pressure to relinquish his Laguna Pueblo worldview in favor of Euro-American science:

> In school the science teacher had explained what superstition was, and then held the science textbook up for the class to see the true source of explanations. [Tayo] had studied those books, and he had no reason to believe the stories any more. The science books explained the causes and effects. But old Grandma always used to say, "Back in time immemorial, things were different, the animals could talk to human beings and many magical things still happened." He never lost the feeling he had in his chest when she spoke those words, as she did each time she told him stories; and he still felt it was true, despite all they had taught him in school—that long long ago things *had* been different, and human beings could understand what the animals said, and once the Gambler had trapped the storm clouds on his mountaintop.[38]

Tayo resists. He holds a space for sacred Laguna Pueblo beliefs. And Indigenous science fiction does the same. For all that it engages directly with Euro-American science and genre fiction, it maintains the sacred. White Buffalo Calf Woman is not reduced to the level of a radiation Creature because these texts respect and even revere Indigenous knowledge. And with that reverence, Indigenous sf expands our definition of the sacred. It encompasses new figures like the Little Little People in *Riding the Trail of Tears* or Sammy and the other children whose lives have been shaped by radiation exposure in *The Ballad of Billy Badass and the Rose of Turkestan*. Rather than rejecting and reframing traditional stories and beliefs, Indigenous science fiction reinforces the relevance and expands the role of Indigenous knowledge, demonstrating its use as a compass to navigate and survive the distinct challenges of the twenty-first century and beyond.

Notes

Introduction

1. Hans Robert Jauss, "Literary History as a Challenge to Literary Theory," trans. Elizabeth Benzinger, *New Literary History* 2, no. 1 (1970): 13.

2. Jauss, "Literary History as a Challenge to Literary Theory," 11.

3. Jauss, "Literary History as a Challenge to Literary Theory," 8.

4. Philip K. Dick, "My Definition of Science Fiction," in *The Shifting Realities of Philip K. Dick: Selected Literary and Philosophical Writings*, ed. Lawrence Sutin (New York: Pantheon Books, 1995), 99.

5. Judith Butler, *Gender Trouble: Feminism and the Subversion of Identity* (New York: Routledge Classics, 1990), 182.

6. Butler, *Gender Trouble*, 181.

7. Rebecca Roanhorse, "Postcards from the Apocalypse," *Uncanny: A Magazine of Science Fiction and Fantasy*, https://uncannymagazine.com/article/postcards-from-the-apocalypse/.

8. Grace L. Dillon, "Imagining Indigenous Futurisms," in *Walking the Clouds: An Anthology of Indigenous Science Fiction* (Tucson: University of Arizona Press, 2012), 2.

9. Dillon, "Imagining Indigenous Futurisms," 4.

10. Rader's *Engaged Resistance* was published before *Walking the Clouds*, but Dillon had already published on the topic of Indigenous science fiction by the time of Rader's book. See, for instance, Dillon's article "*Miindiwag* and Indigenous Diaspora: Eden Robinson's and Celu Amberstone's Forays into 'Postcolonial' Science Fiction and Fantasy," *Extrapolation* 48, no. 2 (2007): 219–43.

11. Although it is true that much canonical science fiction is grounded in plausible or metaphorical applications of science rather than "real" science, the fuzziness that surrounds the concept of reality here is distinct from the way that we understand the reality of Indigenous worldviews. This is in part because the legitimacy of Euro-American science is not threatened simply because it is applied in creative ways in works of science fiction, whereas Native worldviews are already romanticized, critiqued, appropriated, and dismissed by mainstream American culture. But such a categorization also becomes an issue when the "cultural experience of reality" is used to label a text as science fictional. As Dean Rader suggests, it would be inaccurate to categorize "creation stories, shape-shifters, coyotes, and all that is atemporal" as characteristic of sf, because doing so undermines Indigenous worldviews that understand these things as having a very real presence in the world. So, while a work of Indigenous science fiction might well include Coyote, it is not Coyote's presence that qualifies the story as sf. Dean Rader, *Engaged Resistance: American Indian Art, Literature, and Film from Alcatraz to the NMAI* (Austin: University of Texas Press, 2011), 86.

12. Toni Morrison, "An Interview with Toni Morrison, by Christina Davis" in *Conversations with Toni Morrison*, ed. Danille Taylor-Guthrie (Jackson: University Press of Mississippi, 1994), 226.

13. Adrienne Keene, "'Magic in North America': The Harry Potter Franchise Veers Too Close to Home," *Native Appropriations*, March 7, 2016, http://nativeappropriations. com/2016/03/magic-in-north-america-the-harry-potter-franchise-veers-too-close-to-home.html.

14. Keene, "'Magic in North America.'"

15. Keene, "'Magic in North America.'"

16. Rader, *Engaged Resistance*, 86.

17. The allegations about Alexie's behavior toward female writers that came to light in 2018 must be taken into consideration in future discussions of his work. However, both Rader and Dillon published their analyses before those allegations came to light, and I include this discussion here in order to summarize and compare earlier critical conversations, rather than to advocate for Alexie's work as an exemplar of Indigenous science fiction.

For additional information about these allegations, please see Lynn Neary's article, "'It Just Felt Very Wrong': Sherman Alexie's Accusers Go on the Record," NPR, March 5, 2018, https://www.npr.org/2018/03/05/589909379/it-just-felt-very-wrong-sherman-alexies-accusers-go-on-the-record.

18. Dillon, *Walking the Clouds*, 52. Rader, *Engaged Resistance*, 87.

19. Dillon, *Walking the Clouds*, 52–53.

20. Rader, *Engaged Resistance*, 87.

21. Dillon, *Walking the Clouds*, 52–53. Rader, *Engaged Resistance*, 87.

22. Rader, *Engaged Resistance*, 86.

23. Rader, *Engaged Resistance*, 1.

24. Roanhorse, "Postcards from the Apocalypse."

25. James Mooney, *Myths of the Cherokee and Sacred Formulas of the Cherokee* (Washington, DC: Bureau of American Ethnology, 1890), 330.

26. Nalo Hopkinson, introduction to *So Long Been Dreaming: Postcolonial Science Fiction and Fantasy*, ed. Nalo Hopkinson and Uppinder Mehan (Vancouver: Arsenal Pulp Press, 2004), 7.

27. Istvan Csicsery-Ronay Jr., "Science Fiction and Empire," in *Science Fiction Criticism: An Anthology of Essential Writings*, ed. Rob Latham (London: Bloomsbury, 2017), 443.

28. Csicsery-Ronay, "Science Fiction and Empire," 450.

29. Csicsery-Ronay, "Science Fiction and Empire," 453.

30. Jessica Langer, *Postcolonialism and Science Fiction* (New York: Palgrave Macmillan, 2011), 13.

31. Uppinder Mehan, "Final Thoughts" in Hopkinson and Mehan, *So Long Been Dreaming*, 269.

32. Dillon, "*Miindiwag* and Indigenous Diaspora," 237. It is also worth noting, as Dillon points out here, that Hopkinson "identifies with aboriginal thought and emphasizes her own ancestry of Taino and Arawak descent."

33. Langer, *Postcolonial Science Fiction*, 47.

34. Langer, *Postcolonial Science Fiction*, 48.

35. Dillon, "*Miindiwag* and Indigenous Diaspora," 219.

36. Dillon, "*Miindiwag* and Indigenous Diaspora," 221.

37. John Rieder, "On Defining Sf, or Not: Genre Theory, Sf, and History" in Latham, *Science Fiction Criticism*, 79.

38. Csicsery-Ronay, "Science Fiction and Empire," 443–44.

39. Rieder, "On Defining Sf, or Not," 79.

40. Csicsery-Ronay, "Science Fiction and Empire," 448.

41. Roanhorse, "Postcards from the Apocalypse."

42. Rieder, "On Defining Sf, or Not," 87.

43. Rieder, "On Defining Sf, or Not," 80.

44. Carter Meland, "American Indians at the Final Frontiers of Imperial Sf," *Expanded Horizons: Speculative Fiction for the Rest of Us*, no. 1 (2008), http://expandedhorizons.net/magazine/?page_id=150.

45. Meland, "American Indians at the Final Frontiers of Imperial Sf."

46. Dick, "My Definition of Science Fiction," 100.

47. Dick, "My Definition of Science Fiction," 99.

48. Dick, "My Definition of Science Fiction," 99.

49. Acknowledging his immense influence, Rieder uses Suvin as an example of the historical approach to defining sf, noting that "Suvin's definition becomes part of the history of sf, not the key to unraveling sf's confusion with other forms" (Rieder, "On Defining Sf, or Not," 77). While it is useful to remember that Suvin is not the final authority on science fiction, his definitions nonetheless remain a useful starting point for examining science fiction published in the late twentieth and early twenty-first centuries.

50. Darko Suvin, *Metamorphoses of Science Fiction: On the Poetics and History of a Literary Genre* (New Haven: Yale University Press, 1979), 4.

51. Dick, "My Definition of Science Fiction," 100.

52. H. G. Wells, *The Island of Doctor Moreau*, ed. Darryl Jones (Oxford: Oxford University Press, 2017), 123 (see first note for p. 63).

53. Suvin, *Metamorphoses of Science Fiction*, 7–8.

54. Suvin, *Metamorphoses of Science Fiction*, 8.

55. Rieder, "On Defining Sf, or Not," 77.

56. Andrew Milner, *Locating Science Fiction* (Liverpool: Liverpool University Press, 2012), 1.

57. Suvin, *Metamorphoses of Science Fiction*, 66.

58. Suvin, *Metamorphoses of Science Fiction*, 13.

59. Gregory Cajete, *Native Science: Natural Laws of Interdependence* (Santa Fe: Clear Light Publishers, 2000), 3.

60. Cajete, *Native Science*, 3. Suvin, *Metamorphoses of Science Fiction*, 13.

61. Suvin, *Metamorphoses of Science Fiction*, 13.

62. Cajete, *Native Science*, 2.

63. See Channette Romero, *Activism and the American Novel: Religion and Resistance in Fiction by Women of Color* (Charlottesville: University of Virginia Press, 2012), 35–38, for a more detailed discussion of why such terms are problematic. Suvin, *Metamorphoses of Science Fiction*, 4.

64. Suvin, *Metamorphoses of Science Fiction*, 4.

65. Suvin, *Metamorphoses of Science Fiction*, 7.

66. Suvin, *Metamorphoses of Science Fiction*, 6.

67. Ursula K. Le Guin, *The Left Hand of Darkness: 50th Anniversary Edition* (New York: Berkley Publishing Group, 2019), 259.

68. Suvin, *Metamorphoses of Science Fiction*, 7.

69. David M. Higgins, "Toward a Cosmopolitan Science Fiction," *American Literature* 83, no. 2 (2011): 349.

70. Higgins, "Toward a Cosmopolitan Science Fiction," 350.

71. Suvin, *Metamorphoses of Science Fiction*, 7.

72. Vine Deloria Jr., *God Is Red: A Native View of Religion* (Golden, CO: Fulcrum Publishing, 2003), 62.

73. Deloria, *God Is Red*, 102.

74. Deloria, *God Is Red*, 104.

75. While Deloria's argument offers important insights into Native religions, it must be acknowledged that he tends toward broad generalizations, collapsing many different beliefs into a kind of pan-Indian religion. Thus, I rely on Deloria to lay out a broad theoretical argument about Native vs. Euro-American religions in general, but as I examine individual texts in later chapters, I turn to more tribally specific discussions of particular religious beliefs.

76. Deloria, *God Is Red*, 66.

77. Deloria, *God Is Red*, 66.

78. Vine Deloria Jr., *The Metaphysics of Modern Existence* (San Francisco: Harper & Row, 1979), x.

79. Deloria, *Metaphysics of Modern Existence*, x.

80. In fact, because Suvin's condemnation of a static religious approach relies on a Western European understanding of linear time, his criticism must be reconsidered and reframed in a discussion of Native religion. It seems that what Deloria refers to as "religion" is actually more closely related to what Suvin understands as "cognition." Neither thinker champions a fixed and static conception of the world—both privilege the possibilities of change and emphasize the transitory nature of a specific historical moment rather than relying on a fixed or universal system. Ultimately, perhaps Suvin's limited perspective and terminology are simply inadequate to address Indigenous worldviews. He and Deloria value similar characteristics, but the binary Euro-American framework that Suvin employs prevents him from considering an alternate relationship between religion and change, while Deloria's definition demonstrates that the two concepts already coexist.

81. Suvin, *Metamorphoses of Science Fiction*, 5.

82. H. G. Wells, *The Time Machine* (New York: Fawcett Premier, 1968), 65.

83. Wells, *The Time Machine*, 65.

84. Michael Pinsky, *Future Present: Ethics and/as Science Fiction* (Madison, NJ: Fairleigh Dickinson University Press, 2003), 14–15.

85. Pinsky, *Future Present*, 183.

86. Wells, *The Time Machine*, 40.

87. Wells, *The Time Machine*, 42.

88. Wells, *The Time Machine*, 59.

89. Wells, *The Time Machine*, 102.

90. Wells, *The Time Machine*, 72.

91. Wells, *The Time Machine*, 40.

92. Wells, *The Time Machine*, 70.

93. Butler, *Gender Trouble*, 182.

94. Pinsky, *Future Present*, 184.

95. Deloria, *God Is Red*, 107.

96. Vine Deloria Jr., "Reflection and Revelation," in *For This Land: Writings on Religion in America*, ed. James Treat (New York: Routledge, 1999), 250.

97. Deloria, "Reflection and Revelation," 250.

98. Pinsky, *Future Present*, 184.

99. Pinsky, *Future Present*, 185, 186.

100. Le Guin, *The Left Hand of Darkness*, 11.

101. Higgins, "Toward a Cosmopolitan Science Fiction," 347.

102. Le Guin, *The Left Hand of Darkness*, 11.

103. Le Guin, *The Left Hand of Darkness*, 248.

104. Pinsky, *Future Present*, 187.

105. Pinsky, *Future Present*, 187–88.

106. Pinsky, *Future Present*, 188.

107. Deloria, *God Is Red*, 67.

108. Pinsky, *Future Present*, 188.

109. Pinsky, *Future Present*, 188.

110. Pinsky, *Future Present*, 188.

111. Deloria, *God Is Red*, 66.

112. Niigaanwewidam James Sinclair, "A Conversation on Indigenous Ethics with Niigaanwewidam" (presentation at the Annual Convention of the Native American Literature Symposium, Prior Lake, MN, March 21, 2013).

113. Pinsky, *Future Present*, 190.

114. Deloria, *Metaphysics of Modern Existence*, ix.

Part One. Modern Monsters, Modern Borders

1. J. P. Telotte, "Film, 1895–1950," in *The Routledge Companion to Science Fiction*, ed. Mark Bould, Andrew M. Butler, Adam Roberts, and Sherryl Vint (London: Routledge, 2009), 48.

2. Telotte, "Film, 1895–1950," 42.

3. Telotte, "Film, 1895–1950," 50.

4. Aris Mousoutzanis, "Apocalyptic SF," in Bould et al., *The Routledge Companion to Science Fiction*, 459.

5. Mousoutzanis, "Apocalyptic SF," 460.

6. *Godzilla*, directed by Ishiro Honda (Chiyoda, Tokyo: Toho Co., Ltd., 1954). *Them!*, directed by Gordon Douglas (Burbank, CA: Warner Brothers, 1954).

7. Matthew J. Costello, "U.S. Superpower and Superpowered Americans in Science Fiction and Comic Books," in *The Cambridge Companion to American Science Fiction*, ed. Gerry Canavan and Eric Carl Link (Cambridge: Cambridge University Press, 2015), 131.

8. Roland Kelts, "Godzilla Shows Japan's Real Fear Is Sclerotic Bureaucracy Not Giant Reptiles," *The Guardian*, August 21, 2017, https://www.theguardian.com/commentisfree/2017/aug/21/resurgence-shin-godzilla-japanese-culture-film-japan.

9. See Sarah Alisabeth Fox, *Downwind: A People's History of the Nuclear West* (Lincoln: University of Nebraska Press, 2014) for a detailed discussion of the effects of radiation exposure on Native communities.

10. Fox, *Downwind*, 7. See David Rich Lewis, "Skull Valley Goshutes and the Politics of Nuclear Waste: Environment, Identity, and Sovereignty," in *Native Americans and the Environment*, ed. Michael E. Harkin and Judith Antell (Lincoln: University of Nebraska Press, 2007) for an example of the complicated issues surrounding nuclear waste disposal on reservations.

11. Fox, *Downwind*, 19.

12. Fox, *Downwind*, 15.

13. Fox, *Downwind*, 16.

14. Fox, *Downwind*, 15.

15. Fox, *Downwind*, 15.

16. Fox, *Downwind*, 15.

Chapter One. The Yellow Monster: Reanimating Nuclear Fears in *The Ballad of Billy Badass and the Rose of Turkestan*

1. A note on terminology: Fox, *Downwind*, 12, translates the Navajo word *leetso* as "yellow brown" or "yellow dirt" and explains that some Navajo began to refer to *leetso* as "the yellow monster." In science fiction studies, however, a distinction is drawn between Creatures and Monsters, which I discuss in greater detail below. In short, Creatures are those beings that "seem to roam the Earth almost by accident"; they are "less personalized, [have] less of an interior presence than does the Monster. . . . Our sympathy is never evoked by an SF Creature; it remains, always, a thing": Vivian Sobchack, *Screening Space: The American Science Fiction Film* (New Brunswick: Rutgers University Press, 1999), 32. This description echoes the intent of the Navajo phrase, which positions uranium as a "thing" rather than as a nonhuman person that might exist in relationship with the Navajo community. To reflect consistency with sf theory and distinguish from my later discussion of Monsters, I will use the term "Creature" to refer to the being described in *The Ballad of Billy Badass*.

2. Kyoko Matsunaga, "Leslie Marmon Silko and Nuclear Dissent in the American Southwest," *Japanese Journal of American Studies*, no. 25 (2014): 72, http://www.jaas.gr.jp/jjas/PDF/2014/04_Matsunaga.pdf.

3. A. A. Carr, *Eye Killers* (Norman: University of Oklahoma Press, 1995), 155.

4. Carr, *Eye Killers*, 155.

5. Carr, *Eye Killers*, 253.

6. Atomic Heritage Foundation, "The Manhattan Project," May 12, 2017, https://www.atomicheritage.org/history/manhattan-project.

7. Rather ironically in the context of Cherokee removal, the Atomic Heritage Foundation's website notes that, in addition to acquiring the 59,000 acres where Oak Ridge was built, General Leslie Groves "also approved . . . the removal of the relatively few families on the marginal farmland." Atomic Heritage Foundation, "Oak Ridge, TN."

8. Marilou Awiakta, *Abiding Appalachia: Where Mountain and Atom Meet* (Memphis: St. Luke's Press, 1978), 65. In the context of this book, a line such as "we are removed" also echoes the experience of Cherokee removal, which Awiakta addresses explicitly in earlier poems.

9. Meland, "American Indians at the Final Frontiers of Imperial Sf."

10. Higgins, "Toward a Cosmopolitan Science Fiction," 332–33.

11. Higgins, "Toward a Cosmopolitan Science Fiction," 332.

12. Higgins, "Toward a Cosmopolitan Science Fiction," 334–35.

13. Higgins, "Toward a Cosmopolitan Science Fiction," 335.

14. *Independence Day*, directed by Roland Emmerich (1996; Los Angeles: 20th Century Fox, 2013), DVD.

15. Per its title, *Independence Day* is set on July 2–4. It premiered in theaters in late June of 1996, suggesting that American audiences might include the movie in their holiday celebrations—as, indeed, many have done. For instance, the *NPR Politics Podcast* maintains an annual tradition of reading aloud "the climactic speech from the 1996 hit film 'Independence Day' in which President Thomas Whitmore at Area 51 gets up on the back of a truck and gives an inspiring speech through a megaphone." Scott Detrow, Asma Khalid, Ayesha Rascoe, and Mara Liasson, "Weekly Roundup: Tuesday, July 3," *NPR Politics Podcast*, July 3, 2018, MP3 audio, 37:37, https://www.npr.org/transcripts/625807854?storyId=625807854?storyId=625807854.

16. Higgins, "Toward a Cosmopolitan Science Fiction," 332.

17. William Sanders, *The Ballad of Billy Badass and the Rose of Turkestan* (Holicong, PA: Wildside Press, 1999), 7.

18. Sanders, *The Ballad of Billy Badass*, 7.

19. Sanders, *The Ballad of Billy Badass*, 41.

20. Higgins, "Toward a Cosmopolitan Science Fiction," 335.

21. Sanders, *The Ballad of Billy Badass*, 115.

22. Sanders, *The Ballad of Billy Badass*, 115.

23. Sanders, *The Ballad of Billy Badass*, 115.

24. Deloria, *Metaphysics of Modern Existence*, x.

25. Deloria, *God Is Red*, 66.

26. Suvin, *Metamorphoses of Science Fiction*, 5.

27. Brian Burkhart, "Jisdu Goes Decolonial: The Epistemic Resistance of Cherokee Trickster Stories" (paper presentation, Native American Literature Symposium, Prior Lake, MN, March 9, 2019).

28. Sanders, *The Ballad of Billy Badass*, 58.

29. Deloria, *God Is Red*, 55.

30. Sanders, *The Ballad of Billy Badass*, 117.

31. *Godzilla*, dir. Honda.

32. *Godzilla*, dir. Honda.

33. *Godzilla*, dir. Honda.

34. Sanders, *The Ballad of Billy Badass*, 116.

35. *Godzilla*, dir. Honda.

36. *Them!*, dir. Douglas.

37. Sobchack, *Screening Space*, 45.

38. It is true that Serizawa is deeply concerned about the consequences of the military and politicians using his discovery as a weapon. Nonetheless, he agrees to collaborate with both groups so long as he can be solely responsible for the detonation of his Oxygen Destroyer.

39. Sanders, *The Ballad of Billy Badass*, 24.

40. Sanders, *The Ballad of Billy Badass*, 125.

41. Sanders, *The Ballad of Billy Badass*, 86, 93.

42. Sanders, *The Ballad of Billy Badass*, 284–85.

43. Sanders, *The Ballad of Billy Badass*, 40–41.

44. Sanders, *The Ballad of Billy Badass*, 41.

45. Sanders, *The Ballad of Billy Badass*, 46.

46. Sanders, *The Ballad of Billy Badass*, 46.

47. James Wilson, *The Earth Shall Weep: A History of Native America* (New York: Grove Press, 1998), 303–4.

48. Sanders, *The Ballad of Billy Badass*, 43.

49. Sanders, *The Ballad of Billy Badass*, 44.

50. As discussed earlier, Silko makes a similar argument in *Ceremony*.

51. Melanie Benson, *Disturbing Calculations: The Economics of Identity in Postcolonial Southern Literature, 1912–2002* (Athens: University of Georgia Press, 2008), 183.

52. Sanders, *The Ballad of Billy Badass*, 29.

53. Sanders, *The Ballad of Billy Badass*, 29.

54. Sanders, *The Ballad of Billy Badass*, 28–29.

55. Sanders, *The Ballad of Billy Badass*, 35.

56. Sanders, *The Ballad of Billy Badass*, 7.

57. Sanders, *The Ballad of Billy Badass*, 142–43.

58. Sanders, *The Ballad of Billy Badass*, 148.

59. Sanders, *The Ballad of Billy Badass*, 160.

60. Sanders, *The Ballad of Billy Badass*, 160.

61. Sanders, *The Ballad of Billy Badass*, 164.

62. Sanders, *The Ballad of Billy Badass*, 165.

63. Sanders, *The Ballad of Billy Badass*, 166.

64. Sanders, *The Ballad of Billy Badass*, 167.

65. Mooney, *Myths of the Cherokee*, 736.

66. Sanders, *The Ballad of Billy Badass*, 281.

67. Sanders, *The Ballad of Billy Badass*, 279.

68. Sanders, *The Ballad of Billy Badass*, 279.

69. Joseph Erb, "The Beginning They Told," YouTube, October 28, 2016, https://www.youtube.com/watch?feature=youtu.be&v=BUoPB0reYc4&app=desktop. There are many versions of this story, but Erb's short film, told in Cherokee and intended for educational purposes, is a representative example.

70. Sanders, *The Ballad of Billy Badass*, 127.

71. Sinclair, "A Conversation on Indigenous Ethics with Niigaanwewidam."

Chapter Two. Radioactive Rabbits and "Illegal Aliens": Border Crossing in *It Came from Del Rio*

1. Stephen Graham Jones, *It Came from Del Rio* (Colorado: Trapdoor Books, 2010), 27.

2. Theodore C. Van Alst, introduction to *The Faster Redder Road: The Best UnAmerican Stories of Stephen Graham Jones*, ed. Van Alst (Albuquerque: University of New Mexico Press, 2015), 12.

3. Stephen Graham Jones, interview by Billy J. Stratton, "Observations on the Shadow Self," 52, cited in Theodore C. Van Alst, "Lapin Noir: To Del Rio It Went," in *The Fictions of Stephen Graham Jones*, ed. Billy J. Stratton (Albuquerque: University of New Mexico Press, 2016), 332.

4. Stephen Graham Jones, interview by Billy J. Stratton, "Observations on the Shadow Self," in Stratton, *The Fictions of Stephen Graham Jones*, 52.

5. Stephen Graham Jones, "Letter to a Just-Starting-Out Indian Writer—and Maybe to Myself," *Transmotion* 2, nos. 1–2 (2016): 128.

6. A. Robert Lee, "Native Postmodern: Remediating History in the Fiction of Stephen Graham Jones and D. L. Birchfield," in *Mediating Indianness*, ed. Cathy Covell Waegner (East Lansing: Michigan State University Press, 2015), 73–74.

7. Lee, "Native Postmodern," 79.

8. Lee, "Native Postmodern," 75.

9. Jones, *It Came from Del Rio*, 42.

10. Jones, *It Came from Del Rio*, 69.

11. Thomas King, *The Inconvenient Indian: A Curious Account of Native People in North America* (Minneapolis: University of Minnesota Press, 2013), 21.

12. King, *The Inconvenient Indian*, 21.

13. Jones, *It Came from Del Rio*, 21.

14. Jones, *It Came from Del Rio*, 71.

15. Jones, *It Came from Del Rio*, 43.

16. Jones, *It Came from Del Rio*, 27.

17. Jones, *It Came from Del Rio*, 29.

18. Jones, *It Came from Del Rio*, 29.

19. "Star Trek Original Series Intro (HQ)," YouTube, July 23, 2007, https://www.youtube.com/watch?v=hdjL8WXjlGI.

20. Kevin Carey, "Martians Might Be Real: That Makes Mars Exploration Way More Complicated," *Wired*, August 7, 2016, https://www.wired.com/2016/08/shouldnt-go-mars-might-decimate-martians/.

21. Jones, *It Came from Del Rio*, 94.

22. Benjamin Radford, *Tracking the Chupacabra: The Vampire Beast in Fact, Fiction, and Folklore* (Albuquerque: University of New Mexico Press, 2011), 3–4.

23. Radford, *Tracking the Chupacabra*, 3–4.

24. Radford, *Tracking the Chupacabra*, 33.

25. Radford, *Tracking the Chupacabra*, 29.

26. Radford, *Tracking the Chupacabra*, 29.

27. Radford, *Tracking the Chupacabra*, 33.

28. Jones, *It Came from Del Rio*, 93.

29. Jones, *It Came from Del Rio*, 93.

30. Jones, *It Came from Del Rio*, 96.

31. Jones, *It Came from Del Rio*, 199.

32. Wilson, *The Earth Shall Weep*, 206; Fox, *Downwind*, 2–3.

33. Jones, *It Came from Del Rio*, 84.

34. Jones, *It Came from Del Rio*, 178.

35. Butler, *Gender Trouble*, 182.

36. Butler, *Gender Trouble*, 181.

37. Sobchack, *Screening Space*, 30.

38. Sobchack, *Screening Space*, 32.

39. Sobchack, *Screening Space*, 50.

40. Jones, *It Came from Del Rio*, 87.

41. Jones, *It Came from Del Rio*, 95.

42. "Spider-Man (Peter Parker)," *Marvel.com*, https://www.marvel.com/characters/spider-man-peter-parker.

43. Costello, "U.S. Superpower and Superpowered Americans," 131.

44. Costello, "U.S. Superpower and Superpowered Americans," 131.

45. Costello, "U.S. Superpower and Superpowered Americans," 131.

46. Costello, "U.S. Superpower and Superpowered Americans," 136.

47. The dangers of that Christian narrative have been explored in a wide variety of texts, but it is worth noting the especially compelling exploration of this theme in the series *Lovecraft Country*, which draws on the tropes of horror and science fiction to depict the lived experiences of African Americans in the mid-twentieth century. In an episode called "Whitey's on the Moon," the leader of a white supremacist cult imagines himself as a modern Adam who aims to restore God's hierarchy and return to the Garden of Eden. To achieve this goal, he subjects a young Black man named Atticus Freeman to extreme physical torture as part of a mystical, pseudoscientific ceremony.

48. Van Alst, "Lapin Noir," 328, notes "that we'll *not* detour into the wild and wonderful world of the trickster figure here."

49. Jones, *It Came from Del Rio*, 91.

50. Jones, *It Came from Del Rio*, 90, 92.

51. Jones, *It Came from Del Rio*, 97.

52. Jones, *It Came from Del Rio*, 97.

53. Jones, *It Came from Del Rio*, 98.

54. Jones, *It Came from Del Rio*, 98.

55. Jones, *It Came from Del Rio*, 98.

56. Jones, *It Came from Del Rio*, 98.

57. Jones, *It Came from Del Rio*, 98.

58. Jones, *It Came from Del Rio*, 202.

59. Jones, *It Came from Del Rio*, 173.

60. Jones, *It Came from Del Rio*, 174.

61. Jones, *It Came from Del Rio*, 174, 153.

62. Sobchack, *Screening Space*, 50–51.

63. Jones, *It Came from Del Rio*, 208–9.

64. Jones, *It Came from Del Rio*, 107.

65. Jones, *It Came from Del Rio*, 208.

66. Jones, *It Came from Del Rio*, 209.

67. Jones, *It Came from Del Rio*, 108.

Part Two. Reimagining Resistance

1. Rader, *Engaged Resistance*, 76.

2. Dick, "My Definition of Science Fiction," 99.

3. Karen Hellekson, "Alternate History," in Bould et al., *The Routledge Companion to Science Fiction*, 453.

4. Philip K. Dick, *The Man in the High Castle* (Boston: Mariner Books, 2011), 96–99.

5. Hellekson, "Alternate History," 453.

6. Dick, *The Man in the High Castle*, 53.

7. Dick, *The Man in the High Castle*, 53.

8. Hellekson, "Alternate History," 457.

9. Hellekson, "Alternate History," 457.

10. Dick, *The Man in the High Castle*, 234.

11. Dick, *The Man in the High Castle*, 209.

12. Dick, *The Man in the High Castle*, 209.

13. Hellekson, "Alternate History," 454.

14. Roanhorse, "Postcards from the Apocalypse."

15. Hellekson, "Alternate History," 457.

16. See, for instance, novels such as Toni Morrison's *Beloved* or Leslie Marmon Silko's *Ceremony*, both of which are often categorized as "postmodern." Although these books do examine our relationship to history, they also insist upon the objective reality of certain historical events, such as the testing of the atom bomb in the Southwest or the trauma and abuse inflicted on enslaved peoples. They further reinforce the importance of certain values, religious beliefs, and "moral imperatives," though these values are culturally specific rather than universal.

17. Roxanne Dunbar-Ortiz, *An Indigenous People's History of the United States* (Boston: Beacon Press, 2014), 137, 154–55.

18. William Sanders, "Custer Under the Baobab," in *Drakas!*, ed. S. M. Stirling (Riverdale, NY: Baen Books, 2000), https://www.baen.com/Chapters/0671319469/0671319469___2.htm.

19. Hellekson, "Alternate History," 457.

20. Thomas King, *The Truth About Stories* (Minneapolis: University of Minnesota Press, 2003), 2.

Chapter Three. Until the Danger Passes: Dystopian Sovereignty in *Field of Honor*

1. Scott Andrews, "Review of *Of Uncommon Birth: Dakota Sons in Vietnam* by Mark St. Pierre; *Field of Honor*, by D. L. Hirschfield [sic]," *Studies in American Indian Literatures* 17, no. 1 (2005): 90.

2. Rader, *Engaged Resistance*, 86. Tom Mould, *Choctaw Tales* (Jackson: University Press of

Mississippi, 2004), 40.

3. D. L. Birchfield, *Field of Honor* (Norman: University of Oklahoma Press, 2004), 121–25.

4. Birchfield, *Field of Honor*, 104.

5. Birchfield, *Field of Honor*, 11.

6. Birchfield, *Field of Honor*, 10.

7. Birchfield, *Field of Honor*, 11.

8. Birchfield, *Field of Honor*, 24–25.

9. Birchfield, *Field of Honor*, 23.

10. Of course, the Marines are not solely to blame for this obsession: although it seems to have stemmed from the pride and responsibility that Marines are encouraged to feel for the organization, McDaniel has clearly carried that pride to an unhealthy extent. When he finally gets in touch with someone at Marine headquarters, they make several attempts to ease McDaniel's conscience, including trying to convince him to accept treatment at a psychiatric hospital, giving him a promotion and eleven years of back pay, and offering an honorable discharge. Thus, although there is an argument to be made about the long-term effects of patriotic and assimilationist rhetoric, it is worth noting that the Marines are not actively demanding or encouraging McDaniel's behavior.

11. Scott Richard Lyons, *X-Marks: Native Signatures of Assent* (Minneapolis: University of Minnesota Press, 2010), 1.

12. Birchfield, *Field of Honor*, 4.

13. Birchfield, *Field of Honor*, 11.

14. Birchfield, *Field of Honor*, 3.

15. This particular claim is especially noteworthy given the ways that the Mississippi, perhaps more so than any other river, has been viewed as particularly "American" in our collective literary imagination. Consider, for instance, the role of the Mississippi in novels like Mark Twain's *The Adventures of Huckleberry Finn* or songs like "Ol' Man River," from the musical *Showboat*.

16. Birchfield, *Field of Honor*, 41.

17. Gideon Lincecum, *Pushmataha: A Choctaw Leader and His People* (Tuscaloosa: University of Alabama Press, 2004), 29.

18. D. L. Birchfield, *How Choctaws Invented Civilization and Why Choctaws Will Conquer the World* (Albuquerque: University of New Mexico Press, 2007), xvi.

19. Greg O'Brien, introduction to Lincecum, *Pushmataha*, vii–viii, xiv.

20. Lincecum, *Pushmataha*, 26.

21. Birchfield, *Field of Honor*, 110.

22. O'Brien, introduction to Lincecum, *Pushmataha*, x, xii.

23. Lincecum, *Pushmataha*, 30.

24. Lincecum, *Pushmataha*, 90.

25. Wilson, *The Earth Shall Weep*, 155.

26. Lincecum, *Pushmataha*, 90.

27. Wilson, *The Earth Shall Weep*, 155.

28. Lincecum, *Pushmataha*, 90.

29. Birchfield, *Field of Honor*, 20.

30. Birchfield, *Field of Honor*, 22.

31. Birchfield, *Field of Honor*, 23.

32. Birchfield, *How Choctaws Invented Civilization*, 16.

33. Birchfield, *How Choctaws Invented Civilization*, 18.

34. Birchfield, *How Choctaws Invented Civilization*, 18.

35. Birchfield, *How Choctaws Invented Civilization*, 19.

36. Birchfield, *How Choctaws Invented Civilization*, 19.

37. Lincecum, *Pushmataha*, 74.

38. Charles J. Kappler, "Treaty with the Choctaw, 1820," in *Indian Affairs: Laws and Treaties*, ed. Kappler (Washington, DC: Government Printing Office, 1904), 190.

39. Birchfield, *Field of Honor*, 111.

40. Lincecum, *Pushmataha*, 75.

41. Lincecum, *Pushmataha*, 77.

42. Lincecum, *Pushmataha*, 76.

43. Lyons, *X-Marks*, 2–3.

44. Lyons, *X-Marks*, 3.

45. Hellekson, "Alternate History," 453.

46. LeAnne Howe, *Shell Shaker* (San Francisco: Aunt Lute Books, 2001), 196.

47. Howe, *Shell Shaker*, 196.

48. Birchfield, *Field of Honor*, 108.

49. Birchfield, *Field of Honor*, 111.

50. See, for instance, the several versions of the creation story collected by Tom Mould in *Choctaw Tales*.

51. Birchfield, *Field of Honor*, 106, 108.

52. Birchfield, *Field of Honor*, 109–10.

53. Birchfield, *Field of Honor*, 137.

54. Birchfield, *Field of Honor*, 137.

55. Birchfield, *Field of Honor*, 141–42.

56. Birchfield, *Field of Honor*, 105.

57. "Birchfield, Donald," University of Lethbridge Retired Academic Staff Association, September 7, 2012, http://www.uleth.ca/retired-faculty/obituaries/birchfield-donald.

58. Candy Moulton, "It's Gotta Be the Choctaws," *True West*, May 1, 2006, http://www.truewestmagazine.com/its-gotta-be-the-choctaws/.

59. Birchfield, *Field of Honor*, 121.

60. Birchfield, *Field of Honor*, 123.

61. Birchfield, *Field of Honor*, 123.

62. Birchfield, *Field of Honor*, 123.

63. Birchfield, *Field of Honor*, 28.

64. Birchfield, *Field of Honor*, 30.

65. Birchfield, *Field of Honor*, 20.

66. Birchfield, *Field of Honor*, 127.

67. Birchfield, *Field of Honor*, 128.

68. My thanks to Tol Foster, who first suggested that this aspect of the novel deserved more attention.

69. Birchfield, *Field of Honor*, 108.

70. Choctaw Nation of Oklahoma, *The Freedmen Bill: An Act Entitled an Act to Adopt the Freedmen of the Choctaw Nation* (Denison, TX: Murray, 1883).

71. Birchfield, *Field of Honor*, 109.

72. Birchfield, *Field of Honor*, 109.

73. Birchfield, *Field of Honor*, 210.

74. David T. Fortin, "Indigenous Architectural Futures: Potentials for Post-Apocalyptic Spatial Speculation," Architectural Research Centers Consortium Conference Repository (2014): 475–83, http://www.arcc-journal.org/index.php/repository/article/view/301/237.

75. Birchfield, *Field of Honor*, 201. The suggestion of nuclear warfare, especially as brought about by a "mad" scientist or doctor, is a classic science fictional trope. The mad scientist is "a villain who believes that the conventional scientific community . . . [is] needlessly constrained by their petty 'morals' and their self-limiting 'logic'" ("Mad Scientist," TV Tropes, https://tvtropes.org/pmwiki/pmwiki.php/Main/MadScientist). One famous example of the mad scientist occurs in H. G. Wells's novel *The Island of Dr. Moreau*, in which the title character performs gruesome and painful experiments on animals in an attempt to reshape them into human forms. When pressed to justify the infliction of so much pain, Moreau responds that "a mind truly opened to what science has to teach must see that [the pain] is such a little thing" (Wells, *The Island of Dr. Moreau*, 65). He goes on to admit that "I have never troubled about the ethics of the matter" (66). In these moments, Moreau expresses clear contempt for "the conventional scientific community"

and their "petty 'morals,'" which, from his perspective, have kept them from aspiring to the heights of his own experiments. Through Moreau and his unsettling creations, Wells examines the nature of humanity and the boundaries that divide people from other animals.

The trope of the mad scientist also offers a quick shorthand for referring to one of the primary themes of science fiction: a concern with the "combination of apocalyptic destruction and eventual salvation—at the hands of both science and technology" (Telotte, "Film, 1895–1950," 48). In this sense, the mad scientist can be framed as the binary opposite of the "Science Hero," "who uses science, technology, and/or super-science to save the day" ("Science Hero," TV Tropes, https://tvtropes.org/pmwiki/pmwiki. php/Main/ScienceHero). The tension between these opposing concepts—and thus between the Science Hero and the Mad Scientist—comes to a head in the ambivalence surrounding nuclear power in the mid-twentieth century. An especially illustrative example of the genre is Walter M. Miller Jr.'s 1959 novel *A Canticle for Leibowitz*. Miller's story opens in the midst of a dark age several hundred years after humans have nearly destroyed the Earth through nuclear war. In the wake of that war, the survivors blamed "the scientists, leaders, technicians, [and] teachers . . . for having helped to make the Earth what it had become" (Walter M. Miller Jr., *A Canticle for Leibowitz* [New York: Bantam Books, 1997], 63–64). Understandably traumatized after surviving a nuclear holocaust, Leibowitz's masses cast all scientists as "mad." And yet, the novel's protagonists are a small group of monks and priests who pray to Isaac Edward Leibowitz, a mid-twentieth-century scientist and "an expert in the weapons field" who survived the war, joined the priesthood, and founded an order dedicated to the preservation of literature and science (Miller, *A Canticle for Leibowitz*, 65). Reflected in Miller's premise is the mixed admiration and fear inspired by the scientists who discovered and developed nuclear power.

76. Birchfield, *Field of Honor*, 114.
77. Birchfield, *Field of Honor*, 201, 194.
78. Birchfield, *Field of Honor*, 200.
79. Birchfield, *Field of Honor*, 201.
80. Birchfield, *Field of Honor*, 143.
81. Mould, *Choctaw Tales*, 40.
82. Mould, *Choctaw Tales*, 42.
83. Mould, *Choctaw Tales*, 42–43.
84. Birchfield, *Field of Honor*, 226.
85. Suvin, *Metamorphoses of Science Fiction*, 13.

86. Suvin, *Metamorphoses of Science Fiction*, 12.

Chapter Four. The Stories Began to Change: Rewriting Removal in *Riding the Trail of Tears*

1. Blake M. Hausman, *Riding the Trail of Tears* (Lincoln: University of Nebraska Press, 2011), 13.
2. Hausman, *Riding the Trail of Tears*, 51.
3. Hausman, *Riding the Trail of Tears*, 27.
4. Hausman, *Riding the Trail of Tears*, 65, 80.
5. Hellekson, "Alternate History," 453.
6. Elizabeth Grosz, *Architecture from the Outside: Essays on Virtual and Real Space* (Cambridge, MA: MIT Press, 2001), 78.
7. Thomas Foster, "Virtuality," in Bould et al., *The Routledge Companion to Science Fiction*, 319.
8. *The Matrix*, directed by Lana Wachowski and Lilly Wachowski (1999; Burbank, CA: Warner Bros. Pictures), DVD.
9. *The Matrix*, dir. Wachowski and Wachowski.
10. Foster, "Virtuality," 322.
11. *The Matrix*, dir. Wachowski and Wachowski.
12. *TRON*, directed by Steven Lisberger (Burbank, CA: Walt Disney Pictures, 1982).
13. Hopkinson, introduction to Hopkinson and Mehan, *So Long Been Dreaming*, 8.
14. Hausman, *Riding the Trail of Tears*, 94.
15. Hausman, *Riding the Trail of Tears*, 179.
16. Hausman, *Riding the Trail of Tears*, 34.
17. Everett F. Bleiler, with the assistance of Richard J. Bleiler, *Science Fiction: The Gernsback Years. A Complete Coverage of the Genre Magazines "Amazing," "Astounding," "Wonder" and Others from 1926 through 1936* (Kent, OH: Kent State University Press, 1998), xv.
18. "Gone Horribly Wrong," TV Tropes, https://tvtropes.org/pmwiki/pmwiki.php/Main/GoneHorriblyWrong.
19. *Jurassic Park*, directed by Steven Spielberg (Universal City, CA: Universal Pictures, 1993).
20. Hausman, *Riding the Trail of Tears*, 86.
21. "Point of No Return," TV Tropes, https://tvtropes.org/pmwiki/pmwiki.php/Main/PointOfNoReturn.
22. Chris Van Allsburg, *Jumanji* (New York: Houghton Mifflin Harcourt, 1981), 5.

23. *Star Trek: The Next Generation*, season 1, episode 11, "The Big Goodbye," directed by Joseph L. Scanlan, written by Tracy Tormé, aired January 11, 1988, in broadcast syndication.

24. Hausman, *Riding the Trail of Tears*, 86.

25. Mooney, *Myths of the Cherokee*, 331.

26. Suvin, *Metamorphoses of Science Fiction*, 8.

27. Dick, "My Definition of Science Fiction," 8.

28. Hausman, *Riding the Trail of Tears*, 5–6.

29. Hausman, *Riding the Trail of Tears*, 4.

30. Hausman, *Riding the Trail of Tears*, 4.

31. Hausman, *Riding the Trail of Tears*, 5.

32. See, for instance, the documentary film *First Language: The Race to Save Cherokee*, directed by Danica Cullinan and Neal Hutcheson, The Language and Life Project, November 21, 2016, YouTube video, 56:08, https://www.youtube.com/watch?v=e9y8fDOLsO4, which focuses on language revitalization efforts in Cherokee, North Carolina.

33. Hausman, *Riding the Trail of Tears*, 13.

34. Hausman, *Riding the Trail of Tears*, 3.

35. Hausman, *Riding the Trail of Tears*, 13.

36. Cajete, *Native Science*, 3.

37. Mooney, *Myths of the Cherokee*, 331.

38. Eastern Band of Cherokee Indians, "Take a Journey to the Home of the Eastern Band of Cherokee Indians," *Visit Cherokee NC,* https://visitcherokeenc.com/eastern-band-of-the-cherokee/.

39. Cherokee Preservation Foundation, "About the Eastern Band of Cherokee Indians," http://cherokeepreservation.org/who-we-are/about-the-ebci/. Eastern Band of Cherokee Indians, "Take a Journey to the Home of the Eastern Band of Cherokee Indians," *Visit Cherokee NC*, https://visitcherokeenc.com/eastern-band-of-the-cherokee/.

40. Hausman, *Riding the Trail of Tears*, 33.

41. Hausman, *Riding the Trail of Tears*, 33.

42. Pinsky, *Future Present*, 183.

43. Pinsky, *Future Present*, 187.

44. Hausman, *Riding the Trail of Tears*, 57.

45. Hausman, *Riding the Trail of Tears*, 71.

46. Hausman, *Riding the Trail of Tears*, 103.

47. Mooney, *Myths of the Cherokee*, 101.

48. Hausman, *Riding the Trail of Tears*, 167.

49. Mooney, *Myths of the Cherokee*, 101.

50. Hausman, *Riding the Trail of Tears*, 308.

51. Hausman, *Riding the Trail of Tears*, 318.

52. Hausman, *Riding the Trail of Tears*, 57.

53. Hausman, *Riding the Trail of Tears*, 57.

54. Hausman, *Riding the Trail of Tears*, 59.

55. Hausman, *Riding the Trail of Tears*, 335.

56. Hausman, *Riding the Trail of Tears*, 60.

57. Hausman, *Riding the Trail of Tears*, 67.

58. Hausman, *Riding the Trail of Tears*, 286.

59. Hausman, *Riding the Trail of Tears*, 112.

60. Hausman, *Riding the Trail of Tears*, 119.

61. Traditional Cherokee territory spanned a large portion of the Southeast, including parts of what are now recognized as Georgia, North Carolina, South Carolina, Tennessee, Alabama, Virginia, West Virginia, and Kentucky. See C. C. Royce, *Map of the Former Territorial Limits of the Cherokee "Nation of" Indians; Map Showing the Territory Originally Assigned Cherokee "Nation of" Indians* [S.I, 1884], map. https://www.loc.gov/item/99446145/. However, because the only portion of this land retained by the Cherokee people in the twenty-first century is located at Qualla Boundary in the North Carolina mountains, that is the area that the Nunnehi focus on, so that it serves as a kind of synecdoche for the entirety of traditional Cherokee territory. The location also holds special significance for Tallulah, whose Cherokee grandmother "still lives up in Eastern Cherokee country, near the Qualla Boundary reservation in North Carolina" (Hausman, *Riding the Trail of Tears,* 23).

62. Hausman, *Riding the Trail of Tears*, 124.

63. Hausman, *Riding the Trail of Tears*, 124.

64. Hausman, *Riding the Trail of Tears*, 125.

65. Suvin, *Metamorphoses of Science Fiction*, 66.

66. Philip J. Deloria, *Playing Indian* (New Haven: Yale University Press, 1998), 115.

67. Deloria, *Playing Indian*, 115.

68. Deloria, *Playing Indian*, 115.

69. Deloria, *Playing Indian*, 129.

70. Deloria, *Playing Indian*, 115.

71. Hausman, *Riding the Trail of Tears*, 57.

72. Deloria, *Playing Indian*, 115.

73. Deloria, *Playing Indian*, 115.

74. Hausman, *Riding the Trail of Tears*, 361.

75. Hausman, *Riding the Trail of Tears*, 170.

76. Hausman, *Riding the Trail of Tears*, 172.

77. Hausman, *Riding the Trail of Tears*, 178.

78. Hausman, *Riding the Trail of Tears*, 178, 254.

79. Hausman, *Riding the Trail of Tears*, 301.

80. Hausman, *Riding the Trail of Tears*, 74.

81. Hausman, *Riding the Trail of Tears*, 97.

82. Hausman, *Riding the Trail of Tears*, 117.

83. Hausman, *Riding the Trail of Tears*, 83.

84. Hausman, *Riding the Trail of Tears*, 281.

85. Hausman, *Riding the Trail of Tears*, 13.

86. Hausman, *Riding the Trail of Tears*, 12.

87. Hausman, *Riding the Trail of Tears*, 323.

88. Hausman, *Riding the Trail of Tears*, 326.

89. Cajete, *Native Science*, 3.

Coda

1. Lou Cornum, "The Space NDN's Star Map," *The New Inquiry*, January 26, 2015, http://thenewinquiry.com/essays/the-space-ndns-star-map/.

2. Cornum, "The Space NDN's Star Map."

3. William Lempert, "Navajos on Mars: Native Sci-Fi Film Adventures," *Space + Anthropology*, September 21, 2015, https://medium.com/space-anthropology/navajos-on-mars-4c336175d945#.4krdv9s9i.

4. Denise K. Cummings, "Introduction: Indigenous Visualities," in *Visualities: Perspectives on Contemporary American Indian Film and Art*, ed. Denise K. Cummings (East Lansing: Michigan State University Press, 2011), xiii.

5. Cummings, "Introduction," xiii.

6. Michelle H. Raheja, "Visual Prophecies: *Imprint* and *It Starts with a Whisper*," in Cummings, *Visualities*, 4.

7. Cummings, "Introduction," xvii.

8. Raheja, "Visual Prophecies," 5.

9. Cornum, "The Space NDN's Star Map."

10. Nanobah Becker, "The 6th World," directed by Nanobah Becker, season 3, episode 6 of

FutureStates, aired May 8, 2012, https://www.pbs.org/video/futurestates-the-6th-world-a-future-friday-premiere/.

11. Stacy Thacker, "New Navajo Sci-fi Film '6th World' Gives a Glimpse into Navajo Creation Story," *Reznet News*, http://www.reznetnews.org/article/new-navajo-sci-fi-film-6th-world-gives-glimpse-navajo-creation-story.

12. Thacker, "New Navajo Sci-fi Film '6th World.'"

13. Steven Paul Judd, "Neil Discovers the Moon," Vimeo, April 20, 2015, https://vimeo.com/125523619.

14. Judd, "Neil Discovers the Moon."

15. Steven Paul Judd, "The NALS Annual Film Night," presentation at the Annual Convention of the Native American Literature Symposium, Albuquerque, NM, March 17, 2016. Judd has said that the inspiration for this one-minute film was Gary Larson's single-panel comic, *The Far Side*.

16. Skawennati, "Bio," *Skawennati*, last modified December 2015, http://www.skawennati.com/bio/bio.html.

17. "What Is Second Life?," *Second Life*, http://secondlife.com/whatis/.

18. David Gaertner, "'What's a Story Like You Doing in a Place Like This?': Cyberspace and Indigenous Futurism," *Novel Alliances: Allied Perspectives on Literature, Art, and New Media*, March 23, 2015, https://novelalliances.com/2015/03/23/whats-a-story-like-you-doing-in-a-place-like-this-cyberspace-and-indigenous-futurism-in-neal-stephensons-snow-crash/.

19. Jason Edward Lewis and Skawennati, "Opinion: Building a Future in Which Indigenous People Are Present and Thriving," *Montreal Gazette*, April 27, 2016, http://montrealgazette.com/opinion/columnists/opinion-building-a-future-in-which-indigenous-people-are-present-and-thriving.

20. Louis Owens, *I Hear the Train: Reflections, Inventions, Refractions* (Norman: University of Oklahoma Press, 2001), 211.

21. Owens, *I Hear the Train*, 212.

22. Rose Eveleth, "Women Rise in Sci Fi (Again)," *The Atlantic*, November 5, 2014, http://www.theatlantic.com/entertainment/archive/2014/11/women-rise-in-science-fiction-again/382298/.

23. Eveleth, "Women Rise in Sci Fi (Again)."

24. Pamela Rentz, *Red Tape: Stories from Indian Country* (Los Gatos, CA: Smashwords, 2012).

25. Andrea Grant, *Minx: Dream War* (New York: Copious Amounts Press, 2011).

26. See Milner, *Locating Science Fiction*, 115–35, for a more detailed discussion of dystopian science fiction.

27. Stephen Graham Jones, *The Bird Is Gone: A Manifesto* (Tallahassee: FC2, 2003), 168.

28. Jones, *The Bird Is Gone*, 172.

29. Jones, *The Bird Is Gone*, 122.

30. Jones, *The Bird Is Gone*, 43.

31. Jones, *The Bird Is Gone*, 122.

32. Justin Kroll, "Michael Bay Sets '6 Underground,' 'Robopocalypse' as Next Two Films," *Variety*, March 7, 2018, https://variety.com/2018/film/news/michael-bay-new-movies-six-underground-robopocalypse-1202721030/.

33. Cherie Dimaline, *The Marrow Thieves* (Toronto: Cormorant Books, 2017), 24.

34. Louise Erdrich, *Future Home of the Living God* (New York: HarperCollins, 2017), 51.

35. See, for instance, a July 2, 2020 *Newsweek* article by Meghan Roos entitled "Arizona COVID-19 Doctor on Frontlines: 'I Am Scared and You Should Be Too,'" which concludes with this warning: "COVID doesn't discriminate, and it definitely doesn't care who you're going to vote for."

36. Centers for Disease Control and Prevention, "Health Equity Considerations and Racial and Ethnic Minority Groups," July 24, 2020, https://www.cdc.gov/coronavirus/2019-ncov/community/health-equity/race-ethnicity.html.

37. *Star Trek: The Next Generation*, season 3, episode 4, "Who Watches the Watchers," directed by Robert Wiemer, written by Richard Manning and Hans Beimler, aired October 16, 1989, in broadcast syndication, https://www.netflix.com/watch/70177914?trackId=200257859.

38. Leslie Marmon Silko, *Ceremony* (New York: Penguin Classics, 2006), 87.

Bibliography

"About the Eastern Band of Cherokee Indians." Cherokee Preservation Foundation. http://cherokeepreservation.org/who-we-are/about-the-ebci/.

Alexie, Sherman. *Flight.* New York: Black Cat, 2007.

Andrews, Scott. "Review of *Of Uncommon Birth: Dakota Sons in Vietnam*, by Mark St. Pierre; *Field of Honor*, by D. L. Hirschfield [*sic*]." *Studies in American Indian Literatures* 17, no. 1 (2005): 87–90.

Anno, Hideaki and Shinji Higuchi, dirs. *Shin Godzilla.* Chiyoda, Tokyo: Toho Co., Ltd., 2016.

Atomic Heritage Foundation. "The Manhattan Project." May 12, 2017. https://www.atomicheritage.org/history/manhattan-project.

———. "Oak Ridge, TN." https://www.atomicheritage.org/location/oak-ridge-tn.

Awiakta, Marilou. *Abiding Appalachia: Where Mountain and Atom Meet.* Memphis: St. Luke's Press, 1978.

Becker, Nanobah, writer. "The 6th World." Directed by Nanobah Becker. Season 3, episode 6 of *FutureStates.* Aired May 8, 2012. https://www.pbs.org/video/futurestates-the-6th-world-a-future-friday-premiere/.

Benson, Melanie. *Disturbing Calculations: The Economics of Identity in Postcolonial Southern Literature, 1912–2002.* Athens: University of Georgia Press, 2008.

Birchfield, D. L. *Field of Honor*. Norman: University of Oklahoma Press, 2004.

———. *How Choctaws Invented Civilization and Why Choctaws Will Conquer the World*. Albuquerque: University of New Mexico Press, 2007.

———. *The Oklahoma Basic Intelligence Test*. New York: Greenfield Review Press, 1998.

Bleiler, Everett F., with the assistance of Richard J. Bleiler. *Science-Fiction: The Gernsback Years. A Complete Coverage of the Genre Magazines "Amazing," "Astounding," "Wonder," and Others from 1926 through 1936*. Kent, OH: Kent State University Press, 1998.

Burkhart, Brian. "Jisdu Goes Decolonial: The Epistemic Resistance of Cherokee Trickster Stories." Paper presented at the Native American Literature Symposium, Prior Lake, MN, March 9, 2019.

Butler, Judith. *Gender Trouble: Feminism and the Subversion of Identity*. New York: Routledge Classics, 1990.

Cajete, Gregory. *Native Science: Natural Laws of Interdependence*. Santa Fe: Clear Light Publishers, 2000.

Carey, Kevin. "Martians Might Be Real: That Makes Mars Exploration Way More Complicated." *Wired*. August 7, 2016. https://www.wired.com/2016/08/shouldnt-go-mars-might-decimate-martians/.

Carr, A. A. *Eye Killers*. Norman: University of Oklahoma Press, 1995.

Centers for Disease Control and Prevention. "Health Equity Considerations and Racial and Ethnic Minority Groups." July 24, 2020. https://www.cdc.gov/coronavirus/2019-ncov/community/health-equity/race-ethnicity.html.

Choctaw Nation of Oklahoma. *The Freedmen Bill: An Act Entitled an Act to Adopt the Freedmen of the Choctaw Nation*. Denison, TX: Murray, 1883.

Collins, Suzanne. *The Hunger Games*. New York: Scholastic, 2008.

———. *Catching Fire*. New York: Scholastic, 2009.

———. *Mockingjay*. New York: Scholastic, 2010.

Cornum, Lou. "The Space NDN's Star Map." *The New Inquiry*. January 26, 2015. http://thenewinquiry.com/essays/the-space-ndns-star-map/.

Costello, Matthew J. "U.S. Superpower and Superpowered Americans in Science Fiction and Comic Books." In *The Cambridge Companion to American Science Fiction*, edited by Gerry Canavan and Eric Carl Link, 125–38. Cambridge: Cambridge University Press, 2015.

Csicsery-Ronay, Istvan, Jr. "Science Fiction and Empire." In *Science Fiction Criticism: An Anthology of Essential Writings*, edited by Rob Latham, 443–57. London: Bloomsbury, 2017.

Cullinan, Danica, and Neal Hutcheson, dirs. *First Language: The Race to Save Cherokee*. The Language and Life Project. November 21, 2016. YouTube video, 56:08. https://www.youtube.com/watch?v=e9y8fDOLsO4.

Cummings, Denise K. "Introduction: Indigenous Visualities." In *Visualities: Perspectives on Contemporary American Indian Film and Art*, edited by Denise K. Cummings, xiii–xxiv. East Lansing: Michigan State University Press, 2011.

Deloria, Philip J. *Playing Indian*. New Haven: Yale University Press, 1998.

Deloria, Vine, Jr. *God Is Red: A Native View of Religion*. Golden, CO: Fulcrum Publishing, 2003.

———. *The Metaphysics of Modern Existence*. San Francisco: Harper & Row, 1979.

———. "Reflection and Revelation." In *For This Land: Writings on Religion in America*, edited by James Treat, 250–60. New York: Routledge, 1999.

Detrow, Scott, Asma Khalid, Ayesha Rascoe, and Mara Liasson. "Weekly Roundup: Tuesday, July 3." *NPR Politics Podcast*. July 3, 2018. MP3 audio, 37:37. https://www.npr.org/transcripts/625807854?storyId=625807854?storyId=625807854.

Dick, Philip K. *The Man in the High Castle*. Boston: Mariner Books, 2011.

———. *The Shifting Realities of Philip K. Dick: Selected Literary and Philosophical Writings*. Edited by Lawrence Sutin. New York: Pantheon Books, 1995.

Dillon, Grace L., ed. *Walking the Clouds: An Anthology of Indigenous Science Fiction*. Tucson: University of Arizona Press, 2012.

———. "*Miindiwag* and Indigenous Diaspora: Eden Robinson's and Celu Amberstone's Forays into 'Postcolonial' Science Fiction and Fantasy." *Extrapolation* 48, no. 2 (2007): 219–43.

Dimaline, Cherie. *The Marrow Thieves*. Toronto: Cormorant Books, 2017.

Douglas, Gordon, dir. *Them!* 1954; Burbank, CA: Warner Brothers.

Dunbar-Ortiz, Roxanne. *An Indigenous People's History of the United States*. Boston: Beacon Press, 2014.

Eastern Band of Cherokee Indians. "Take a Journey to the Home of the Eastern Band of Cherokee Indians." *Visit Cherokee NC*. https://visitcherokeenc.com/eastern-band-of-the-cherokee/.

Emmerich, Roland, dir. *Independence Day*. 1996; Los Angeles: 20th Century Fox, 2013. DVD.

Erb, Joseph. "The Beginning They Told." YouTube. October 28, 2016. https://www.youtube.com/watch?feature=youtu.be&v=BUoPB0reYc4&app=desktop.

Erdrich, Louise. *Future Home of the Living God*. New York: HarperCollins, 2017.

Eveleth, Rose. "Women Rise in Sci Fi (Again)." *The Atlantic*. November 5, 2014. http://www.theatlantic.com/entertainment/archive/2014/11/women-rise-in-science-fiction-again/382298/.

Fortin, David T. "Beyond Architecture: New Intersections and Connections," University of Hawai'i at Manoa, 2014. ARCC/EAAE Architectural Research Conference hosted by the University of Hawai'i at Manoa, February 12–15, 2014, ARCC conference repository, 475–83. https://www.arcc-journal.org/index.php/repository/article/view/301/237.

Foster, Thomas. "Virtuality." In *The Routledge Companion to Science Fiction*, edited by Mark Bould, Andrew M. Butler, Adam Roberts, and Sherryl Vint. London: Routledge, 2009.

Fox, Sarah Alisabeth. *Downwind: A People's History of the Nuclear West*. Lincoln: University of Nebraska Press, 2014.

Gaertner, David. "'What's a Story Like You Doing in a Place Like This?': Cyberspace and Indigenous Futurism." *Novel Alliances: Allied Perspectives on Literature, Art, and New Media*. March 23, 2015. https://novelalliances.com/2015/03/23/whats-a-story-like-you-doing-in-a-place-like-this-cyberspace-and-indigenous-futurism-in-neal-stephensons-snow-crash/.

"Gone Horribly Wrong." TV Tropes. https://tvtropes.org/pmwiki/pmwiki.php/Main/GoneHorriblyWrong.

Grosz, Elizabeth. *Architecture from the Outside: Essays on Virtual and Real Space*. Cambridge, MA: MIT Press, 2001.

Groves, Leslie. "The First Nuclear Test in New Mexico." *American Experience*. PBS.org. http://www.pbs.org/wgbh/americanexperience/features/primary-resources/truman-bombtest/.

Hausman, Blake M. *Riding the Trail of Tears*. Lincoln: University of Nebraska Press, 2011.

Hellekson, Karen. "Alternate History." In *The Routledge Companion to Science Fiction*, edited by Mark Bould, Andrew M. Butler, Adam Roberts, and Sherryl Vint, 453–57. London: Routledge, 2009.

Higgins, David M. "Toward a Cosmopolitan Science Fiction." *American Literature* 83, no. 2 (2011): 331–54.

Honda, Ishiro, dir. *Godzilla*. Chiyoda, Tokyo: Toho Co., Ltd., 1954.

Hopkinson, Nalo. *Midnight Robber*. New York: Warner Books, Inc., 2000.

Hopkinson, Nalo, and Uppinder Mehan, eds. *So Long Been Dreaming: Postcolonial Science Fiction and Fantasy*. Vancouver: Arsenal Pulp Press, 2004.

Howe, LeAnne. *Miko Kings: An Indian Baseball Story*. San Francisco: Aunt Lute Books, 2007.

———. *Shell Shaker*. San Francisco: Aunt Lute Books, 2001.

Jauss, Hans Robert. "Literary History as a Challenge to Literary Theory." Translated by Elizabeth Benzinger. *New Literary History* 2, no. 1 (1970): 7–37.

Jemisin, N. K. *The Fifth Season*. New York: Orbit Books, 2015.

———. *The Obelisk Gate*. New York: Orbit Books, 2016.

———. *The Stone Sky*. New York: Orbit Books, 2017.

Jones, Stephen Graham. *The Bird Is Gone: A Manifesto*. Tallahassee: FC2, 2003.

———. *It Came from Del Rio*. Colorado: Trapdoor Books, 2010.

———. *The Last Final Girl*. Portland: Lazy Fascist Press, 2012.

———. *Ledfeather*. Tuscaloosa: University of Alabama Press, 2008.

———. "Letter to a Just-Starting-Out Indian Writer—and Maybe to Myself." *Transmotion* 2, nos. 1–2 (2016): 124–30.

———. "Observations on the Shadow Self." In *The Fictions of Stephen Graham Jones*, edited by Billy J. Stratton, 14–59. Albuquerque: University of New Mexico Press, 2016.

———. *Zombie Sharks with Metal Teeth*. Portland: Lazy Fascist Press, 2013.

Judd, Steven Paul. "Neil Discovers the Moon." Vimeo. April 20, 2015. https://vimeo.com/125523619.

———. "The NALS Annual Film Night." Presentation at the Annual Convention of the Native American Literature Symposium, Albuquerque, NM, March 17, 2016.

Kappler, Charles J. "Treaty with the Choctaw, 1820." In *Indian Affairs: Laws and Treaties*, ed. Kappler, 2:191–95. Washington, DC: Government Printing Office, 1904.

Kaufman, Scott. "Noam Chomsky: Zombies Are the New Indians and Slaves in White America's Collective Nightmare." *The Raw Story*. February 14, 2014. http://www.rawstory.com/2014/02/noam-chomsky-zombies-are-the-new-indians-and-slaves-in-white-americas-collective-nightmare/.

Keene, Adrienne. "'Magic in North America': The Harry Potter Franchise Veers too Close to Home." *Native Appropriations*. March 7, 2016. http://nativeappropriations.com/2016/03/magic-in-north-america-the-harry-potter-franchise-veers-too-close-to-home.html.

Kelts, Roland. "Godzilla Shows Japan's Real Fear Is Sclerotic Bureaucracy Not Giant Reptiles." *The Guardian*. August 21, 2017. https://www.theguardian.com/commentisfree/2017/aug/21/resurgence-shin-godzilla-japanese-culture-film-japan.

King, Thomas. *The Inconvenient Indian: A Curious Account of Native People in North America*. Minneapolis: University of Minnesota Press, 2013.

———. *The Truth about Stories*. Minneapolis: University of Minnesota Press, 2003.

Kroll, Justin. "Michael Bay Sets '6 Underground,' 'Robopocalypse' as Next Two Films." *Variety*. March 7, 2018. https://variety.com/2018/film/news/michael-bay-new-movies-six-underground-robopocalypse-1202721030/.

Kubrick, Stanley, dir. *2001: A Space Odyssey*. Film. 1968; Burbank, CA: Warner Home Video, 2011. DVD.

Langer, Jessica. *Postcolonialism and Science Fiction*. New York: Palgrave Macmillan, 2011.

Le Guin, Ursula K. *The Left Hand of Darkness: 50th Anniversary Edition*. New York: Berkley Publishing Group, 2019.

Lee, A. Robert. "Native Postmodern: Remediating History in the Fiction of Stephen Graham Jones and D. L. Birchfield." In *Mediating Indianness*, edited by Cathy Covell Waegner, 73–88. East Lansing: Michigan State University Press, 2015.

Lempert, William. "Navajos on Mars: Native Sci-Fi Film Futures." *Space + Anthropology*. September 21, 2015. https://medium.com/space-anthropology/

navajos-on-mars-4c336175d945#.4krdv9s9i.

Lewis, David Rich. "Skull Valley Goshutes and the Politics of Nuclear Waste: Environment, Identity, and Sovereignty." In *Native Americans and the Environment*, edited by Michael E. Harkin and Judith Antell, 304–42. Lincoln: University of Nebraska Press, 2007.

Lewis, Jason Edward, and Skawennati. "Opinion: Building a Future in Which Indigenous People Are Present and Thriving." *Montreal Gazette*. April 27, 2016. http://montrealgazette.com/opinion/columnists/opinion-building-a-future-in-which-indigenous-people-are-present-and-thriving.

Levinas, Emmanuel. *Otherwise than Being*. Pittsburgh: Duquesne University Press, 1998.

Lincecum, Gideon. *Pushmataha: A Choctaw Leader and His People*. Tuscaloosa: University of Alabama Press, 2004.

Lisberger, Steven, dir. *TRON*. Burbank, CA: Walt Disney Pictures, 1982. DVD.

Lyons, Scott Richard. *X-Marks: Native Signatures of Assent*. Minneapolis: University of Minnesota Press, 2010.

"Mad Scientist." TV Tropes. https://tvtropes.org/pmwiki/pmwiki.php/Main/MadScientist.

Manning, Richard, and Hans Beimler, writers. *Star Trek: The Next Generation*. Season 3, episode 4, "Who Watches the Watchers." Directed by Robert Wiemer. Aired October 16, 1989, in broadcast syndication.

Matsunaga, Kyoko. "Leslie Marmon Silko and Nuclear Dissent in the American Southwest." *Japanese Journal of American Studies*, no. 25 (2014): 67–88.

Meland, Carter. "American Indians at the Final Frontiers of Imperial Sf." *Expanded Horizons: Speculative Fiction for the Rest of Us*, no. 1 (2008). http://expandedhorizons.net/magazine/?page_id=150.

———. "The Possibilities (and Problems) of Indigenizing SF." *Expanded Horizons: Speculative Fiction for the Rest of Us*, no. 5 (2009). http://expandedhorizons.net/magazine/?page_id=95.

———. "The Trickster Is History: Tribal Tricksters and American Cultural History in Contemporary Native Writing." PhD Diss, University of Minnesota, 2002.

Miller, Bruce, creator. *The Handmaid's Tale*. Directed by Mike Barker et al. Beverly Hills: MGM Television, 2017–.

Miller, Walter M., Jr. *A Canticle for Leibowitz*. New York: Bantam Books, 1997.

Milner, Andrew. *Locating Science Fiction*. Liverpool: Liverpool University Press, 2012.

Mooney, James. *Myths of the Cherokee and Sacred Formulas of the Cherokee*. Washington, DC: Bureau of American Ethnology, 1890.

Morrison, Toni. "An Interview with Toni Morrison, by Christina Davis." In *Conversations with Toni Morrison*, edited by Danille Taylor-Guthrie, 223–33. Jackson: University Press of

Mississippi, 1994.

Mould, Tom. *Choctaw Tales*. Jackson: University Press of Mississippi, 2004.

Moulton, Candy. "It's Gotta Be the Choctaws." *True West*. May 1, 2006. http://www. truewestmagazine.com/its-gotta-be-the-choctaws/.

Mousoutzanis, Aris. "Apocalyptic SF." In *The Routledge Companion to Science Fiction*, edited by Mark Bould, Andrew M. Butler, Adam Roberts, and Sherryl Vint, 458–62. London: Routledge, 2009.

Neary, Lynn. "'It Just Felt Very Wrong': Sherman Alexie's Accusers Go on the Record." *NPR*. March 5, 2018. https://www.npr.org/2018/03/05/589909379/it-just-felt-very-wrong-sherman-alexies-accusers-go-on-the-record.

Northrup, Jim. *Rez Road Follies: Canoes, Casinos, Computers, and Birch Bark Baskets*. Minneapolis: University of Minnesota Press, 1999.

———. *Walking the Rez Road*. Minneapolis: Voyageur Press, 1993.

O'Brien, Greg. Introduction to *Pushmataha: A Choctaw Leader and His People*, by Gideon Lincecum. Tuscaloosa: University of Alabama Press, 2004.

Owens, Louis. *I Hear the Train: Reflections, Inventions, Refractions*. Norman: University of Oklahoma Press, 2001.

Pinsky, Michael. *Future Present: Ethics and/as Science Fiction*. Madison, NJ: Fairleigh Dickinson University Press, 2003.

"Point of No Return." TV Tropes. https://tvtropes.org/pmwiki/pmwiki.php/Main/PointOfNoReturn.

Rader, Dean. *Engaged Resistance: American Indian Art, Literature, and Film from Alcatraz to the NMAI*. Austin: University of Texas Press, 2011.

Radford, Benjamin. *Tracking the Chupacabra: The Vampire Beast in Fact, Fiction, and Folklore*. Albuquerque: University of New Mexico Press, 2011.

Raheja, Michelle H. "Visual Prophecies: *Imprint* and *It Starts with a Whisper*." In *Visualities: Perspectives on Contemporary American Indian Film and Art*, edited by Denise K. Cummings, 3–40. East Lansing: Michigan State University Press, 2011.

Rentz, Pamela. *Red Tape: Stories from Indian Country*. Los Gatos, CA: Smashwords, 2012.

Rieder, John. "On Defining Sf, or Not: Genre Theory, Sf, and History." In *Science Fiction Criticism: An Anthology of Essential Writings*, edited by Rob Latham, 74–93. London: Bloomsbury, 2017.

Roanhorse, Rebecca. "Postcards from the Apocalypse." *Uncanny: A Magazine of Science Fiction and Fantasy*. https://uncannymagazine.com/article/postcards-from-the-apocalypse/.

Roberts, Adam. *Science Fiction*. New York: Routledge, 2000.

Roos, Meghan. "Arizona COVID-19 Doctor on Frontlines: 'I Am Scared and You Should Be Too.'"

Newsweek. July 2, 2020. https://www.newsweek.com/arizona-covid-19-doctor-frontlines-i-am-scared-you-should-too-1515095.

Romero, Channette. *Activism and the American Novel: Religion and Resistance in Fiction by Women of Color.* Charlottesville: University of Virginia Press, 2012.

Roth, Veronica. *Allegiant.* New York: HarperCollins, 2013.

———. *Divergent.* New York: HarperCollins, 2011.

———. *Insurgent.* New York: HarperCollins, 2012.

Rowling, J. K. *Harry Potter and the Sorcerer's Stone.* New York: Scholastic, 1997.

Royce, C. C. *Map of the Former Territorial Limits of the Cherokee "Nation of" Indians; Map Showing the Territory Originally Assigned Cherokee "Nation of" Indians.* [S.I, 1884]. Map. https://www.loc.gov/item/99446145/.

Sackheim, Daniel, dir. *Lovecraft Country.* Season 1, episode 2, "Whitey's on the Moon." Aired August 23, 2020, on HBO.

Sanders, William. *Are We Having Fun Yet?* Holicong, PA: Wildside Press, 2005.

———. "Custer under the Baobab." In *Drakas!,* edited by S. M. Stirling. Riverdale, NY: Baen Books, 2000. https://www.baen.com/Chapters/0671319469/0671319469___2.htm.

———. *The Ballad of Billy Badass and the Rose of Turkestan.* Holicong, PA: Wildside Press, 1999.

"Science Hero." TV Tropes. https://tvtropes.org/pmwiki/pmwiki.php/Main/ScienceHero.

"What Is Second Life?" *Second Life.* http://secondlife.com/whatis/.

Shelley, Mary. *Frankenstein or The Modern Prometheus.* Edited by M. K. Joseph. London: Oxford University Press, 1969.

Silko, Leslie Marmon. *Ceremony.* New York: Penguin Classics, 2006.

Sinclair, Niigaanwewidam James. "A Conversation on Indigenous Ethics with Niigaanwewidam." Presentation at the Annual Convention of the Native American Literature Symposium, Minneapolis, MN, March 21, 2013.

Skawennati. *Time Traveller.* http://www.timetravellertm.com/.

———. "Bio." *Skawennati.* December 2015. http://www.skawennati.com/bio/bio.html.

Sobchack, Vivian. *Screening Space: The American Science Fiction Film.* New Brunswick, NJ: Rutgers University Press, 1999.

"Spider-Man (Peter Parker)." *Marvel.com.* https://www.marvel.com/characters/spider-man-peter-parker.

Spielberg, Steven, dir. *Jurassic Park.* Universal City, CA: Universal Pictures, 1993.

Stableford, Brian. *Opening Minds: Essays on Fantastic Literature.* San Bernardino: Borgo Press, 1974.

"Star Trek Original Series Intro (HQ)." YouTube. July 23, 2007. https://www.youtube.com/

watch?v=hdjL8WXjlGI.

Suvin, Darko. *Metamorphoses of Science Fiction: On the Poetics and History of a Literary Genre*. New Haven: Yale University Press, 1979.

Swain, Molly, and Chelsea Vowell, *Métis in Space*. February 17, 2016. http://www.indianandcowboy.com/metis-in-space/.

Telotte, J. P. "Film, 1895–1950." In *The Routledge Companion to Science Fiction*, edited by Mark Bould, Andrew M. Butler, Adam Roberts, and Sherryl Vint, 42–51. London: Routledge, 2009.

Thacker, Stacy. "New Navajo Sci-fi Film '6th World' Gives a Glimpse into Navajo Creation Story." *Reznet News*. http://www.reznetnews.org/article/new-navajo-sci-fi-film-6th-world-gives-glimpse-navajo-creation-story.

Tormé, Tracy, writer. *Star Trek: The Next Generation*. Season 1, episode 11, "The Big Goodbye." Directed by Joseph L. Scanlan. Aired January 11, 1988, in broadcast syndication.

U.S. Department of Agriculture. "Food Distribution Program on Indian Reservations." Food and Nutrition Service. May 11, 2016. http://www.fns.usda.gov/fdpir/food-distribution-program-indian-reservations.

University of Lethbridge. "Birchfield, Donald." University of Lethbridge Retired Academic Staff Association. September 7, 2012. http://www.uleth.ca/retired-faculty/obituaries/birchfield-donald.

Van Allsburg, Chris. *Jumanji*. New York: Houghton Mifflin Harcourt, 1981.

Van Alst, Theodore C. Introduction to *The Faster Redder Road: The Best UnAmerican Stories of Stephen Graham Jones*, edited by Theodore C. Van Alst, xiii–xix. Albuquerque: University of New Mexico Press, 2015.

———. "Lapin Noir: To Del Rio It Went." In *The Fictions of Stephen Graham Jones*, edited by Billy J. Stratton, 327–42. Albuquerque: University of New Mexico Press, 2016.

Wachowski, Lana, and Lilly Wachowski, dirs. *The Matrix*. Burbank, CA: Warner Bros. Pictures, 1999.

Walters, Anna Lee. *Ghost Singer*. Albuquerque: University of New Mexico Press, 1994.

Weaver, Jace, Craig Womack, and Robert Warrior. *American Indian Literary Nationalism*. Albuquerque: University of New Mexico Press, 2006.

Wells, H. G. *The Island of Dr. Moreau*. Edited by Darryl Jones. Oxford: Oxford University Press, 2017.

———. *The Time Machine*. New York: Fawcett Premier, 1968.

Wilentz, Amy. "A Zombie Is a Slave Forever." *New York Times*. October 30, 2012. http://www.nytimes.com/2012/10/31/opinion/a-zombie-is-a-slave-forever.html?_r=0.

Wilson, Daniel. *Robogenesis*. New York: Vintage Books, 2015.

———. *Robopocalypse*. New York: Vintage Contemporaries, 2011.

Wilson, James. *The Earth Shall Weep: A History of Native America*. New York: Grove Press, 1998.

Womack, Craig. *Red on Red: Native Literary Separatism*. Minneapolis: University of Minnesota Press, 1999.

Index

AMERICAN INDIAN STUDIES SERIES